Conrad's Marlow

MANCHESTER
1824

Manchester University Press

Conrad's Marlow

Narrative and death in 'Youth',
Heart of Darkness, *Lord Jim*
and *Chance*

Paul Wake

Manchester University Press
Manchester and New York
distributed exclusively in the USA by Palgrave

Published by Manchester University Press
Oxford Road, Manchester M13 9NR, UK
and Room 400, 175 Fifth Avenue, New York, NY 10010, USA
www.manchesteruniversitypress.co.uk

Distributed exclusively in the USA by
Palgrave, 175 Fifth Avenue, New York,
NY 10010, USA

Distributed exclusively in Canada by
UBC Press, University of British Columbia, 2029 West Mall,
Vancouver, BC, Canada V6T 1Z2

British Library Cataloguing-in-Publication Data
A catalogue record for this book is available from the
British Library

Library of Congress Cataloging-in-Publication Data applied for

ISBN 978 0 7190 7490 5 *hardback*

First published 2007

16 15 14 13 12 11 10 09 08 07   10 9 8 7 6 5 4 3 2 1

Typeset
by Florence Production Ltd, Stoodleigh, Devon
Printed in Great Britain
by Biddles Ltd, King's Lynn

Contents

Acknowledgements

It's only those who do nothing that make no mistakes, I suppose. (Joseph Conrad, *An Outcast of the Islands*)

My first debt of gratitude is to Simon Malpas who I would like to thank for his supervision of this work in its early stages and for his unfailingly optimistic support and encouragement throughout. I would also like to record my thanks to Barry Atkins, Margaret Beetham, Michael Bell, Tanya Gokulsing and Kate McGowan who all read and commented on parts of the manuscript, and to Laurence Coupe for bringing a number of useful articles on Hermes to my attention.

I am grateful to my colleagues at the Department of English at Manchester Metropolitan University for their kind support over the past years, to the English Research Institute for the research post that allowed me some time at a crucial stage in my work, and to Mary Garland for her tireless and meticulous proofreading. Thanks are also due to those members of the Joseph Conrad Society who responded so generously to a conference paper that would later be incorporated into the third chapter, to my editor at Manchester University Press, and to MUP's two anonymous readers for their most helpful comments on early drafts of my work.

Finally, I offer my thanks to my family who have been immensely supportive as always, and to Christine Kessler to whom this book is dedicated.

A note on the texts

All citations from Conrad's works, with the exception of *The Secret Agent* which appeared as the first volume of the Cambridge Edition of the Works of Joseph Conrad (Cambridge University Press, 1990-), are from the Dent Collected Edition (1946–55).

Preface

That was how it began. How it was that it ended as we know it did end, is not so easy to state precisely. (Joseph Conrad, *Victory*)

Conrad's Marlow: Narrative and Death in Joseph Conrad's 'Youth', *Heart of Darkness, Lord Jim* and *Chance*

As the title of this book makes clear, this is a study of Joseph Conrad's narrator-character Marlow who is introduced properly in the first chapter. In the meantime, the subtitle, 'Narrative and Death in Joseph Conrad's "Youth", *Heart of Darkness, Lord Jim* and *Chance*', indicates the trajectory that this investigation will follow. Through a series of close readings of Conrad's four Marlow texts, each of which will be discussed in a chapter of its own, this study explores the relation between narrative and death and the ways in which this relationship impacts on our readings of Conrad's fiction. The Marlow texts, which are not only littered with death, both literal and figurative, but whose very structure evinces a concern with questions of narration, provide the ideal ground for an investigation with such a double concern. In this analysis Marlow, who frequently traverses the border between narrator and character, becomes the key figure affording useful reflection on the process of narrating which, in this study, is conducted at the philosophically problematic border, or more properly the limit, between life and death.

The structure of this volume

No book-length study of Conrad's work, and certainly not one that takes as its object the four texts narrated by Marlow, can sensibly proceed without entering into a dialogue of some kind with the vast amount of Conrad scholarship that it follows and this one is no exception. In the case of Charlie Marlow this body of work includes Bernard J. Paris's recent monograph *Conrad's Charlie Marlow* (2005) which, by taking a psychological approach to Marlow, reveals a very different aspect of Conrad's narrator to that considered here, and a far larger number of shorter studies, a number of which have been collected in Harold Bloom's *Marlow* (1992). In addition to the diverse body of criticism that takes Marlow as its subject, there are a far larger number of studies of Conrad's work in general that offer insightful comment on a character who is quite probably the most famous of Conrad's literary creations. Notable examples of these that are picked up in this study include, and this list is by no means exhaustive; Peter Brooks's *Reading for the Plot*, Anthony Fothergill's *Heart of Darkness*, Jeremy Hawthorn's *Joseph Conrad: Narrative Technique and Ideological Commitment*, Susan Jones's *Conrad and Women*, Jakob Lothe's *Conrad's Narrative Method*, J. Hillis Miller's *Poets of Reality*, and Ian Watt's *Conrad in the Nineteenth Century*.

These texts are mentioned here not just in an attempt to offer an acknowledgement of my sources, although it does of course serve this purpose, but also to indicate that my intention in this volume is to stage a series of interventions into some of these important, and still vital, critical debates. At no point is this an exercise in the finding and setting up of straw men (or women), instead my reading of Marlow operates through the interrogation of the positions that he occupies in these earlier readings with the intention of both furthering the understanding of Conrad's use of this character and of reflecting on the critical practices that take him as their object. In this my study deliberately adopts the methodology of Paul Ricoeur's hermeneutics, which is discussed in the introductory chapter, by following his suggestion that any interpretative endeavour must start with certain presuppositions, and that the interpretative process itself must involve recognising the position from which it begins. In this I follow, and concur with, Fothergill who, noting 'how readily metaphors used to describe critical practice – "density", "getting to the heart of", "penetrating to the core", "casting light on" – mimic many of the gestures we "discover" in Conrad's story itself', advises that as readers of *Heart of Darkness* 'we should try to be as aware as possible of our own (and other's) critical procedures as we go along.'[1] So, entering wilfully into what I hope will prove to be a 'virtuous [critical] circle', I take these prior discussions of Marlow as the starting point for a study of Conrad's narrator-character which also seeks to provide a reflection on, and refiguration of, that starting point. This reflection, as will be seen from the brief chapter outline below, begins by applying to the work of a number of writers and philosophers, some of which might not be immediately connected with Conrad studies. So Conrad's work, and that of his critics, is approached here in relation to the work of Walter Benjamin, Jacques Derrida, Gérard Genette and Frank Kermode, all of whom will be familiar in the context of Conrad studies, along with that of Maurice Blanchot, G.W.F. Hegel, Martin Heidegger and Paul Ricoeur, whose work is perhaps less readily associated with Conrad's but which, having found useful application in other areas of literary studies, will no doubt be familiar to many readers.

The introduction begins by contextualising the Marlow texts, which are considered in terms of their original publication in *Blackwood's Edinburgh Magazine* before being explored in relation to Victorian realism and modernist experimentation. With this intention, Conrad's work is situated at the intersection of Victorianism and modernism, a literary-historical context that introduces the possibility of approaching the two literary movements in terms of their points of similarity rather than in their points of divergence. In making this argument I approach the Marlow texts in terms of a narrative hermeneutics that emerges from the work of Ricoeur and Kermode and which is concerned with the manner in which literary narratives approach the representation of truth.

The first chapter, following Lothe's example, draws on Genette's narrative theory in order to locate Marlow in the dual position of narrator and character through close readings of 'Youth' and *Heart of Darkness*, investigating the idea that Conrad's narratives are structured around the transmission of story, and questioning the possibility of sustaining the distinction between that which is transmitted and the means of transmission. With this established, Marlow's role as a narrator in the oral tradition is read alongside Benjamin's 'The Storyteller' in order to introduce a connection between narrative authority and death that will be developed in detail over the course of the book. The chapter concludes with a reading of 'Youth' in which the narrative frame becomes central to a reading of Marlow's 'central' story.

Questions surrounding the instant of death form the basis of the second chapter which offers a reassessment of two influential readings of *Heart of Darkness*, those of Miller and Brooks. These readings, which are linked by a common recognition of the significance of death with regards to meaning (specifically, in the case of *Heart of Darkness*, the death of Kurtz) are approached with reference to Heidegger's notion of Dasein as Being-towards death and his formulation of death as the 'possibility of impossibility' both of which appear in *Being and Time*.[2] Through a close analysis of death in *Heart of Darkness*, Miller and Brooks's readings are then critiqued in relation to Derrida's *Aporias* which examines the possibility of the experience that is denoted by the phrase 'my death' and which poses a radical challenge to Heidegger's notion of death.[3]

The idea of death as it has been set out in Derrida's reading of Heidegger is revisited in the third chapter which begins by examining the numerous suicides that are found in Conrad's work before offering a close reading of what might be called 'structures of suicide' in *Lord Jim*. Following an explication of Blanchot's work on suicide that focuses on his formulation of the 'double death' and his contention that literary language is similarly 'doubly negative', I consider the structural implications of suicide for narrative. This proceeds through an investigation into Conrad's biographers' attempts to narrate his supposed suicide attempt in 1898, an investigation that leads to the identification of similar narrative structures in *Lord Jim*. Through a reading of *Lord Jim* that focuses on the absence of Jim's jump from the stricken *Patna* I undertake to investigate the ways in which Conrad's text demonstrates a similar unwillingness to offer, or the impossibility of offering, the completion demanded by both narrative and suicide.

The fourth chapter, continuing the close textual reading of Conrad's texts, focuses on the last Marlow novel, *Chance*. Through a consideration of the implications of a narratology that has its basis in the double negation of literary language I argue that rather than rendering literature meaningless Blanchot's doubling of death generates the possibility of locating meaning in the narrating act itself. Accordingly, this final chapter sees a shift of emphasis away from death as impossibility towards a reading of *Chance* in terms of truth and gender that engages with a number of critical readings that both challenge and exemplify this emphasis on narrative structure over, and as, the content of story.

The book closes with an epilogue that returns to the questions with which it began, asking once again, 'who is Marlow?' in order to offer a final consideration of his function within Conrad's texts. Figuring Marlow in terms of the liminality that allows him to occupy an ever-shifting position within, and across, the four texts affords the possibility of approaching narrative, for which he might be said to stand, in the same way. Thus an informational sense of literature, which might attempt to somehow fix the meaning of a text, is challenged by a more dynamic sense of narrative as a continuing process of exchange.

The study of the Marlow texts

There are a number of practical considerations that a narratological study of the Marlow texts must take into account. First, there is a question of terminology. Of the four texts 'Youth' and *Heart of Darkness* are, properly speaking, novellas. In order to avoid unnecessary complication the four texts, when discussed together, are referred to as 'the Marlow texts'. The second difficulty is that of quoting from these texts, a difficulty that arises from the many levels of narrative and specifically from the fact that the bulk of each of the texts is presented as the narrative of an unnamed, first, narrator-character who, more often than not, is directly quoting Marlow, who, in turn, also makes extensive use of quotation. Purely for practical reasons I have, unless otherwise noted, omitted the quotation marks that signify the first narrator's reproduction of Marlow's storytelling. A final minor issue regards the publication dates of the four texts which were all serialised for journal or newspaper publication before being published in book form, and to complicate matters further the dates of their British publication differ from those of their American publication. In an attempt at standardisation, dates quoted will, unless otherwise stated, refer to the date of their first publication.

Finally, it is necessary to note some of the omissions from my discussion. As a result of the scope of my project, the analysis I offer of the individual Marlow novels is far from exhaustive. In attempting to trace a philosophically rigorous narratology, I have approached the individual texts with specific concerns in mind in order to develop the central thread of my argument. This has necessarily meant that I have been unable to consider the whole range of issues that surround Conrad's fictions; hence the notable omissions of postcolonial and gender theory, except in instances where such approaches are germane to my overall argument. More significant, perhaps, are those texts that, for reasons of brevity, I do not mention at all. There are numerous literary theorists and philosophers whose work would have enriched my argument; two significant figures that have been omitted are Emmanuel Levinas whose writings on the philosophy of death could have been usefully employed in my reading of Heidegger, and Jacques Lacan whose discussions of subjectivity, specifically in relation to his 'symbolic order', seem a natural continuation of my narrative theory.

Notes

1   Anthony Fothergill, *Heart of Darkness* (Milton Keynes: Open University Press, 1989), p. 6.
2   Martin Heidegger, *Being and Time*, trans. J. Macquarrie and E. Robinson (Oxford: Blackwell, 1962).
3   Jacques Derrida, *Aporias*, trans. Thomas Dutoit (Stanford, CA: Stanford University Press, 1993).

Introduction: Marlow, realism, hermeneutics

To a teacher of languages there comes a time when the world is but a place of many words and man appears a mere talking animal not much more wonderful than a parrot. (Joseph Conrad, *Under Western Eyes*)

Marlow, realism, hermeneutics

Charlie Marlow, whose forename is given on only two occasions, is the most celebrated of Conrad's narrator-characters. Variously described as 'not in the least typical', 'the average pilgrim', a 'wanderer', and 'a Buddha preaching in European clothes', Marlow is the voice behind 'Youth' (1898), *Heart of Darkness* (1899), *Lord Jim* (1900) and *Chance* (1912).[1] All four stories, whose texts are supposedly faithful reproductions of his words, are transcribed by an unnamed and largely unobtrusive narrator, or narrators, of whom we learn little beyond the fact that he has, like Marlow, some connection to the sea and, we are invited to believe, quite remarkable powers of recall. Of Marlow himself we learn far more: over the course of the four books he appears as both a narrator and as a character and it is the duality of this role that makes it possible to discuss him both in relation to the specifics of the texts in which he appears and in terms of a broader narratological investigation into the connection between narrative and literary truth.

Marlow made his first appearance in *Blackwood's Edinburgh Magazine* where 'Youth' was first published in September 1898 alongside articles on, among other things, 'The Spaniard at Home', 'Louise-Ulrique, Queen of Sweden', and 'The Great Elk of Grönvand'.[2] Described by Jocelyn Baines as 'a conservative, traditionalist magazine that liked to give its readers good fare in masculine storytelling,' *Blackwood's* had published many of the great Victorian novelists, including George Eliot, Margaret Oliphant, James Hogg and Anthony Trollope.[3] Conrad would join this illustrious list of names when he became a regular contributor after the success of 'Youth', which David Meldrum, *Blackwood's* literary editor, described as 'the most notable book we have published since George Eliot'.[4] Marlow continued to feature in *Blackwood's* which serialised both *Heart of Darkness*, the first instalment of which appeared as 'The Heart of Darkness' in its thousandth issue in February 1899, and *Lord Jim* which ran in instalments from October 1899 until November 1900. There is also evidence to suggest that Conrad intended a fourth short story featuring Marlow for *Blackwood's*, presumably an embryonic version of what would become *Chance*. A letter to Edward Garnett written in late May/early June 1898 mentions plans for 'Dynamite', a 5,000 word story to be published alongside 'Lord Jim' (at that point envisaged at around 20,000 words) and 'Youth'. In February of the following year Conrad would again make reference to what is again very likely an early version of *Chance*, this time as 'the one about a Captains wife' [sic], in a letter to Meldrum.[5] However, by the time *Chance* came to be serialized in 1912, Conrad's close professional relationship with *Blackwood's* had come to an end: his '*Blackwood* period' which began with 'Karain: A Memory' in November 1897 concluded with the publication of *The End of the Tether* in December 1902, and Marlow's final tale would be first serialised in the *New York Herald* (January-June 1912) before being published in England by Methuen in 1913.[6]

The importance of *Blackwood's* for Conrad's literary development should not be underestimated. The magazine not only provided Conrad with a much needed-sense of financial stability, it also provided him with a clear sense of his readership – recognising just this, he'd comment in a letter to James Pinker, his long-term literary agent, 'One was in decent company there [*Blackwood's*] and had a good sort of public'.[7] This heightened awareness of his English readership and Marlow's appearance in the magazine has prompted productive discussion of Conrad's negotiation of his own identity in terms of his adopted Englishness. Marlow is, argues John Batchelor, 'the Englishman that Conrad would have liked to have been' and, whether this is accepted or not, there is a clear sense that the dramatisation of his storytelling locates him, and his story, in relation to his new-found audience.[8] It was presumably with an eye to his new audience that 'Youth', the first of Conrad's stories to be written specifically for *Blackwood's*, begins 'This could have occurred nowhere but in England' before going on to indicate those men that hear Marlow's tale: the 'Director of companies', the Lawyer, 'a fine crusted Tory, High Churchman, the best of old fellows', and the narrator himself.[9] As Allan Simmons has noted, by entering into this dialogic relation with these men, an imagined cross-section of *Blackwood's* English readership, Marlow exemplifies Conrad's own attempts to inscribe himself into Englishness.[10] The complexities of his relation to his new homeland and its language were felt keenly by Conrad, who complained to his compatriot Marguerite Poradowska in 1907, 'English is still for me a foreign language' and who was so sensitive to criticism that emphasized his Polish roots that he remarked, in response to reviews of *The Secret Agent*, 'I've been so cried up of late as a sort of freak, an amazing bloody foreigner writing in English'.[11] Conrad's relation to English literature and language, so readily apparent in the Marlow texts, has met with mixed response: the *Times Literary Supplement* would describe him as 'an alien of genius' in 1907 and his obituary there, penned by Virginia Woolf seventeen years later, would continue to insist on his foreignness, lamenting his death as the departure of one of England's 'guests', whilst F. R. Leavis, placing Conrad as the successor to Austen, Eliot and James in the 'great tradition' of the English novel, nonetheless stresses 'his foreignness'.[12] This increased consciousness of the presence of his audience, exacerbated by Conrad's apparent desire to write himself into the English literary tradition, had a significant effect on the structuring of the Marlow texts.

The publishing history of the Marlow texts is significant not only for the implications of the place of original publication, which suggest a number of productive avenues of research, but also, rather more obviously, for the dates of their publication which locates them, with the exception of *Chance*, both as examples of late-Victorian fiction and, given their appearance at the turn of the century, as immediate predecessors to twentieth-century modernism. John Lyon summarises the sense of an emerging modernism in Conrad's fiction concisely in the introduction to his edition of *Youth/Heart of Darkness/The End of the Tether*:

> *Heart of Darkness* has come to stand as preface to an entire century . . . this work has a convoluted form and self-conscious style which are predictive of the array of difficult styles and forms which dominate the succeeding century. As 'an unreadable report', *Heart of Darkness* bears witness to what the influential German critic Walter Benjamin saw, earlier in the century, as a primary symptom of modernity – a decline in the communicability of experience.[13]

It is unsurprising that this position has become a standard approach to Conrad's work, and *Heart of Darkness* in particular. Straddling the nineteenth and twentieth centuries the Marlow texts are conveniently placed as markers of a shifting literary environment and, more significantly, Conrad's literary 'impressionism' and the often complex structural forms of his texts would appear to support claims that seek to figure him as an early modernist writer.[14] However, the case should not be overstated. Conrad's work is, as Lyon says, a 'preface' to modernism.

Similarly, Fredric Jameson sees in Conrad's work 'the *emergence* . . . of what will be contemporary modernism' [my emphasis] and not modernism itself, recognising signs of what was to come but stopping short of including Conrad in the modernist canon.[15] It is, in fact, equally possible to argue for Conrad's status as a novelist in the Victorian tradition, as Ian Watt does in *Conrad in the Nineteenth Century* – a convincing contextualising account that figures Conrad not as 'incidentally, loosely situated in the nineteenth century' but rather as 'exactly *of* that time.'[16] The framed nature of the Marlow tales, which can be used to demonstrate a modernist emphasis on questions of identity and the subjective nature of experience, provides an equally viable link to Conrad's Victorian forbears – indeed the lineage of the structure is easily traced from *The Arabian Nights*, Chaucer's *Canterbury Tales* and Shakespeare's *The Taming of the Shrew*, through Tennyson and Browning to Emily Brontë's *Wuthering Heights*. Similarly, George Levine, in *The Realistic Imagination*, argues that Conrad, along with Gissing, Hardy and James, 'rejected the "experimental novel" and . . . wrote within the English tradition and sought to reconcile form and art with an appeal both to truth and to [his] audience' whilst Watt argues that, 'both Conrad and Freud defend a practical social ethic based on their fairly similar reformulations of the Victorian trinity of work, duty, and restraint.'[17] My reason for invoking Conrad's position at this fault-line between Victorian realism and modernist fiction is not to argue for his inclusion in either position (it is undeniable that both positions have their merits), nor is it to suggest modernism's points of divergence from the literature that preceded it, but rather to suggest a certain continuity of concern between the two.[18] Despite their different formal properties, both Victorian realism and modernist experimentation demonstrate a concern with the relation to, and depiction of, what, for want of a better term, I shall call 'reality'.

For Victorian writers this concern manifests itself most clearly in the realist project: the artistic attempt to render the real world as faithfully as possible, while for modernist writers this takes on the guise of a more self-conscious literary endeavour to discover a form suitable to the realities of the early twentieth century. This commonality of aim provides a connection between Victorian and modernist literature that allows Levine to argue for 'a direct historical continuum between the realists who struggled to make narrative meaningful and modern critics who define themselves by virtue of their separation from realism and even from narrativity itself.'[19] This similarity can be seen, despite their clear points of difference, in the critical work of two key figures of Victorianism and modernism: George Eliot and Virginia Woolf. Eliot offers something approximating a manifesto of literary realism in her famous comments on John Ruskin, another nineteenth-century thinker and writer:

> The truth of infinite value that he teaches is *realism* – the doctrine that all truth and beauty are to be attained by a humble and faithful study of nature, and not by substituting vague forms, bred by imagination on the mists of feeling, in place of definite substantial reality.[20]

According to Eliot, 'all truth and beauty are to be attained by a humble and faithful study of nature': the 'faithfulness' of this study might be read as its being true to nature – in other words realistic. Just as significant is the word 'humble' – which precludes the subjectivity of the author to suggest a kind of fiction that moves away from being the very individualistic vision that might be associated with Romanticism. Instead this 'humble', which could be read as 'discreet' or 'objective', author is intended to present what Eliot describes as a 'definite substantial reality'. This definition of realism can usefully be read alongside Woolf's essay 'Modern Fiction' which evinces a determination to define modern fiction as a clear epistemological break with the literature of its predecessors that is typical of the theorising of modernism that appears in the critical work of its practitioners. Woolf hazards the opinion that 'at this moment the form of fiction most in vogue more often misses than secures the thing we seek. Whether we call it life or spirit, truth or reality, this, the essential thing, has moved off, or on, and refuses to be contained any longer in such ill-fitting vestments as we provide.'[21] For a theory of modernism insistent on the dualism of the then and the now, Eliot's 'humble and faithful study' becomes the 'ill-fitting vestments' of an attempt to express 'truth or reality' of the early twentieth century. Michael H. Levenson, arguing against such a confidently dualistic definition of modernism quotes Eliot's *Middlemarch* in which she writes of the 'suppressed transitions which unite all contrasts': the point of 'transition' is not necessarily a stylistic development but could equally be located in a common relation between literature (both Victorian and modern) and the elusive 'truth' of which both Eliot and Woolf write.[22] In effect, according to Woolf, it is the shifting nature of this truth that prompts developments in literary form. With this in mind, Woolf's claim that 'the essential thing, has moved off, or on' would support Randall Stevenson's cautious claim that 'if contemporary novelists "changed everything" in their work, as Thomas Hardy suggests, it would be reasonable to suppose that this was simply because they perceived everything around them as changed'.[23] This suggestion would certainly make sense of Conrad's stylistic innovations; as Watt remarks, 'between Conrad's arrival in England in 1878, and the writing of *Heart of Darkness* twenty years later, it had become increasingly evident that the Victorian world order was collapsing.'[24]

Conrad, sometime-Victorian sometime-modernist, is, perhaps, better approached in terms of the connection between literature and truth that appears in both his fiction and his critical writing. The 1897 'Preface' to *The Nigger of the 'Narcissus'*, described by Watt as 'the most reliable, and the most voluntary, single statement of Conrad's general approach to writing', is helpful in this respect.[25] There art is defined as,

> a single-minded attempt to render the highest kind of justice to the visible universe, by bringing to light the truth, manifold and one, underlying its every aspect. It is an attempt to find in its forms, in its colours, in its light, in its shadows, in the aspects of matter and in the facts of life what of each is fundamental, what is enduring and essential – their one illuminating and convincing quality – the very truth of their existence.[26]

Conrad makes a similar claim in his 1920 'Author's Note' to *Within The Tides* where he identifies his literary aims as the 'conscientious rendering of truth in thought and fact'.[27] In Conrad's work, and the Marlow novels are exemplary in this case, 'the rendering of truth' is not only a question of representation but also of the transmission of meaning: 'My task which I am trying to achieve is, by the power of the written word to make you hear, to make you feel – it is, before all, to make you *see*. That – and no more, and it is everything.'[28] Readings of this oft-quoted passage from the 'Preface' to *The Nigger of the 'Narcissus'* tend to focus on Conrad's emphasis on seeing, on his 'impressionism'. Taking a different approach to the same material, this study instead pays attention to the emphasis Conrad places on the role of the 'written word' in a process of transmission that negotiates the connection between the author/narrator and the reader.

There is a clear sense in Conrad's writing, seen famously by J. Hillis Miller as nihilism, of the difficulty, if not the impossibility, of communication. In Miller's view, 'The special place of Joseph Conrad in English literature lies in the fact that in him the nihilism covertly dominant in modern culture is brought to the surface and shown for what it is.'[29] Whether or not this charge of nihilism is accepted, the possibility of communication, both spoken and written, is a constant feature of Conrad's major work. Anthony Fothergill, attributing this in part to Conrad's historical position, sees the author,

> Standing at a historical crux between a moment of narration confident in its audience's shared assumptions and one cut off from it and uncertain of (if not deeply sceptical about) the very existence of such shared truths, Conrad would have been centrally preoccupied with how a story could be told and how, even whether, it could be heard.[30]

It is easy to find support for such a position in Conrad's work: as Marlow famously says in *Heart of Darkness*, in an important passage to which I shall return:

'It seems to me I am trying to tell you a dream – making a vain attempt,
because no relation of a dream can convey the dream-sensation, that
commingling of absurdity, surprise, and bewilderment in a tremor of
struggling revolt, that notion of being captured by the incredible which is
the very essence of dreams . . . .
    He was silent for a while.
    'No, it is impossible; it is impossible to convey the life-sensation of any
given epoch of one's existence – that which makes its truth, its meaning – its
subtle and penetrating essence. It is impossible. We live, as we dream – alone
. . . .'[31]

Marlow's words echo Conrad's recognition that 'written words can
only form a sort of translation' and that he must contend with 'the
commonplace surface of words: of the old, old words, worn thin, defaced
by ages of careless usage.'[32] In other words, he must necessarily employ
a language that offers no direct connection to the 'real', words whose
'careless' and repeated 'usage' implies a failure to connect with the reality
that they attempt to describe. This is the problem that is at the heart
of the realist project: realism, writes Levine, 'implies an attempt to use
language to get beyond language, to discover some non-verbal truth out
there.'[33] In this definition of realism, which resonates with Conrad's
description of words as a 'translation', there appears a kind of circularity
of argument, an impasse in the literary endeavour. This impasse, if impasse
it is, becomes a question of narrative hermeneutics that is enacted in
Conrad's deployment of Marlow in 'Youth', *Heart of Darkness*, *Lord
Jim* and *Chance*, questioning, through a structure that at all points
interrogates its own possibility of meaningful transmission, the connection
between language and truth. This approach to the Marlow texts, which I
am describing as a narrative hermeneutics, picks up on Allon White's
suggestion that Conrad's writing, which 'defies the reader to remain at the
literal level of story', 'solicits a hermeneutic approach' in its recognition
that those narratives themselves are concerned with interpretation.[34]
Whilst hermeneutics was traditionally concerned with the interpretation of (initially biblical) texts, Martin Heidegger's phenomenological
hermeneutics in *Being and Time* shifted this focus from textual analysis
to questions of Being, a move that influenced Paul Ricoeur whose
hermeneutics refigures 'text' as the more dynamic, and temporally inflected,
'narrative'. Narratives thus become the site of a dialogue between discourse
and interpretation: 'wherever a man dreams or raves, another man arises
to give interpretation; what was already discourse, even if it was incoherent, is brought into coherent discourse by hermeneutics.'[35] Envisaged
in such a way Marlow becomes a figure who enacts both sides of this
dialogue, delivering and interpreting the stories in which he appears.

From realism to hermeneutics: Marlow and Hermes

> I was on the point of interrupting Marlow when he stopped of himself, his eyes fixed on vacancy, or – perhaps – (I wouldn't be too hard on him) on a vision. He has the habit, or, say, the fault, of defective mantelpiece clocks, of suddenly stopping in the very fullness of the tick. If you have ever lived with a clock afflicted with that perversity, you know how vexing it is – such a stoppage. I was vexed with Marlow.[36]

Marlow is, according to this outburst, 'faulty', 'defective', 'afflicted', 'perverse' and, above all, 'vexing'. It is this aspect of the loquacious ex-mariner that marks him as a site at which to consider the connection between literary narrative and truth: Marlow may have a 'propensity to spin yarns' but their transmission and reception, always dramatised, is not straightforward.[37] Like the unnamed-narrator of *Chance*, readers have found Marlow's stoppages equally vexing: a young Cedric Watts found them 'infuriating', Edward Garnett described Marlow as 'a tiresome, garrulous, philosophising bore', and W. L. Courtney, in his *Daily Telegraph* review of *Lord Jim*, complained that 'the constant wandering from the point, [and] the recurrent introductions of incidents which do not affect the main issue, are distinctly weakening to the general end and aim of the book'.[38] Readings such as these reveal as much about the demands placed on narrative as they do about the personality of Marlow. Regarding such stoppages as defective, as 'weakening' a book's 'end and aim', suggests a theory of narrative that is premised by the expectation of ending and that with that ending will come meaning. To continue with Conrad's metaphor, this understanding of narrative insists that the 'fullness of the tick' be followed by an equally resounding 'tock' of narrative closure. The apparent perversity of the disruption of narrative and the 'vacancy' that arises from the refusal, or impossibility, of pronouncing the final 'tock' is the point from which this discussion really begins.[39]

   Marlow's narrator would certainly find support in narrative theory for his expectation that narrative should impose meaning on its material. The notion of narrative as a structuring activity can be traced back to Aristotle's discussion of tragedy in his *Poetics* in which plot, 'the most important thing of all', is described as 'the organization of events' by which tragedy finds its form as 'a complete, i.e. whole, action, possessing a certain magnitude'.[40] As Ricoeur writes, for Aristotle *muthos* (variously translated as plotting or narrative) is 'the organization of the events [that] first emphasizes concordance'.[41] 'Wholeness', the appropriate deployment of beginning, middle and end, is key to Aristotle's analysis and has become a central tenet of narratology: Paul Cobley summarises, 'nearly all analysis of narrative has been devoted to the way that narrative forecloses reality.'[42] This notion of foreclosure, which implies a prior expectation (fore) of ending (closure) as well as the delimiting, and necessarily limiting, of reality is what makes possible a narrative desire that is premised on the awareness of ending. Thus Roland Barthes's 'hermeneutic code', 'the various (formal) terms by which an enigma can be distinguished, suggested, formulated, held in suspense, *and finally disclosed*' [my emphasis], is at once 'enigma' and 'solution'.[43] Narrative becomes a more explicitly hermeneutic act in the work of Peter Brooks who suggests that plots are 'a viable and a necessary way of organizing and interpreting the world', recalling Conrad's recognition that narrative is a form of 'translating' experience into transmissible form, and that in working through plots both writers and readers engage in an 'irreducible act of understanding how human life acquires meaning'.[44] This approach to narrative, which appears to hinge on the demand that narratives generate coherent meaning, will be explored and questioned in relation to Conrad's fiction in the chapters that follow.

A useful approach to the 'stoppages' that characterise Marlow's narratives is found in the narrative hermeneutics of Paul Ricoeur and Frank Kermode. Ricoeur, in his hugely-influential *Time and Narrative*, defines narrative as 'the organization of the events [that] first emphasizes concordance.'[45] Kermode argues a similar position, offering a clear account of the vexing nature of narrative 'stoppages' in *The Sense of an Ending* where, using the same metaphor as Conrad's narrator, the clock's 'tick-tock' is used to great effect as a model of narrative. It is, he argues, essential to 'maintain within that interval between *tick* a lively expectation of *tock*, and a sense that however remote *tock* may be, all that happens happens as if *tock* were certainly following.'[46] For Kermode, as for the narrator of *Chance*, 'Tock' is analogous with the sense of an ending that makes narrative meaningful.

In making this argument for the organizational aspect of narrative both Kermode and Ricoeur draw on the Aristotelian idea of '*emplotment*' which Ricoeur describes as 'an eminently verbal experience where concordance mends discordance', or more plainly as 'the organizing of events'.[47] That this is 'eminently verbal' is significant, for both Ricoeur and Kermode the structuring of human experience becomes possible through the action of narrative. Ricoeur and Kermode, in effect, connect narrative, which figures both writing and reading as structuring activities, with a way of interpreting, or in Kermode's terms 'making sense of', the world. Kermode suggests such a reading of both literary narrative and literary criticism, beginning his book with the claim that 'It is not expected of critics as it is of poets that they should help us make sense of our lives; they are bound only to attempt the lesser feat of making sense of the ways we try to make sense of our lives'.[48] In other words, *The Sense of an Ending* is premised on the belief that narrative fulfils a hermeneutic function and that the study of literature is necessarily a hermeneutic activity. Similarly, Ricoeur concludes that 'life needs to be understood through literature . . . because "life in the raw" is beyond our reach.'[49] Essentially, for both Kermode and Ricoeur, hermeneutics is a theory of narrative; moving from a consideration of specific literary/historical texts to a position that regards our experience of the world itself in terms of narratives. This is not to say that textual narrative is somehow identical to life – Ricoeur is explicit about this: 'the ideas of beginning, middle, and end are not taken from experience. They are not features of some real action but the effects of the ordering of the poem' – rather the world might be said to be comprehended through narrative activity in that human existence is expressed through discourse, a discourse through and in which individuals must situate themselves.[50] In Ricoeur's words, human 'action is already symbolically mediated; literature, in the largest sense of the word, including history as well as fiction, tends to reinforce a process of symbolization already at work.'[51] In this description there is already a hint of the hermeneutic circle that characterises Ricoeur's work: a circularity that arises from the same linguistic source that leads realism, as it is defined by Levine, to the apparently aporetic position in which the extra-linguistic must be rendered in a language that it precedes. As Heidegger tells us, hermeneutics, 'is that exposition which brings tidings because it can listen to a message. Such exposition becomes an interpretation of what has been said earlier.'[52] The circularity in which 'exposition becomes an interpretation' is a central feature of the hermeneutics which for Ricoeur 'proceeds from a prior understanding of the very thing that it tries to understand by interpreting it.'[53] Ricoeur argues that this is a productive circle, which might be better imagined as a spiral, through which human beings are able to gain a better understanding of their existence. Dermot Moran summarises this productive circle well:

> In order to pose an intelligent question, something about the nature of the subject matter of the question must already be understood . . . But the answers to the questions force us to revise the presuppositions with which we began. Thus there is a 'circle', but not a vicious circle.[54]

Conceived in this way narrative is dynamic, it both structures discourse and, by entering into a dialogue that reflects on its own processes, makes the presuppositions from which it proceeds transparent.

It is this idea that is explored in what follows through a consideration of Conrad's Marlow novels which constantly reflect on their own status as narratives and, in doing so, on the connection between the process of transmission and the truths that they attempt to convey. Framed as he is as both character and narrator, as a participant in as well as a producer and reader of his own narratives, Marlow can be readily figured in terms of hermeneutics. Just as, in *On the Way to Language*, Heidegger makes the 'playful' connection between hermeneutics and Hermes, the herald of the Olympian gods, Marlow might be connected with Hermes in the sense that he too is both a source and an interpreter of narrative.[55] The identity and function of Conrad's sailor, like that of the ancient Greek god, is tied up with his relation to the texts that he delivers – he exists neither wholly 'inside' nor 'outside' them but rather, occupying both positions simultaneously, is himself delivered by the texts. Marlow must, like Hermes, constantly renegotiate his position. As Richard E. Palmer writes, Hermes 'is the messenger between Zeus and mortals, also between Zeus and the underworld and between the underworld and mortals. Hermes crosses these ontological thresholds with ease ... Liminality or marginality is his very essence.'[56] Marlow is a similarly liminal figure, repeatedly crossing the thresholds between character and narrator, deliverer and interpreter of narrative in each of the texts in which he appears. It is in this sense that he will be considered in the discussion of 'Youth' – his is a liminality that reflects, and explores, the relation between exposition and interpretation, or, to use the terms that will be employed in the next chapter, 'story' and 'narration'. With this in mind, the Marlow texts might be described, in the words of Barthes, as 'broken texts'; texts that not only invite, but already include, their own commentary. A commentary that,

> based on the affirmation of the plural, cannot therefore work with 'respect' to the text; the tutor text will ceaselessly be broken, interrupted without any regard for its natural divisions ... the work of the commentary, once it is separated from any ideology of totality, consists precisely in *manhandling* the text, *interrupting* it.[57]

According to such a reading Conrad's Marlow texts come to reflect on the process of refiguration, to use Ricoeur's terminology, itself an interruption of a narrative that purports to function because of its own relation to its *pre*figured (in other words already existing) status; a status that appears most clearly in its relation to its own, 'sense making', ending. It is this constant awareness of its own interpretative function, be it vexing or otherwise, that guarantees the productivity of narrative's hermeneutic circle.

Notes

1   Joseph Conrad, *Youth, Heart of Darkness, The End of the Tether* (London:
    J. M. Dent and Sons Ltd, 1946), p. 58; Joseph Conrad, *Lord Jim* (London:
    J. M. Dent and Sons Ltd, 1946), p. 34; Conrad, *Youth, Heart of Darkness,
    The End of the Tether*, pp. 48, 50.

2   *Blackwood's Edinburgh Magazine*, vol. 164, no. 995 (Sept 1898) (Edinburgh
    & London). In addition to 'Youth' this volume contained: 'The Company and
    the Individual', W. L. Watson; 'The Spaniard at Home', Hannah Lynch; 'On
    Friendships', Ida A. Taylor; 'An Orkney Foray', J. Storer Clouston; 'Louise-
    Ulrique, Queen of Sweden', Felicia M. F. Skene; 'A Good Turn', Hilda C.
    Gregg; 'The Great Elk of Grönvand', Percy Stephens; 'A Pilgrimage to La
    Verna', H. D. Rawnsley; 'The End of an Old Song: Confessions of a Cuban
    Governor', David Hannay; and 'The Looker On' (No. VII), Frederick
    Greenwood.

3   Jocelyn Baines, *Joseph Conrad: A Critical Biography* (London: Wiedenfeld,
    1993), p. 281.

4   William Blackburn (ed.), *Joseph Conrad: Letters to William Blackwood and
    David S. Meldrum* (Durham, NC: Duke University Press, 1958), p. 172.

5   Frederick R. Karl and Laurence Davies (eds), *The Collected Letters of Joseph
    Conrad, Volume Two 1898–1902* (Cambridge: Cambridge University Press,
    1986), pp. 62, 169.

6   Despite this move to other publications, *Blackwood's* would publish 'Her
    Captivity' (September 1905), which would be collected as 'In Captivity' in
    The Mirror of the Sea (1906), and 'Initiation' (January 1906).

7   Karl and Davies (eds), *The Collected Letters of Joseph Conrad, Volume Two
    1898–1902*, p. 401; Frederick R. Karl and Laurence Davies (eds), *The
    Collected Letters of Joseph Conrad, Volume Four 1908–1911* (Cambridge:
    Cambridge University Press, 1990), p. 506.

8   John Batchelor, *The Life of Joseph Conrad: A Critical Biography* (Oxford:
    Blackwell, 1994), p. 110.

9   Conrad, *Youth, Heart of Darkness, The End of the Tether*, p. 3.

10 Allan H. Simmons, 'The Art of Englishness: Identity and Representation in
    Conrad's Early Career', *The Conradian*, 29:1 (Spring 2004), pp. 1–26.

11 Frederick R. Karl and Laurence Davies (eds), *The Collected Letters of Joseph
    Conrad, Volume Three 1903–1907* (Cambridge: Cambridge University Press,
    1988), p. 488.

12 Simmons, 'The Art of Englishness: Identity and Representation in Conrad's
    Early Career', pp. 19, 2; F. R Leavis, *The Great Tradition: George Eliot,
    Henry James, Joseph Conrad* (London: Chatto & Windus, 1962), p. 17.

13 John Lyon, 'Introduction' to Conrad, *Youth/Heart of Darkness/The End of
    the Tether*, ed. John Lyon (London: Penguin, 1995) pp. vii-viii.

14 Kenneth Graham offers an overview of Conrad's relation to modernism in
    'Conrad and Modernism', in J. H. Stape (ed.), *The Cambridge Companion
    to Joseph Conrad* (Cambridge: Cambridge University Press, 1996), pp.
    203–22. See also his chapter on Conrad in his *Indirections of the Novel:*

James, Conrad, and Forster (Cambridge: Cambridge University Press, 1988), pp. 93–153, Randall Stevenson's *Modernist Fiction: An Introduction* (London: Prentice Hall, 1998), and Allon White's *The Uses of Obscurity: The Fiction of Early Modernism* (London: Routledge & Kegan Paul, 1981). For a fuller discussion of Conrad's relation to impressionism see: Ian Watt, *Conrad in the Nineteenth Century* (London: Chatto and Windus, 1980), pp.169–80; Bruce Johnson, 'Conrad's Impressionism and Watt's "Delayed Decoding"', in Ross C. Murfin (ed.), *Conrad Revisited: Essays for the Eighties* (Alabama: Alabama University Press, 1985), pp. 51–70.

15 Fredric Jameson, *The Political Unconscious: Narrative as a Socially Symbolic Act* (London: Methuen, 1981), p. 206.

16 Robert L. Caserio, 'Joseph Conrad, Dickensian Novelist of the Nineteenth Century: A Dissent from Ian Watt', *Nineteenth Century Fiction*, vol. 36, no. 3 (Dec 1981), pp. 337–47, p. 337.

17 George Levine, *The Realistic Imagination: English Fiction from Frankenstein to Lady Chatterley* (Chicago and London: University of Chicago Press, 1981), p. 6; Watt, *Conrad in the Nineteenth Century*, p. 167.

18 For a detailed discussion of the emergence of literary modernism and its relation to earlier forms of literature see Michael H. Levenson's *A Genealogy of Modernism: A Study of English Literary Doctrine 1908–1922* (Cambridge: Cambridge University Press, 1984), which offers a detailed and productive analysis of Conrad's relation to modernism through a reading of *The Nigger of the 'Narcissus'*.

19 Levine, *The Realistic Imagination*, p. 4.

20 George Eliot, 'Art and Belles Lettres: Review of *Modern Painters* III', *Westminster Review*, April 1856. Quoted in John Rignall (ed.), *Oxford Reader's Companion to George Eliot* (Oxford: Oxford University Press, 2000), p. 324.

21 Virginia Woolf, *The Common Reader* (London: Hogarth Press, 1975), p. 188.

22 Levenson, *A Genealogy of Modernism*, p. ix

23 Stevenson, *Modernist Fiction*, pp. 8–9.

24 Watt, *Conrad in the Nineteenth Century*, p. 161.

25 Ian Watt, 'Conrad's Preface to *The Nigger of the "Narcissus"*', *Novel*, Vol. 7, No. 2 (Winter 1974), pp. 101–15, p. 103.

26 Joseph Conrad, *The Nigger of the 'Narcissus'* (London: J. M. Dent and Sons Ltd, 1950), p. vii.

27 Joseph Conrad, *The Shadow-Line and Within the Tides* (London: J. M. Dent and Sons Ltd, 1950), p. vi.

28 Conrad, *The Nigger of the 'Narcissus'*, p. x.

29 J. Hillis Miller, *Poets of Reality: Six Twentieth Century Writers* (Cambridge, MA: The Belknap Press of Harvard University Press, 1966), p. 5.

30 Anthony Fothergill, *Heart of Darkness* (Milton Keynes: Open University Press, 1989), p. 114.

31 Conrad, *Youth, Heart of Darkness, The End of the Tether*, p. 82.

32   Conrad, *The Shadow-Line and Within the Tides*, p. viii; Conrad, *The Nigger of the 'Narcissus'*, p. ix.

33   Levine, *The Realistic Imagination*, p. 6.

34   White, *The Uses of Obscurity*, p. 108.

35   Paul Ricoeur, *The Symbolism of Evil*, trans. Emerson Buchanan (Boston: Beacon Press, 1969), p. 350.

36   Joseph Conrad, *Chance: A Tale in Two Parts* (London: J. M. Dent and Sons Ltd, 1949), p. 283.

37   Conrad, *Youth, Heart of Darkness, The End of the Tether*, p. 48.

38   Cedric Watts, 'Introduction' to Conrad, *Lord Jim*, ed. Robert Hampson (London: Penguin, 1989), p. 11; Norman Sherry (ed.), *Conrad: The Critical Heritage* (London: Routledge & Kegan Paul, 1973), pp. 118, 114–15.

39   Anthony Fothergill notes the apparent paradox that is implied by critical responses to *Heart of Darkness*: 'There is a paradox here. The readerly desire to arrest the play of multiple meanings by settling on a "closed" one characteristically takes as its object works whose "classic" quality lies precisely in their demonstrable capacity to engender a variety of readings in the historical course of their reception. *Heart of Darkness* is not alone in being a work which powerfully exhibits multivalency of meaning. Is it possible that it has become a seminal work in the twentieth century precisely because of this paradox? It seems to answer the felt need for works both to exemplify a broader cultural preoccupation with the relativity of "truth", with scepticism, and ambiguity, yet to entice with the dangled hope of an end to all that.' Anthony Fothergill, *Heart of Darkness* (Milton Keynes: Open University Press, 1989), p. 4.

40   Aristotle, *Poetics*, trans. Malcolm Heath (London: Penguin, 1996), pp. 11, 13.

41   Paul Ricoeur, *Time and Narrative: Volume One*, trans. Kathleen McLaughlin and David Pallauer (Chicago: Chicago University Press, 1984), pp. 36, 38.

42   Paul Cobley, *Narrative* (London: Routledge, 2001), p. 216.

43   Roland Barthes, *S/Z*, trans Richard Miller (Oxford: Blackwell, 1990), pp. 19, 17.

44   Peter Brooks, *Reading for the Plot: Design and Intention in Narrative* (Oxford: Clarendon, 1984), p. xii.

45   Ricoeur, *Time and Narrative: Volume One*, p. 38.

46   Frank Kermode, *The Sense of an Ending: Studies in the Theory of Fiction, With a New Epilogue* (Oxford: Oxford University Press, 2000), p. 46.

47   Ricoeur, *Time and Narrative: Volume One*, pp. 31, 34.

48   Kermode, *The Sense of an Ending*, p. 3.

49   David Wood (ed.), *On Paul Ricoeur: Narrative and Interpretation* (London: Routledge, 1991), pp. 181–2.

50   Ricoeur, *Time and Narrative: Volume One*, p. 38–9.

51   Wood, *On Paul Ricoeur*, p. 182.

52   Martin Heidegger, *On The Way to Language*, trans. Peter D. Hertz (New York: Harper & Row, 1971), p. 29.

53 Ricoeur, *The Symbolism of Evil*, p. 352.
54 Dermot Moran, *Introduction to Phenomenology* (London: Routledge, 2000) pp. 276–7.
55 Heidegger, *On The Way to Language*, p. 29.
56 Richard E. Palmer, 'The Liminality of Hermes and the Meaning of Hermeneutics', *MacMurray College Homepage* <http://www.mac.edu/faculty/richardpalmer/liminality.html> (2001) [Accessed 23 April 2006]
57 Barthes, *S/Z*, p. 15.

1

Marlow: 'Youth' and the oral tradition

For a long time already he, sitting apart, had been no more to us than a voice. (Joseph Conrad, *Heart of Darkness*)

Marlow: character or narrator?

The description of Marlow given in the *Oxford Reader's Companion to Conrad*, distilling, as it does, decades of critical discussion, provides a useful place from which to begin a study of his role, its authors tell us:

> He has often been seen as Conrad's autobiographical alter ego, since his narratives are based on Conrad's own experiences in the ill-fated *Palestine* ('Youth') or in the Congo ('Heart of Darkness'). At the same time, Conrad and Marlow differ fundamentally in their ethnic background (Marlow is an Englishman, without Slavic origins) and their marital status (Marlow never marries, and becomes increasingly misogynist).[1]

Contained in this short passage are two ideas that have been central to critical approaches to Marlow. The first is the suggestion of a biographical link between Conrad and his fictional creation. The second is the implicit understanding that Marlow is a fictional character (with an ethnic background, a marital status, and an *increasingly* misogynist outlook that implies a mappable psychology) in addition to being a narrator (it is 'his narrative'). Whilst it is the second of these approaches that will be adopted here, the biographical reading of Marlow indicates the direction that this narratological approach to Marlow will take. The *Oxford Reader's Companion to Conrad* connects Conrad and his character through near identical experiences (aboard the *Palestine* and in the Congo), but for the purposes of this study, the point of interest in this suggestion of autobiography lies not in the correspondence of events in the lives of Conrad and Marlow but rather in their shared position as storytellers. This chapter, which concerns itself with storytellers and storytelling, will argue that the Marlow texts, and in this sense they might be said to be autobiographical, dramatise concerns about the writing process itself.[2]

On occasion, the question of how to position Marlow has revealed rather divided approaches to the works in which he appears. The texts can be shown to support, on the one hand, a narratological approach that regards Marlow in terms of his narrating activity, and, on the other, a more character-driven analysis that regards Marlow as a character in his own right. As I will go on to suggest, this is a division that is made possible by the framed structure of the four texts which effectively creates two distinct 'Marlows': the Marlow who narrates and the younger Marlow who is the subject, or at least *a* subject, of that narration. In essence prioritising one Marlow over the other, narrator or character, becomes a question of emphasis that is best understood by an exploration of the relation between these two figures. In any case, before Marlow is approached in his duality it is useful to briefly rehearse the critical approaches that privilege just one of his roles: Pierre Vitoux, Richard Curle, Alan Warren Friedman, and Bernard J. Paris provide clear examples.

Vitoux, in 'Marlow: The Changing Narrator of Conrad's Fiction', argues that Marlow is not a character in the proper sense and his reading emphasizes Marlow's own act of narration, arguing that, 'He is part of the tale not as a character in it, but as the narrator of it, merging into his role.'[3] For Vitoux the relative successes of the four texts depend on the narrating Marlow's relation to his tales rather than his actions within those tales as a character. Indeed, writing of *Chance*, Vitoux suggests that 'the reader's impression at the end is still likely to be that there is too much Marlow in the novel . . . smothering it in his general view of life.'[4] Richard Curle, goes further, describing Marlow as, 'a literary device' by which 'the narrative can be carried on.'[5] This tendency to regard Marlow as a narrator rather than a character is neither new nor unusual: Conrad himself responded to suggestions that Marlow is 'a clever screen, a mere device' in his 1917 'Author's Note' to 'Youth', offering a view that could readily be used to support the notion of Marlow as narrator, he is 'not an intrusive person' and is 'most discreet'.[6]

The 'Author's Note' also gestures towards the opposite reading: Conrad talks fondly of his creation, 'the man Marlow and I came together in the casual manner of those health-resort acquaintances which sometimes ripen into friendships. This one has ripened', he recognizes a certain 'assertiveness in matters of opinion' and suspects his narrator of 'vanity'.[7] It is Marlow the 'man', assertive and possibly vain, that is the centre of Friedman's study 'Conrad's Picaresque Narrator'. Coining the term 'Marlovian', Friedman reads the four Marlow novels together, arguing that Marlow should be read as the character central to the quartet and suggesting that when read in this way the texts 'differ markedly from what they are in isolation. In the four works taken together, Marlow himself becomes the moving centre of an episodic, larger fiction in which characters and incidents spin off and revolve around him'.[8] Friedman goes on to suggest that the four tales exist 'perhaps most fundamentally, certainly most organically – as temporal stages in the development of Marlow himself' continuing with the suggestion that, 'it is our task, then, to consider how this oddly constructed tetralogy – growing much longer and more cumbersome each step of the way – negotiates the personal, moral, and esthetic evolution of its central spokesman.'[9] Cedric Watts would appear to agree, writing: 'Cumulatively, Marlow was to become the fullest, most sophisticated, and most convincing character in the whole of Conrad's literary work', a statement that is based on a reading of all four texts.[10] Publishing history bears such a reading out: the order of Marlow's experiences in 'Youth,' *Heart of Darkness*, *Lord Jim*, and *Chance* coincides with their order of publication. Further to that, Blackwood's 1902 volume *Youth: A Narrative; and Two Other Stories*, was originally envisaged as a triptych united by Marlow, under the title 'Three Tales of Sea and Land', comprised of 'Youth', *Heart of Darkness* and *Lord Jim*. However, when it became clear that *Lord Jim* was growing beyond the confines of the short story it was replaced by 'The End of the Tether'.[11] This character-based approach to Marlow finds what is perhaps its most detailed consideration in Bernard J. Paris's recent book *Conrad's Charlie Marlow*, an extended psychological study of the character that regards the Marlow of 'Youth', *Heart of Darkness* and *Lord Jim* as 'a single continuously evolving character who is profoundly affected by his experiences and develops inner conflicts in the course of these works', and goes on to argue that 'seeing him predominantly in functional terms obscures his psychological complexity.'[12]

Despite their apparent polarity these two positions, at the extremes of which we find Curle and Paris, are by no means mutually exclusive. Rather it is possible to situate Marlow in either position, as narrator or character, or, more plausibly, as occupying both positions simultaneously within each text. It is undeniable that this duality caused a certain amount of anxiety, or dismay, in Conrad's early readers; John Masefield's 1903 review of *Heart of Darkness* is perhaps not untypical in its complaint that 'the author is too much cobweb, and fails, as we think, to create his central character.'[13] More recent responses to Conrad's work tend to evince an openness to the fluidity of Marlow's dual positioning. Wayne C. Booth, who also describes *Heart of Darkness* as a 'web', pauses to question the validity of the questions that have been asked of the text:

Is *Heart of Darkness* the story of Kurtz or the story of Marlow's experience of Kurtz? Was Marlow invented as a rhetorical device for heightening the meaning of Kurtz's moral collapse, or was Kurtz invented in order to provide Marlow with the centre of his experience in the Congo? Again a seamless web, and we tell ourselves that the old-fashioned question 'Who is the protagonist?' is a meaningless one.[14]

Booth neatly illustrates Marlow's dual role as storyteller and as the subject of story. Emerging from this rejection of the over-simplistic, and often reductive, question 'who is the protagonist?' is another question: it becomes necessary to ask, what remains in the absence of an easily identifiable protagonist? Booth's description of the narrative of *Heart of Darkness* as a 'seamless web' is one with which many readers will concur, understanding it to indicate a radical complication of the relative positions of the narrator and the narrated. Booth's notion of *Heart of Darkness* as a narrative in which the merging of narrator and character is seamless, with its questioning of the legitimacy, and possibility, of prioritising one over the other, suggests a way of reading Marlow that can be usefully extended across the four texts in which he appears. Picking up on the questions raised by the recognition of this 'seamless web,' this chapter will examine the ways in which Marlow can be read both as a narrator *and* as a character whose primary action within the stories is often the act of narration.

Marlow and narrative structure

This structural reading of Marlow's dual role owes much to Jakob Lothe's *Conrad's Narrative Method* and Watts's *The Deceptive Text*, two texts which demonstrate very successfully the richly productive connection between form and content in Conrad's fiction. By mapping the divided narrator/narrated across onto the more familiar form/content division it is possible to regard the use of Marlow as both narrator and narrated, as both a character who narrates and as a character of that narration, as an essential element of Conrad's artistic achievement. In this way, I will go on to explore the ways in which Lothe's comment that 'when the relationship is productive and successful, as in "Heart of Darkness", it becomes particularly difficult to discriminate between constituent aspects of form and content' might be applied to the various ways in which Marlow is deployed.[15] Following Lothe's example, I will proceed by offering an overview of the narrative structures common to the four Marlow texts, examining the processes of narrating they employ with reference to Gérard Genette's work on narratology, before exploring a reading of 'Youth' in which the relation between the two Marlow's, the form if you like, is central to the story's ostensible 'content'.

Genette's *Narrative Discourse*, a key text of narrative theory, begins by identifying three distinct ways in which the word 'narrative' is commonly used:

> A first meaning [narrative] – the one nowadays most evident and most central in common usage – has *narrative* refer to the narrative statement, the oral or written discourse that undertakes to tell of an event or a series of events . . . A second meaning [story] . . . has *narrative* refer to the succession of events, real or fictitious, that are the subjects of this discourse . . . A third meaning [narrating], apparently the oldest, has *narrative* refer once more to an event: not, however, the event that is recounted, but the event that consists of someone recounting something: the act of narrating taken in itself.[16]

To avoid the confusion that might result from the inherent ambiguity of the word 'narrative', containing as it does these three meanings, Genette deploys his own terminology: the first version of 'narrative' retains the title 'narrative', the second becomes 'story' and the third 'narrating'. All three aspects of narrative are related, and their relation is a central concern of this chapter: specifically, and adhering to Genette's terminology, my primary concern is with the relation between 'narrating' and 'story'. In other words, this study will investigate the relation between Marlow's two roles: as a storyteller and as a character of both his own stories and those of the unnamed narrator.

Structural analyses of the Marlow texts soon reveal both the complexity of Conrad's narratives and the precarious nature of Genette's 'narrative', 'story' and 'narrating'. This is something that Genette himself acknowledges, making direct reference to *Lord Jim* as a narrative 'where the entanglement reaches the bounds of general intelligibility', words which Lothe echoes in his remark that 'the narrative discourse of *Lord Jim* . . . is indeed so complicated that no analysis of it can do it justice'.[17] Genette's use of the word 'entanglement' is a key to understanding the way that 'narrative', 'story' and 'narrating', defined so painstakingly in *Narrative Discourse*, co-exist – the common root of the three terms, the single word 'narrative', indicating the way in which each term is always already inhabited by the terms against which it is defined. Genette's answer to the 'entangled' and 'inhabited' nature of his terminology is to view narrative as comprised of different 'levels', defining the difference of level by saying that, '*any event a narrative recounts is at a diegetic level immediately higher than the level at which the narrating act producing this narrative is placed.*'[18] Diegesis, a Platonic term, refers to the narrative content that Genette terms story, 'with the same meaning ["story"], I will also use the term *diegesis*', so it becomes possible to identify numerous stories in a single text.[19] Genette's system employs a series of spatial metaphors that allow him to divide a single text into multiple narratives that are conceived as being above/below or outside/within one another, and allows the terms narrative, story and narrating a certain mobility across the levels whilst retaining their specific identities on any single plain. Genette helpfully avoids ascribing value to any narrative level and thus his approach, by recognizing that the narrating act of one level can be the story of another, suggests a way of approaching texts that need not focus on either the purely functional aspects of narrative technique or simply on the events of story.

Recognizing the multiple levels of narrative in Conrad's texts is to recognise what one reviewer of *Chance* described as 'Mr Conrad's unmistakable method of telling a story . . . he hides behind one man at first and then puts a second in front of the first, and perhaps a third in front of the second.'[20] This method is apparent from the most cursory analysis of the four Marlow texts which display common structural traits that go beyond simply having a narrator with the same name. 'Youth', *Heart of Darkness*, *Lord Jim* and *Chance* share a narrative structure in that Marlow's narrative is embedded within the narrative of another unnamed character who retells in written form Marlow's earlier oral narrative. Reading this structure according to Genette's terminology, there is an immediate doubling at each stage. On one level Marlow can be seen to be narrating (telling) a story, in which he appears as a character. At a second level the narrating act is performed by the unnamed narrator. Marlow features again in this story, but in this instance he appears as a character who tells a story. In this manner, which is clearly linked to the temporal positioning of Conrad's character, Marlow simultaneously functions in terms of both story and narrating. The two aspects of Genette's definition of narrative meet in this figure much as they did in the more general term narrative from which they are derived. Given this doubling it might make sense to figure Marlow as two entities: he is at once the generator and subject of story. Closer analysis of the texts makes this clear.

'Youth' is introduced by an unnamed character who sets a scene that Conrad will later reuse, with slight variation, in *Heart of Darkness*. Five men – the unnamed narrator, Marlow, a director of companies, an accountant, and a lawyer – are seated around a table drinking. The five men, we learn, are connected by 'the strong bond of the sea':

> The director had been a *Conway* boy, the accountant had served four years at sea, the lawyer – a fine crusted Tory, High Churchman, the best of old fellows, the soul of honour – had been chief officer in the P. & O. service in the good old days when mail-boats were square-rigged at least on two masts,

and used to come down the China Sea before a fair monsoon with stun'-sails set alow and aloft. We all began life in the merchant service.[21]

Aside from this brief introduction, and a revisiting of this same scene at the story's conclusion, the narrator provides no further description of either these characters or the location, withdrawing and presenting Marlow's speech, supposedly verbatim. Marlow then proceeds to tell his story, which continues uninterrupted, with the exception of his own interjections, to its conclusion and the final revisiting of the scene around the polished mahogany table that effectively closes the narrative's frame.

Reading 'Youth' with attention to its narrative structure it soon becomes clear that the short story, which Frederick R. Karl describes rather disparagingly as 'a small job neatly performed', is extremely complex in its construction.[22] The narrative operates on two levels: that of the first narrator whose story bears on the scene of the transmission of an earlier narrative, and Marlow's story itself which comprises the second narrative level. Accordingly there are two parallel stories, that in which Marlow is a character telling a story, and that in which the young Marlow appears as a character of this narrative which recounts his youthful adventures as second mate of the *Judea*. Read in isolation, the first narrative, the frame around Marlow's tale, is relatively straightforward. This narrative is what Genette terms 'homodiegetic': the unnamed narrator, 'plays only a secondary role, which almost always turns out to be a role as observer and witness'.[23] To this definition it is necessary, given the emphasis here on narrating, to add that this narrator, Marlow's observer and auditor, is also a creator of narrative. Similarly, Marlow's narrative is straightforward when read in isolation from this frame narrative. In direct contrast to the first narrative, this second narrative is both narrated by Marlow and features him as its central character: a type of narrative that Genette terms 'autodiegetic', to designate those stories in which the narrator appears as the 'hero' or 'star'.[24] The Marlow encountered in 'Youth' is, in a way that cannot be said of his later narratives, very clearly the centre of narrative interest. It is when the two narrative levels are read together, a reading that the text demands, that these categories become increasingly problematic and, as I will go on to discuss, it is through the interaction of these two levels that 'Youth' functions as a meaningful narrative.

The unnamed narrator of 'Youth', whose characterisation does not even extend to the act of naming, is apparently, in the four short paragraphs that frame Marlow's tale, positioned in such a way as to minimise his intervention into the tale that he introduces. Although fictive this character operates at a level 'outside' the story, and it is at this 'extradiegetic' level that he comments, 'This could have occurred nowhere but in England'.[25] Remaining 'outside' Marlow's story, the narrator is able to present it as if it were a literal transcript of his words which are 'reported'. As Genette says, this is 'the most "mimetic" form [of narrative] ... where the narrator pretends literally to give the floor to his character'.[26] At no point does Marlow's narrator speak or interact with the other listeners, his presence is simply given in the framing device and later inferred from Marlow's own comments.

Despite the withdrawal of the first narrator, the primal scene of transmission is constantly present, appearing in Marlow's own relation to the story that he tells. Unlike his narrator, Marlow's intervention into, and his obvious creation of, his narrative is constant. At all points he 'is present as source, guarantor, and organizer of the narrative, as analyst and commentator, as stylist (as "writer" in Marcel Muller's vocabulary) and particularly – as we well know – as producer of "metaphors".'[27] This intervention is most obvious in the refrain 'Pass the bottle' with which Marlow repeatedly interrupts, and disrupts, the second narrative, recalling its position within the first and introducing a very physical connection between the tale, its teller and his group of listeners.[28] In addition to this repeated line Marlow frequently addresses the four men seated around the mahogany table with rhetorical questions and explanations, demanding, in a phrase that is central to Conrad's literary endeavour, 'Do you see', implicating both Marlow's listeners and Conrad's readers in the tale that unfolds: 'Her youth was where mine is – where yours is – you fellows who listen to this yarn'.[29] Thus, in the absence of intervention from the frame narrator it is Marlow's narrative that insists on the connection between the two narrative levels, repeatedly drawing attention to his act of storytelling by locating himself and his tale in relation to his audience.

If the narrative of 'Youth' turns out to be more involved than Karl's 'small job neatly performed' might imply, then *Heart of Darkness* is more complex still. The novella follows the pattern established in 'Youth': an unnamed narrator retells a story that has been told by Marlow including in his narrative the moment of its original transmission. The scene is similar to that of 'Youth'; once again Marlow addresses a group comprised of the first narrator, the director of companies, the lawyer and the accountant, this time on the cruising yawl the *Nellie*, anchored on the Thames. The homodiegetic narrative of the unnamed narrator is, as before, a clear example of reported narrative – an uncluttered and unobtrusive reproduction of Marlow's narrative. Marlow himself begins his story with the disclaimer, 'I don't want to bother you much with what happened to me personally,' in effect promising to tell the story of Kurtz: in structural terms, he intends his narrative to be homodiegetic, to exclude himself as a character, although of course this is not the case and his own story soon overtakes that of Kurtz. [30] As in 'Youth' Marlow is both narrator *and* central character in this second level of narrative, however in this later text Marlow's narrative style more obviously emphasizes its status as narrative and is what Genette would term, with characteristic precision, 'autodiegetic narratized narrative'.

The scene of Marlow's storytelling in *Heart of Darkness* is evoked throughout the novel. It is notable that the first narrator's interjections increase in number compared to those in 'Youth' where references to the situation of the first narrative came only from Marlow himself. After the initial situation on board the *Nellie* has been set, the first narrator returns repeatedly: 'he began again, lifting one arm from the elbow, the palm of the hand outwards, so that, with his legs folded before him, he had the pose of a Buddha preaching in European clothes'; 'He was silent for a while.'; 'It had become so pitch dark that we listeners could hardly see one another. For a long time already he, sitting apart, had been no more to us than a voice'; ' "Try to be civil, Marlow," growled a voice, and I knew there was at least one listener awake besides myself'; 'There was a pause of profound stillness, then a match flared, and Marlow's face appeared, worn, hollow, with downward folds and dropped eyelids, with an aspect of concentrated attention'; 'Marlow ceased, and sat apart, indistinct and silent, in the pose of a meditating Buddha.'[31] Such interjections reiterate the oral nature of Marlow's storytelling; he preaches in a darkness that makes seeing, and therefore reading, impossible. Marlow is a voice, his silences are noted and are significant because they belong to the first narrative, the narrative which takes narrating as its story and for which silence is a failure of that story.

Identifying the two narrative levels in 'Youth' and *Heart of Darkness*, both linked by the character of Marlow, makes it clear that there can be more than one story in a single text. So, in each of the Marlow texts, there is the story that Marlow ostensibly tells – stories that are understandably prioritised in readings of the texts. Alongside this is a second story, that of Marlow's storytelling and here he appears as a distinct character, no longer as the *Judea*'s second mate or as the young 'freshwater sailor' in the Congo, he is now an older man, the product of these earlier (life) stories and the primary action of this character is the telling of stories. What makes distinguishing these two levels productive is not recognizing them in isolation but in the manner in which they interact. The co-existence of these two narratives immediately suggests that the way in which Marlow tells his story may be as significant as what happens in his story. In this way Conrad's complex narratives make it necessary for a narratological reading to recognize, and contend with, a number of different narrative levels that inhabit one another just as Genette's three readings of the word 'narrative' might be said to inhabit one another.

Marlow and Benjamin's storyteller

Close structural analysis of the four texts demonstrates that each tells a story at one narrative level whilst dramatising the transmission of that story at another. In dramatising the transmission of story as story in itself, and more exactly in dramatising the connection between the transmission of story and the story that is being transmitted, Conrad's Marlow narratives might be seen to explore similar concerns to those that impel Walter Benjamin's hugely-influential 1936 essay 'The Storyteller'.[32] Benjamin's essay, which starts out as a discussion of Nikolai Leskov's stories, goes on to interpret oral storytelling, the novel and, finally, 'information' in the context of specific historical conditions of production. Following a productive line of argument about the development of modern narrative, 'The Storyteller' offers insights into the relation between the storyteller (narrating) and the tale (story), a connection that insists on a productive relation between the telling and the reception (as retelling) of stories. This aspect of Benjamin's argument could usefully be read in terms of a narrative hermeneutics that necessarily 'starts from speech that has already taken place, and in which everything has already been said in some fashion,' and for which 'the first task is not to begin but from the midst of speech to remember; to remember with a view to beginning'.[33] In this way Ricoeur's description of the productive hermeneutic circle describes Benjamin's notion of storytelling for which meaning emerges through retelling.

It is easy to make a number of literal connections between the Marlow narratives and the 'storyteller' that Benjamin describes. Benjamin, with a nostalgic emphasis on pre-capitalist models of production, associates storytelling proper with the artisan class, determining that 'peasants and seamen were past masters of storytelling'.[34] As sailors, both Marlow and his unnamed narrator (and indeed Conrad himself) resemble his idealised storyteller perfectly. From the outset the technique of both Marlow and the unnamed narrator fits well with Benjamin's description of the tradition, and his contention that: 'Storytellers tend to begin their story with a presentation of the circumstances in which they themselves have learned what is to follow' can be readily adapted as a description of the texts.[35] In this vein, 'Youth' opens with a page that sets the scene of Marlow's storytelling in which both the unnamed narrator and then Marlow himself indicate the sources of the tale that they will share:

> We were sitting round a mahogany table that reflected the bottle, the claret-glasses, and our faces as we leaned on our elbows . . . Marlow (at least I think that is how he spelt his name) told the story, or rather the chronicle, of a voyage.[36]

The narrative is then picked up by Marlow who begins with his own introduction, 'Yes, I have seen a little of the Eastern seas; but what I remember best is my first voyage there.'[37] In his introduction to the Penguin edition of 'Youth', John Lyon comments on this scene:

> In both *Youth* and *Heart of Darkness*, Marlow is given a particular context in which he tells his tale – a particular place and occasion, and a particularized audience. In *Youth* such details are largely embellishment; in *Heart of Darkness* these same details have assumed a primary role in that work's struggle for meaning.[38]

Lyon is right to assert that in *Heart of Darkness* the inclusion of this primary scene is more detailed: in that text it articulates, as Anthony Fothergill has so clearly demonstrated, a 'network of thematic concerns' that reverberate throughout the whole novel.[39] However, whilst the struggle for meaning is central to the later Marlow texts, the inclusion of this scene in 'Youth' is, as I shall go on to argue, far from being functionless embellishment, but is in fact central to reading the text in which the return to this initial scene, the closing of the frame, becomes very much part of the central story.

Perhaps the clearest connection, at least on first glance, between Conrad's Marlow and Benjamin's storyteller is the emphasis on the oral, spoken, mode.[40] Each of the Marlow texts is presented as a written account of the reception of an earlier oral narrative and in his repeated return to oral storytelling Marlow is not unlike the captain of the *Judea* who 'didn't care for writing at all'.[41] He is a narrator in the oral tradition whose listeners come to expect a story who has, according to the narrator of *Heart of Darkness*, a 'propensity to spin yarns'.[42] This propensity for excessive verbiage has been the subject of no little critical mockery, with critics questioning the plausibility, and possibility, of such lengthy outpourings. Conrad answered such complaints, not without humour, in his 1917 'Author's Note' to *Lord Jim*:

> When this novel first appeared in book form a notion got about that I had been bolted away with. Some reviewers mentioned the fact that the work starting as a short story had got beyond the writer's control . . . They argued that no man could have been expected to talk all that time, and other men to listen so long. It was not, they said, very credible.
>
> After thinking it over for something like sixteen years I am not so sure about that. Men have been known, both in the tropics and in the temperate

zone, to sit up half the night 'swapping yarns'. This, however, is but one yarn, yet with interruptions affording some measure of relief; and in regard to the listeners' endurance, the postulate must be accepted that the story *was* interesting. It is the necessary preliminary assumption. If I hadn't believed that it *was* interesting I could never have begun to write it. As to the mere physical possibility we all know that some speeches in Parliament have taken nearer six hours than three hours in delivery; whereas all that part of the book which is Marlow's narrative can be read through aloud, I should say, in less than three hours. Besides – though I have kept strictly all such insignificant details out of the tale – we may presume that there must have been some sort of refreshments on that night, a glass of mineral water of some sort to help the narrator on.[43]

This critical disbelief further ties Marlow to the figure of the storyteller, a figure whose decline, argues Benjamin, is tied to an increasing demand for abbreviation:

> We have witnessed the evolution of the 'short story,' which has removed itself from the oral tradition and no longer permits that slow piling up, one on top of the other, of thin, transparent layers which constitutes the most appropriate image of the way in which the perfect narrative is revealed through the layers of various retellings.[44]

Whilst 'Youth', at around 13,500 words in length, clearly falls into the category of the short story it retains something of the layering of which Benjamin speaks, functioning, to a large extent, as a result of its levels of retelling.

It is made clear in the opening pages of 'Youth' that the translation of oral into written narrative is to be a significant part of the story. This manifests itself immediately as a problem with proper names, a problem that is repeated across the four texts. When the narrator of 'Youth' writes, 'Marlow (at least I think that is how he spelt his name)', he simultaneously underlines the oral nature of the original narrative and, while emphasizing that his is a written account, instigates a measure of doubt into his own narrative.[45] Marlow, the narrator informs us, 'told the story, or rather the chronicle of a voyage', and again there is an uncertainty of voice that draws attention away from the story to the act of narration.[46] The difficulty with naming persists in Marlow's narrative, again with the effect of revealing the narrative act, in this case it is a reversal of the first narrator's problem, as Marlow remarks: 'his name was Mahon, but he insisted that it should be pronounced Mann.'[47] Shortly after this Marlow finds his ship: 'Her name was the *Judea*. Queer name, isn't it. She belonged to a man Wilmer, Wilcox – some name like that; but he has been bankrupt and dead these twenty years or more, and his name don't matter.'[48] They later pass a steamer in the mist: 'They shouted at us some name – a woman's name, Miranda or Melissa – or some such thing.'[49] The act of naming, of ascribing proper names to objects, people and places, foregrounded here by a rather deliberate lack of precision, introduces a concern with the function and uses of language that is characteristic of the Marlow narratives which perhaps finds its clearest expression in *Heart of Darkness*.

This concern with the possibility of translating individual experience into a common language is also at the heart of 'The Storyteller': for Benjamin, the key to storytelling is to be found in the transmission of stories from one narrator to another and the repetition of this process. '[S]torytelling' writes Benjamin, 'is always the art of repeating stories.'[50] If Marlow, as he appears in the four novels, has one defining characteristic it might be this: he is clearly a character who likes to tell stories, and one of the few things that we discover about the unnamed narrator, if it is assumed that he is the same character across the four texts, is that he has a tendency to repeat the stories that he hears. There is almost an audible groan when, in *Heart of Darkness*, the narrator says, 'we knew we were fated, before the ebb began to run, to hear about one of Marlow's inconclusive experiences.'[51] Similarly there is a certain sense of good-natured weariness when the narrator of *Lord Jim* remarks, 'And later on, many times, in distant parts of the world, Marlow showed himself willing to remember Jim, to remember him at length, in detail and audibly.'[52] Lothe gives an attentive reading of this crucial passage, noting the 'many times' that Marlow will tell Jim's story, reaching the conclusion that this constant repetition makes the novel 'more open' to interpretation, a fact that can be linked to the specifics of this repeated narrating act.[53] Genette calls narratives of this kind 'pseudo-iterative': 'scenes presented, particularly by their wording in the imperfect, as iterative, whereas their richness and precision of detail ensure that no reader can seriously believe they occur and reoccur in that manner, several times, without any variation.'[54] Indeed, it is made clear in these texts that Marlow retells and revises his tales.

Whilst the iterative nature of Marlow's storytelling might mark him as a storyteller in Benjamin's mould, the repetition of which Benjamin writes is not the repetition of story by the *same* storyteller as much as its transmission to, and repetition by, *subsequent* storytellers: 'The storyteller takes what he tells from experience – his own or that reported by others. And he in turn makes it the experience of those who are listening to his tale.'[55] Up to this point little mention has been made of the anonymous narrator who recounts Marlow's stories. Like Marlow, he is a seaman and, again like Marlow, he continues the telling of tales that he has heard, effectively performing the same act as Marlow at a higher narrative level.

Benjamin's claim that 'the perfect narrative is revealed through the layers of various retellings' could find few better examples than those provided by Conrad which, employing numerous narrative layers, clearly display the marks of their retelling.[56] This emphasis on the transmission of the story, Genette's narrating, is the defining feature of the storyteller for Benjamin, and this is what he claims distinguishes storytelling from novelistic, written, narrative. The contrast he draws between the novel and oral storytelling is directly comparable to the contrast drawn by the narrator of *Heart of Darkness* between the 'yarns of seamen' which have a 'direct simplicity, the whole meaning of which lies within the shell of a cracked nut' and the narrative technique of Marlow for whom, 'the meaning of an episode was not inside like a kernel but outside, enveloping the tale which bought it out only as a glow brings out a haze, in the likeness of one of these misty halos that sometimes are made visible by the spectral illumination of moonshine.'[57] Understood in narratological terms Marlow's words suggest that meaning will be found not in the story so much as in that which surrounds it, in the narrating act. Thus recognizing, and responding to, narrating (the act of storytelling) as a constitutive part of story, as a story at a second narrative level and not as a separate distinct element of the storytelling process, affords valuable insight into the Marlow texts.

The functional value of reintegrating 'narrating' and 'story', an integration that Genette recognises, which must somehow maintain the two terms as distinct and yet in a state of constant play, can be clearly seen in reading 'Youth'. Commenting, in the 1902 'Author's Note', on the relation between his own life story and Marlow's tale, Conrad remarks that '*Youth* is a feat of memory. It is a record of experience.'[58] That experience came when Conrad was second mate of the *Palestine*, a ship which sank off the coast of Sumatra in March of 1883, five years before he penned the story. The key events are recreated in 'Youth': as second mate of the *Judea*, a young and inexperienced Marlow sets off on an ill-fated voyage from London to Bangkok, enduring a long and troublesome voyage which ends in the sinking of his ship after its cargo of coal explodes just south of Java Head. 'Youth' is also a feat of memory for both of its storytellers, Marlow and his unnamed narrator, and the text is structured in such a way that this is foregrounded and made an essential part of its interpretation. Just as Conrad is able to remember and reuse this early experience so, too, does Marlow and the connection between the narrator and his younger self, what narrative theory would term the 'focalizer' (a visual term that distinguishes between the one who speaks and the one who sees/experiences), parallels very directly the relation between Conrad and the youth that he remembers as second mate of the *Palestine*.

In 'Youth' the distinction between focalizer and narrator is not only very clear but is also an extremely productive device in the interpretation of the story.

As became apparent in the earlier discussion of the text's narrative structure, 'Youth' is a retelling of a story told by Marlow to a group of friends. Conrad's use of this framing device allows for the appearance of a certain temporal dislocation between experience and expression that is central to reading the text. In setting up his tale Marlow tells us, 'It was twenty-two years ago; and I was just twenty. How time passes!' and in so doing he positions the 'two Marlows' very precisely: Marlow aged 20, the focalizer; and, Marlow aged 42, the narrator.[59] Marlow creates his younger self as a character, this Marlow no longer exists: in effect the translation of this self into character is what allows the older Marlow the authority to conclude his tale. The way in which the structure of the text is reinforced by the narrative technique indicates that the transmission of the story will be crucially important to an understanding of the story itself. The situation of Marlow's storytelling, and thus the story's dual temporality, is evoked repeatedly from the moment that Marlow's story is placed inside the quotation marks that anchor it unobtrusively to the first narrative of the first narrator. Marlow's repeated calls to the four men around the mahogany table to 'Pass the bottle' and the frequent rhetorical questions with which he addresses them locate his narrative within that of the first narrator and introduce a temporal gap between the narrating act and the events of the story. This temporal disjunction serves a thematic purpose in 'Youth', which is concerned with the passing of time, substantiating the reading indicated by the title that the story will be concerned with passed youth.

'Youth' is, on one level at least, a sentimental tale about the vigour and optimism of youth. Karl regards the story as 'a work bursting with sentimentality' with, 'the aura of a sentimental story for a family magazine'.[60] Watts writes in a similar vein: 'The nostalgia is frank and unashamed: a middle-aged Marlow looks back indulgently on the ardent optimism of his younger self and, licensed by the claret-bottle, veers finally towards a sentimentality which the anonymous narrator endorses.'[61] This short quotation from Watts contains the germs of two distinct approaches to the text: there is a youthful 'looking forward', exemplified here by the word optimism, and the 'looking back' that is necessitated by the story's temporal structure. Jocelyn Baines's description of 'Youth' contains a similar division; 'Conrad's most consistently cheerful story' carries with it, he writes, 'a taste of ashes'.[62] Refiguring 'Youth' as a text that is concerned not so much about the vigour of youth as it is about the passing of youth opens up the possibility of reading it in a manner that responds to Karl's suggestion that Conrad's 'similes and metaphors are frequently somber [sic] and dark for a lightly recalled memory'.[63]

This 'lightly recalled memory is, as James Hansford has pointed out, 'about growing up and growing old' and, with this in mind, the narrator's initial stumbling designation of Marlow's tale as a 'chronicle', which he prefers over 'story', might not seem so accidental, drawing attention, as it does, to a word that has at its heart the Greek *chronos* meaning time.[64] Marlow's refrain, 'Pass the bottle' and his direct address to his auditors, constantly remind the reader of the passage of time by playing off the passivity of the scene of this middle-aged storytelling against the activity of youth that is being recalled. The recognition that Marlow's auditors, and Conrad's readers, are the subjects of this narrative on aging may be an uncomfortable one in a text that continually reflects on death, both metaphorically and in a literal sense. At a linguistic level, examples of the 'dark and sombre' language of 'Youth' are easy to find: shifting ballast in the hold, 'gloomy like a cavern', is 'gravedigger's work', as the *Judea* fills with water, the sailors man the pumps, 'for dear life . . . as though we had been dead', and when the *Judea* reaches Falmouth, she is a 'carcass of a ship' with a Captain that 'looked like the ghost of a Geordie skipper'.[65] Death appears just as frequently on a more literal level. The older, reflecting Marlow clearly connects the passage of time with the passing away of the characters that populate his story, his 'Pass the bottle' is perhaps not the innocent phrase that it might appear, and Wilmer (or Wilcox), Mrs Beard, Captain Beard, Mahon, Jermyn, all old when they are encountered by the young Marlow, will all be dead by the time of its telling. As is Marlow's younger self:

> Oh the glamour of youth! Oh, the fire of it, more dazzling than the flames of the burning ship, throwing a magic light on the wide earth, leaping audaciously to the sky, presently to be quenched by time, more cruel, more pitiless, more bitter than the sea . . .[66]

The realization of the loss of youth emerges through a narrative structure that insists on the distinction between Marlow the narrator and the *Judea*'s young second mate, who, in recalling, he consigns to the past.

In this 'Youth' can again be approached in terms of Benjamin's storyteller. For Benjamin, 'Death is the sanction of everything that the storyteller can tell. He has borrowed his authority from death.'[67] He continues, 'His gift is the ability to relate his life; his distinction, to be able to tell his *entire* life. The storyteller: he is the man who could let the wick of his life be consumed completely by the gentle flame of his story.'[68] Benjamin's suggestion that the wisdom of the storyteller stems from completeness, from his telling an 'entire life', can be connected to the structure of Conrad's short story. To be more specific, what Benjamin might term 'wisdom' emerges in the relation between the older, narrating Marlow (who occupies the framing apparatus of the story as a character, and the twenty-two-year-old story that he tells and in which a younger version of himself appears as the central character. In the Marlow texts full meaning is disclosed by a narrator who has already experienced events. This becomes apparent in the very 'symmetrical' nature of the frame that surrounds Marlow's tale – or, more properly, in the very slight asymmetry of that final framing scene. What first appears as the most straightforward closing scene of the four Marlow texts, turns out to be deceptive in its apparent simplicity. The opening scene is mirrored: the group of five men is revealed once again, seated, as they were when Marlow began his tale, around the mahogany table and, as before, the polished surface of the table reflects their faces. However, at this point we are allowed to see more in the reflection:

> And we all nodded at him: the man of finance, the man of accounts, the man of law, we all nodded at him over the polished table that like a still sheet of brown water reflected our faces, lined, wrinkled; our faces marked by toil, by deceptions, by success, by love; our weary eyes looking still, looking always, looking anxiously for something out of life, that while it is expected is already gone – has passed unseen, in a sigh, in a flash – together with the youth, with the strength, with the romance of illusions.[69]

In the structuring of the story towards this end, to the revealing of the aged and lined faces of Marlow's auditors, 'Youth' attains full meaning. 'Do or Die', the motto of the *Judea*, must be reread in the light of the passage both of time and of narrative, the youthful assumptions which allowed the focalizing Marlow to read it as a spirited affirmation of life are now revealed – it is no longer a question of 'doing or dying' but as Hansford so eloquently puts it, 'doing *is* dying'.[70]

Such revelation can come only at the end. Marlow, like Benjamin's storyteller, is aware of the story in its completeness and it is this authority that allows the forty-two year old Marlow to comment in the opening pages: 'Mrs Beard is dead, and youth, strength, genius, thoughts, achievements, simple hearts – all dies . . . No matter.'[71] According to Benjamin, it is the authority of death that distinguishes the storyteller from the novelist, allowing him to share wisdom rather than imparting information. In this the scene reflected in the table becomes more significant still, the reflection encompasses the group as a whole – reflecting 'our faces' – implicates them in the exchange of this wisdom. Marlow's refrain 'Pass the bottle' which, in the words of Andrea White, 'marks him as one with the others around the table' also condemns them to accede to the storyteller's vision of the relation between experience and past (passed away) youth.[72]

Notes

1 Owen Knowles and Gene M. Moore (eds), *Oxford Reader's Companion to Conrad* (Oxford: Oxford University Press, 2000), p. 219.

2 A great deal of work has been done to indicate the relation between Conrad's life and his fictions, most notably by Norman Sherry in his book *Conrad's Western World* (Cambridge: Cambridge University Press, 1971).

3 Pierre Vitoux, 'Marlow: The Changing Narrator of Conrad's Fiction', *Cahiers Victoriens et Édouardiens*, 2 (1975), pp. 83–102, p. 94.

4 Vitoux, 'Marlow: The Changing Narrator of Conrad's Fiction', pp. 100–1.

5 Richard Curle, *Joseph Conrad and his Characters: A Study of Six Novels* (New York: Russell & Russell, 1957), p. 62.

6 Joseph Conrad, *Youth, Heart of Darkness, The End of the Tether* (London: J. M. Dent and Sons Ltd, 1946), p. vi.

7 Conrad, *Youth, Heart of Darkness, The End of the Tether*, p. vi.

8 Alan Warren Friedman, 'Conrad's Picaresque Narrator: Marlow's Journey from "Youth" through *Chance*', *Joseph Conrad: Theory and World Fiction – Proceedings of the Comparative Literature Symposium, Vol. VII*, eds Wolodmymyr T. Zyla and Wendell M. Aycock (Lubbock, Texas: Inter-departmental Committee on Comparative Literature, Texas Tech University, 1974), p. 18.

9 Friedman, 'Conrad's Picaresque Narrator', p. 19.

10 Cedric Watts, 'Introduction' to Conrad, *Heart of Darkness and Other Tales*, ed. Cedric Watts (Oxford: Oxford University Press, 1998), p. xiii.

11 In his 'Author's Note' Conrad remarks, 'The three stories in this volume lay no claim to unity of artistic purpose. The only bond between them is that of the time in which they were written.' (Conrad, *Youth, Heart of Darkness, The End of the Tether*, p. v).

12 Bernard J. Paris, *Conrad's Charlie Marlow: A New Approach to 'Heart of Darkness' and Lord Jim* (Houndmills, Basingstoke: Palgrave Macmillan, 2005), pp. 5, 4.

13 Norman Sherry (ed.), *Conrad: The Critical Heritage* (London: Routledge & Kegan Paul, 1973), p. 142.

14 Wayne C. Booth, *The Rhetoric of Fiction* (Chicago and London: Chicago University Press, 1961), p. 346.

15 Jakob Lothe, *Conrad's Narrative Method* (Oxford: Clarendon, 1989), p. 2.

16 Gérard Genette, *Narrative Discourse: An Essay in Method*, trans. Jane E. Lewin (Oxford: Blackwell, 1980), pp. 25–6. For clarity I have added these terms in parenthesis to this quotation.

17 Genette, *Narrative Discourse*, p. 232; Lothe, *Conrad's Narrative Method*, p. 133.

18 Genette, *Narrative Discourse*, p. 228.

19 Genette, *Narrative Discourse*, p. 27n.
20 Sherry (ed.), *Conrad: The Critical Heritage*, p. 274.
21 Conrad, *Youth, Heart of Darkness, The End of the Tether*, p. 3.
22 Frederick R. Karl, *A Reader's Guide to Joseph Conrad* (Syracuse, NY: Syracuse University Press, 1997), p. 133.
23 Genette, *Narrative Discourse*, p. 245.
24 Genette, *Narrative Discourse*, p. 245.
25 Conrad, *Youth, Heart of Darkness, The End of the Tether*, p. 3.
26 Genette, *Narrative Discourse*, p. 172.
27 Genette, *Narrative Discourse*, p. 167.
28 The refrain 'Pass the bottle' appears throughout the text. See Conrad, *Youth, Heart of Darkness, The End of the Tether*, pp. 10, 12, 16, 21, 24.
29 Conrad, *Youth, Heart of Darkness, The End of the Tether*, pp. 28, 17.
30 Conrad, *Youth, Heart of Darkness, The End of the Tether*, p. 51.
31 Conrad, *Youth, Heart of Darkness, The End of the Tether*, pp. 50, 82, 83, 94, 114, 162.
32 Benjamin's essay has been taken up by a number of critics working on Conrad. Notable examples include Peter Brooks (whose work on *Heart of Darkness* in *Reading for the Plot* is discussed in my second chapter), Peter Fothergill (1989) and Jakob Lothe (1989).
33 Paul Ricoeur, *The Symbolism of Evil*, trans. Emerson Buchanan (Boston: Beacon Press, 1969), pp. 348–9.
34 Walter Benjamin, *Selected Writings: Volume Three 1935–1938*, trans. Edmund Jephcott, Howard Eiland *et al.*, ed. Howard Eiland and Michael W. Jennings (Cambridge, MA: The Belknap Press of Harvard University Press, 2002), p. 144.
35 Benjamin, *Walter Benjamin: Selected Writings Volume Three*, p. 149.
36 Conrad, *Youth, Heart of Darkness, The End of the Tether*, p. 3.
37 Conrad, *Youth, Heart of Darkness, The End of the Tether*, p. 3.
38 John Lyon, 'Introduction' to Conrad, *Youth/Heart of Darkness/The End of the Tether*, ed. John Lyon (London: Penguin 1995), p. xv.
39 Anthony Fothergill, *Heart of Darkness* (Milton Keynes: Open University Press, 1989), p. 22.
40 Before examining this further, however, a word of caution must be sounded/ recognised. Conrad's novels are not oral narratives (although they purport to repeat a fictional oral narration) and the storytellers that Benjamin discusses are not, in fact, confined to the oral mode. Notably, Benjamin finds 'the incomparable aura that surrounds the storyteller, in Leskov as in Hauff, in Poe and in Stevenson' all of whom produced written narrative (Benjamin, *Walter Benjamin: Selected Writings Volume Three*, p. 162). It becomes apparent that Benjamin is using his discussion of oral storytelling as a way of approaching written narrative, a realisation that recalls Marie Maclean's claim that the study of narrative has 'convinced so many distinguished theorists of the genre (Propp, Todorov, Brémond, Prince, Greimas), that the basic problems of narrative can, in the first instance, be better understood in

relation to oral narration.' Marie Maclean, *Narrative as Performance: The Baudelairean Experiment* (London: Routledge, 1988), p. 1.

41 Conrad, *Youth/Heart of Darkness, The End of the Tether*, p. 5.
42 Conrad, *Youth, Heart of Darkness, The End of the Tether*, p. 48.
43 Joseph Conrad, *Lord Jim* (London: J. M. Dent and Sons Ltd, 1946), p. vii.
44 Benjamin, *Walter Benjamin: Selected Writings Volume Three*, p. 150.
45 Conrad, *Youth, Heart of Darkness, The End of the Tether*, p. 3.
46 Conrad, *Youth, Heart of Darkness, The End of the Tether*, p. 3.
47 Conrad, *Youth, Heart of Darkness, The End of the Tether*, p. 5.
48 Conrad, *Youth, Heart of Darkness, The End of the Tether*, p. 5.
49 Conrad, *Youth, Heart of Darkness, The End of the Tether*, p. 8.
50 Benjamin, *Walter Benjamin: Selected Writings Volume Three*, p. 149.
51 Conrad, *Youth, Heart of Darkness, The End of the Tether*, p. 51.
52 Conrad, *Lord Jim*, p. 33.
53 Lothe, *Conrad's Narrative Method*, p. 146.
54 Genette, *Narrative Discourse*, p. 121.
55 Benjamin, *Walter Benjamin: Selected Writings Volume Three*, p. 146.
56 Benjamin, *Walter Benjamin: Selected Writings Volume Three*, p.150.
57 Conrad, *Youth, Heart of Darkness, The End of the Tether*, p.48.
58 Conrad, *Youth, Heart of Darkness, The End of the Tether*, p. vii.
59 Conrad, *Youth, Heart of Darkness, The End of the Tether*, p. 4.
60 Karl, *A Reader's Guide to Joseph Conrad*, p. 133.
61 Watts, 'Introduction' to Conrad, *Heart of Darkness and Other Tales*, p. xiv.
62 Jocelyn Baines, *Joseph Conrad: A Critical Biography* (London: Weidenfeld, 1993), p. 211.
63 Karl, *A Reader's Guide to Joseph Conrad*, p. 133. Reconciling the sentimental with the sombre has certainly led to some very productive readings of the story. See, for example, James Hansford's 'Reflection and Self Consumption in "Youth"', *The Conradian*, 12.2 (1987), pp. 150–65, and also Richard Niland's 'Aging and Individual Experience in "Youth" and "Heart of Darkness"', *The Conradian*, 29.1 (2004), pp. 99–118.
64 Hansford, 'Reflection and Self Consumption in "Youth"', p. 150.
65 Conrad, *Youth, Heart of Darkness, The End of the Tether*, pp. 6, 11–12, 14, 15.
66 Conrad, *Youth, Heart of Darkness, The End of the Tether*, p. 30.
67 Benjamin, *Walter Benjamin: Selected Writings Volume Three*, p. 151.
68 Benjamin, *Walter Benjamin: Selected Writings Volume Three*, p. 162.
69 Conrad, *Youth, Heart of Darkness, The End of the Tether*, p. 42.
70 Hansford, 'Reflection and Self Consumption in "Youth"', p. 152.
71 Conrad, *Youth, Heart of Darkness, The End of the Tether*, p. 7.
72 Andrea White, *Joseph Conrad and the Adventure Tradition: Constructing and Deconstructing the Imperial Subject* (Cambridge: Cambridge University Press, 1993), p. 180.

2

Heart of Darkness and death

I have wrestled with death. It is the most unexciting contest you can imagine. It takes place in an impalpable greyness, with nothing underfoot, nothing around, without spectators, without clamour, without glory, without the great desire of victory, without the great fear of defeat, in a sickly atmosphere of tepid scepticism, without much belief in your own right, and still less in that of your adversary. If such is the form of ultimate wisdom, then life is a greater riddle than some of us think it to be. (Joseph Conrad, *Heart of Darkness*)

Introduction

Heart of Darkness, as even the most cursory of readings will reveal, is a novel that is preoccupied with death: its 118 pages are littered with representations of the dying and the dead, and death is referred to on almost every second page. From the moment that Marlow steps into the shoes of Fresleven, his murdered predecessor, 'killed in a scuffle with the natives', the death toll rises: Marlow variously recalls: a Swede who hangs himself, discarded slaves 'dying slowly . . . in the greenish gloom', an 'invalid agent from up-country' dying in a corner of the accountant's office, a 'middle-aged negro, with a bullet-hole in the forehead', the 'fool-helmsman' killed in a battle with the 'natives', the 'heads on the stakes' that ornament Kurtz's dilapidated house, the death of Kurtz himself, 'Mistah Kurtz – he dead', and finally, returning from the Inner Station, his own 'wrestle' with death.[1] These deaths are mirrored by Marlow's language – cognates of death ('dead', 'deadened', 'deadly', 'death', 'deathlike', 'death-mask', 'die', 'died' and 'dying') occur throughout the text and, ignoring the references to darkness which become synonymous with death, are supplemented by a great deal of mortuary imagery with words such as 'buried', 'catacomb', 'cemetery', 'corpse', 'decaying', 'funeral', 'ghost', 'grave', 'morbidly', 'mourn', 'mourned', 'mournful', 'mournfully', 'mourning', 'murder', 'sepulchre' and 'wraith' working with cumulative effect to associate every aspect of Marlow's tale with death.

Critics have not been slow to pick up on this prevalence of death imagery, Albert J. Guerard describes *Heart of Darkness* as 'a novel depending on mortuary imagery from beginning to end' and Peter J. Glassman describes it as being 'before anything else about death' going on to read the novel as a journey towards authenticity in which Kurtz's death becomes a moment of victory that allows him to reach full understanding of himself.[2] Thomas Moser offers a similar reading:

> [*Heart of Darkness* is] principally concerned with the theme of self-knowledge: we must recognise our potential weaknesses, our plague spots, in order to achieve a perceptive, moral life . . . Only Kurtz, in Marlow's eyes, achieves self recognition . . . On his deathbed he looks into his soul, sees the truth about himself, and pronounces judgement: 'The horror! The horror!' Through Kurtz, Marlow too gains self-knowledge, comes to recognise Kurtz's 'deficiencies' are potentially his own.[3]

Advancing a similar argument in *Poets of Reality*, J. Hillis Miller who approaches *Heart of Darkness* through a reading of Kurtz's death, more specifically Marlow's relation to that death, reaches the conclusion that, 'the truth of the universe can only be recognized by those who have entered the realm of death'.[4] Peter Brooks, in his hugely-influential *Reading for the Plot*, is also explicitly concerned with Kurtz's death and his reading of the novel explores the possibility of Marlow, for whom 'Kurtz is doubly such a deathbed figure and a writer of obituary', locating and retrieving meaning from that death.[5]

In making a connection between death, narrative and meaning, works like those of Glassman, Moser, Miller and Brooks express similar concerns and ideas to those set out by Walter Benjamin in his essay 'The Storyteller', introduced in the previous chapter, and specifically to his claims that the authority of the storyteller is derived from a certain privileged relation to death. Moser's claims for the novel, set out in the quotation above, are immediately reminiscent of Benjamin, who tells us:

> Dying was once a public process in the life of the individual, and a most exemplary one; think of the mediaeval pictures in which the deathbed has turned into a throne that people come toward through the wide-open doors of the dying person's house . . . it is not only a man's knowledge or wisdom, but above all his real life – and this is the stuff that stories are made of – which first assumes transmissible form at the moment of his death.[6]

Accordingly, we can read *Heart of Darkness* as Marlow's journey to this deathbed scene and his retrieval, and repetition of, the truths that he discovers there. Moser argues, as becomes clear when his work is read alongside Benjamin's essay, for a connection between meaning and death and for the possibility of transmitting this meaning. Moreover, the

constant presence of death in *Heart of Darkness* suggests a way of reading
Conrad's novel that focuses not only on the much discussed death of Kurtz
but also on the questions generated by its juxtaposition with so many
other deaths. Questions thus arise about the possibility of speaking
(writing) of the experience of death and, given the weight that critical
readings of *Heart of Darkness* place on Marlow's relation to Kurtz's
death, further recall the importance of the transmission of wisdom in
Benjamin's definition of the storyteller. It becomes necessary to ask, how
can the death of the other be experienced?

These questions point up the fact that whilst so much criticism of
Heart of Darkness focuses on death, little attempt is made to establish
the nature of death itself. Jacques Derrida makes a similar complaint
of history, revealing, in what he terms 'radically absent questions', the
presuppositions with which analyses of *Heart of Darkness* often begin. He
writes:

> the historian knows, thinks he knows, or grants to himself the unquestioned
> knowledge of what death is, of what being-dead means . . . The question of
> the meaning of death and of the word 'death,' the question 'What is death
> in general?' or 'What is the experience of death?' and the question of
> knowing *if* death 'is' – and *what* death 'is' – all remain radically absent *as
> questions*.[7]

Demonstrating an awareness that similar criticism could be levelled at
literary studies, Peter Brooks writes, 'the further we inquire into the
problem of ends, the more it seems to compel a further inquiry into its
relation to the human end.'[8] This chapter, then, begins this 'further
enquiry' reading *Heart of Darkness*, and readings of *Heart of Darkness*,
alongside a close analysis of Martin Heidegger's phenomenological
account of death.

Heart of Darkness, meaning and Being

Heidegger's *Being and Time*, in the connection it posits between death and
Being, offers a striking parallel to the connection between meaning and
death made by critics of *Heart of Darkness*. Whilst Brooks, for example,
doesn't mention Heidegger by name, his interest in 'the problem of
temporality: man's time-boundedness, his consciousness of existence
within the limits of mortality' describes elements of *Being and Time*
closely.[9] Heidegger's phenomenology works through the implications of
man's (or in his more specific term Dasein's) consciousness of his own
existence, refigured as a concern with the question of (her/his own) Being,
before, in the passages that concern us here, examining the essential role

of death in the access to Being. Heidegger's hermeneutic phenomenology locates Being in the movement towards, and recognition of, death and it is this structuring of the approach to meaning that allows a connection to be made between his philosophy and critical readings that attempt to locate the 'meaning' of *Heart of Darkness*. What is variously termed 'sense' (Kermode), 'wisdom' (Benjamin), 'reality' (Miller), and 'meaning' (Brooks) can therefore be located in the relation to some form of completion whether this be the movement towards narrative closure or the end of life. Or, as is often the case in discussions of *Heart of Darkness*, both: in many readings of the novel, narrative closure and the disclosure of narrative meaning take place at, and are sanctioned by, the instant of death.

Heidegger's work on Being begins with a lengthy exposition on the choice of the correct subject for study. Dasein, which literally translates as 'there being', is not so much selected as defined as the *only* entity from which the nature of Being might be deduced, it is distinguished from other entities by the fact that it is the only entity for which its own Being is an issue. It has an ontical priority in that at all times it relates itself to its own Being, and from this issues an ontological priority: Dasein has an implicit understanding of its relation to its own Being. The essence of Dasein is effectively in its existence: 'Dasein always understands itself in terms of its existence – in terms of a possibility of itself: to be itself or not itself. Dasein has either chosen these possibilities itself, or got itself into them, or grown up in them already.'[10] Because of its inescapable capacity for self-definition through existence Dasein's true name might be 'possibility'.

In Heidegger's reading, death is Dasein's ultimate possibility and it is on this point of Heidegger's argument that Derrida focuses his attention in *Aporias* where he argues, through a meticulously executed close reading of *Being and Time*, that any logical 'problems' located here will 'infect' the entire enterprise. In other words, if Dasein cannot be distinguished as a distinct entity at this border then it is, always already, indistinguishable from other orders of Being. Derrida claims, on behalf of Heidegger, that, 'The difference between nature and culture, indeed between biological life and culture, and, more precisely, between the animal and the human is the relation *to* death ... The relation to death *as such*.'[11] It is in Heidegger's existential analytic of Dasein that the central role of death in the analysis of Being becomes apparent. In section 46 of *Being and Time*, Heidegger poses the question of whether it is possible to grasp the Being of Dasein in its totality, concluding that it is an essential part of Dasein's Being that its 'wholeness' will not be defined by the 'completion' of its physical end: 'As long as Dasein *is* as an entity, it has never reached its 'wholeness'. But if it gains such 'wholeness', this gain becomes the utter loss of Being-in-the-world. In such a case, it can never again be experienced *as an entity*.'[12] The implications of this claim are that Dasein can never experience its own death and that if it is ever to be 'whole' then this cannot be understood in the sense of some final 'completion'. For Heidegger Dasein's wholeness must therefore be located in the manner of its approach to death, on what he will describe as the 'this side' that is in life. The death of Dasein is therefore characterised by its relation to death and this relation is in turn conditioned by its particular mode of Being. Dasein has been defined as that for which its Being is an issue and as living with the 'not yet' of its own potentiality. Heidegger clarifies the idea of Dasein's 'not yet' by drawing out a comparison, which functions by contrast, between this not-yet and the not-yet of ripening fruit. Unlike the Being of Dasein, the Being of ripening fruit hinges on the specific possibilities (ripening) that are 'present-at-hand in it and with it': its totality is answered by its potential to ripen, it is 'not-yet' ripe.[13] Its movement towards ripeness is a movement towards predetermined wholeness. In contrast Dasein possesses no what-Being, its 'not yet' is the capacity for self-interpretation. Rather than being possessed of an already determined nature Dasein's 'not yet' is a continual process of self-definition.

It is the certainty of the inevitability of its own death that guarantees Dasein the ontico-ontological priority that makes it unique: the omnipresent threat of annihilation makes Dasein aware that its Being is at issue and this awareness allows the assumption of responsibility for each individual's life. Heidegger's understanding of the term 'dying' is here revealed, in contrast to what he terms 'perishing' and 'demise', as Dasein's authentic relation to its end: 'The full existential-ontological conception of death may now be defined as follows: *death, as the end of Dasein, is Dasein's ownmost possibility – non-relational, certain and as such indefinite, not to be outstripped. Death is*, as Dasein's end, in the Being of this entity *towards* its end.'[14] The untranslatable nature of the experience denoted by 'my death' is crucial: it is impossible to die for the other or to experience the other's death. The expression 'my death' is, as Derrida suggests, 'a concept or a reality that would constitute the object of an indisputably determining experience.'[15] In other words 'my death', if one can in fact say 'my death', is the guarantee that every other is absolutely other. It is impossible to die in the place of the other or to experience the death of the other, leading to the conclusion that one can only live one's own life and has the responsibility to do so.

This conception of death is crucial to Heidegger when he writes that, for Dasein, '[d]eath is the possibility of the absolute impossibility of Dasein.'[16] By this he understands death to be Dasein's 'ownmost' possibility and, the influence of all other Daseins being stripped away, it becomes Dasein's ultimate and most authentic possibility. And yet, it is also impossibility because at the moment of this ultimate and most authentic possibility Dasein is no longer present to lay claim to it. The acceptance of death as Dasein's ultimate possibility leads Heidegger to conclude that Dasein, as Dasein, can be grasped in its wholeness:

> In Dasein, as being towards its death, its own uttermost 'not-yet' has already been included – that 'not-yet' which all others lie ahead of. So if one has given an ontologically inappropriate Interpretation of Dasein's 'not-yet' as something still outstanding, any formal inference from this to Dasein's lack of totality will not be correct.[17]

This notion of wholeness, of the inclusion of the 'not yet', refutes the idea of a purely linear connection between Dasein's beginning and end which is replaced by the understanding that both beginning and end are complicit in allowing Being to appear. By its ever-present threat of annihilation death makes clear not just the particulars of Dasein's existence but the fact that existence *itself* is an issue for Dasein. Without what Joshua Schuster terms the 'mineness' of Dasein, that is the ownmost possibility of death, which relies on an always already present, pre-theoretical understanding of 'mineness' and 'death', there can be no access to Being.[18]

Differentiating between the end of Dasein and the end of all other entities is essential to Heidegger's project which must establish that 'the kind of ending which Dasein can have is distinguished from the end of a life.'[19] The 'ending of anything that is alive, is denoted as "perishing" [*Verenden*]', a term which recalls the example of the ripening fruit and which denotes a physical entity's bodily end, is set against the modes of ending specific to Dasein which Heidegger terms 'demise' [*ableben*] and 'dying' [*sterben*].[20] Demise, which *'is "only" empirically certain'*, is the bodily end, distinguished from perishing by its relation to 'dying', 'that *way of Being* in which Dasein *is towards* its death' and which Dasein knows as a certainty.[21] For Derrida Heidegger's existential analysis of Dasein rests upon this distinction:

> [I]f the attestation of this 'properly dying' or if the property of this death proper to *Dasein* was compromised in its rigorous limits, then the entire apparatus of these edges would become problematic, and along with it the very project of an analysis of *Dasein*, as well as everything that, with its professed methodology, the analysis legitimately [*en droit*] conditions.[22]

When Heidegger claims that the existential interpretation of death precedes, is presupposed by, and founds all other discourses on death (be they anthropological, biological or religious) Derrida agrees with the logic of his methodology, describing it as, 'undeniable, impossible to dismantle, and invulnerable . . . except perhaps in this particular case called death'.[23]

It is, according to Derrida, undeniable because all discourses on death other than the existential analysis of Dasein always already presuppose a knowledge of death. The problem that Derrida locates 'in this particular case called death', the point at which the undeniability of Heidegger's methodology is challenged, arises in the aporetic requirement that the analysis of death precedes all analysis, including, impossibly, the analysis of death.

Death, seen as a limit at which Heidegger's 'invulnerable' methodology should somehow be brought into question recalls the title of Derrida's essay, *Aporias*. Taken from the Greek *'aporia'*, meaning a stalling point in argument which seemingly possesses no solution, it is the non-passage and non-place, the point at which logic and truth disappear. It is Derrida's contention that death is the aporia par excellence, and he makes no claim to be able to solve the problem, nor does he necessarily regard reaching a solution as desirable should it even be possible. Rather Derrida enacts a series of questions that may allow the better understanding of this particular aporia and, to this end, his analysis is focused on Heidegger's insistence on the ontico-ontological priority of the existential analysis of Dasein.

It is the possibility of dying 'as such' that distinguishes Dasein not only from other orders of Being but also each individual Dasein from every other Dasein: Dasein enjoys a certain access to death. Logically this demands that the analysis of Dasein must be able to rely on the possibility of the 'as such' of death:

> For if one must assume that the difference between a mortal (whoever dies in the sense of 'properly dying') and an animal incapable of dying is a certain access to death *as* death, to death *as such*, then this access will condition every distinction between these two ends, *perishing* and *dying*. By the same token, it will condition the very possibility of an analysis of *Dasein*, that is, of a distinction between *Dasein* and another mode of Being, and of a distinction to which *Dasein* may *testify* by *attesting* to its proper being-able. It is therefore on the possibility of the *as such* of death that the interrogation would have to bear.[24]

In what develops as an argument against the logic of *Being and Time*, Derrida begins by way of an examination of the importance of death for Heidegger's analysis of Dasein. He takes as his first axiom:

> If being-possible is the being proper to *Dasein*, then the existential analysis of the death of *Dasein* will have to make of this possibility its theme. Like an example, the analysis of death is submitted to the ontological law that rules the being of *Dasein*, whose name is 'possibility.' But death is possibility par excellence. Death exemplarily guides the existential analysis.[25]

Death, which Heidegger defines as Dasein's 'ownmost' possibility, is the guarantor of all possibilities. Understanding this, Derrida argues that the possibility of death must submit to the same ontological laws that govern all the possibilities of Dasein: if it cannot be shown to do so then the entirety of Heidegger's existential analysis will be brought into question.[26]

With this position made clear Derrida undertakes his analysis of death which is itself an analysis of Dasein's possibility. He selects Heidegger's problematic formulation of death as 'the possibility of the absolute impossibility of Dasein' and poses the question: how can one think this aporia?[27] His response deserves quoting at length:

> we will have to ask ourselves how a (most proper) possibility as impossibility can still appear *as such* without immediately disappearing, without the 'as such' already sinking beforehand and without its essential disappearance making *Dasein* lose everything that distinguished it – both from other forms of entities and even from the living animal in general, from the animal [*bête*]. And without its *properly-dying* being originally contaminated and parasited by the *perishing* and the *demising*.[28]

In other words, can Dasein, which is distinguished by its unique access to death, remain distinct from other orders of Being when at the moment that it would realise its ultimate distinguishing possibility it is no longer present to do so. Its ownmost possibility manifests itself as the impossibility of possibility. Derrida suggests that death is in fact Dasein's *least proper* possibility in that, at the moment of its realisation, that before which it would appear is no longer there. With this introduction of a non-access to the 'as such' of death the most proper possibility of Dasein becomes instead the most improper and inauthenticating one.

Through his close reading of *Being and Time* Derrida shows that Heidegger's position is absolutely dependent upon the possibility of impossibility. Without it Dasein can no longer be so clearly distinguished from the other orders of Being and Heidegger's whole argument, which places so much emphasis on its ontological foundations, is called into question according to the terms of its own logic. A second quotation makes Derrida's position clear:

> According to Heidegger, it is therefore the impossibility of the 'as such' that, *as such*, would be possible to *Dasein* and not to any form of entity and living thing. But if the impossibility of the 'as such' is indeed the impossibility of the 'as such,' it is also what cannot appear as such. Indeed, this relation to the disappearing as such of the 'as such' – the 'as such' that Heidegger makes the distinctive mark and the specific ability of *Dasein* – is also the characteristic common *both* to the inauthentic *and* to the authentic forms of the existence of *Dasein*, common to all experiences of death (properly dying, perishing, and demising), and also, outside of *Dasein*, common to all

living things in general. Common characteristic does not mean homogeneity, but rather the impossibility of an absolutely pure and rigorously uncrossable limit (in terms of existence or of concepts) between an existential analysis of death and a fundamental anthropo-theology, and moreover between anthropological cultures of death and animal cultures of death.[29]

This passage sets out the implications of the denial of Dasein's 'properly dying'; once access to death, understood as the possibility of impossibility, has been denied then the distinction Heidegger set up between 'dying', 'perishing' and 'demise' collapses. Without this distinction it becomes impossible to distinguish Dasein from other orders of Being. In other words, the non-relation to death is a characteristic common to all forms of life. Derrida has no need to argue for homogeneity from this common relation, it is enough that he has collapsed the distinction between Dasein and other entities to this slight degree. Whilst Heidegger regards death as the possibility of the appearance of the impossibility of possibility (Dasein) as such, Derrida regards this formulation of death as the primary and originary example of the aporia. The aporia that is death arises from the impossibility of experiencing one's own death: it is the disappearance of the 'as such'. In posing the question: 'What difference is there between the possibility of appearing as such of the possibility of an impossibility and the impossibility of appearing *as such* of the same possibility?' Derrida argues for the denial of any difference and concludes that the distinction between Dasein and other entities cannot be sustained and that Dasein never has a relation to death 'as such' but only to perishing, demise and the death of the other.[30] The relation to the death of the other, which Derrida says 'is not the other', is an idea that will be examined further in relation to Maurice Blanchot's reading of 'the possibility of impossibility' in the next chapter.[31]

This reading of *Aporias* suggests several ways in which the philosophical discussion of death can be used to allow insights into the reading of death in *Heart of Darkness*. The first point that should be drawn from *Aporias* is the suggestion, or possibly insistence, that any discourse (whether historical, religious, or in this case literary) should question the very terms with which it approaches the object of its study. Secondly, *Aporias* introduces a two-fold way of regarding death: first, there is 'my death' regarded by Heidegger as central to authentic Being; and secondly, there is the 'experience' of the death of the other which Derrida argues is the only possible relation to death. This distinction can be seen to operate in the approaches Miller and Brooks make to *Heart of Darkness* and makes possible the rereading of their work that I shall undertake in the remainder of this chapter. Heidegger's writing of 'my death', as allowing access to authentic Being, and Derrida's subsequent denial of the term, is particularly useful when applied to the work of Miller. The discussion of Miller's work on *Heart of Darkness* as it relates to the idea of 'my death' introduces the discussion of the death of the other that emerges when Brooks's work on the novel is read alongside *Aporias*. Finally, the tentative connection between death and language made by Heidegger in *Being and Time*, and furthered by Derrida in *Aporias*, will form an equally tentative conclusion to this chapter and gesture towards the next.

J. Hillis Miller, *Heart of Darkness* and the death of the other

Miller's *Poets of Reality*, which contains his influential reading of *Heart of Darkness*, begins by situating the late-nineteenth and early twentieth-century authors it considers in relation to a nihilism that is figured as characteristic of the modern period. This is a nihilism born of the collapse of religion-based systems of belief by which 'Man has killed God by separating his subjectivity from everything but itself. The ego has put everything in doubt, and has defined all outside itself as the object of its thinking power . . . Nothing now has any value except the arbitrary value he sets on things as he assimilates them into his consciousness.'[32] This is a Nietzschean nihilism which Miller defines as, 'the nothingness of consciousness when consciousness becomes the foundation of everything'.[33] This egotistical subject-object relationship takes the form of the denial of an objective reality outside the self to which Miller responds with the demand that it be overcome by something originating beyond the self. With this position established Miller attempts to figure an appropriate response to this nihilism, his analysis mirroring what Simon Critchley describes as 'the task of *philosophical* modernity', which, 'in its peak experiences – Hegel, Nietzsche, Heidegger – is a thinking through of the death of God in terms of the problem of finitude.'[34] Accordingly, *Poets of Reality* explores 'the possibility of an escape from subjectivism' where 'both mind and things are present in a single realm of proximity.'[35] This discussion of meaning, an attempt to recover reality in its immediacy, recalls Heidegger's arguments for the possibility of Dasein's wholeness in *Being and Time* in which it is the authentic relation to death that allows the thinking of Dasein's Being to emerge.

Miller's express intention is to read *Heart of Darkness* in terms of the nihilism of modernism, with the understanding that his project will ultimately explore the attempts made by other writers to reclaim some form of meaning by moving beyond this nihilism. *Heart of Darkness*, which is figured as an expression of the impossibility of moving beyond the subjective, is approached in terms of the opposition between the

fictions of the light of Western civilisation and the darkness of Africa. In
Miller's reading, it is only when light and darkness co-exist, neither
supplanting the other, that meaning will be accessed: only the impossible
union of the two will allow the 'Being' of the world to be apprehended
in itself. Miller explores this impossible union through the discussion
of Kurtz's death, and his attempt to bring darkness into light parallels
Heidegger's idea of death as the possibility of impossibility in its
apparently aporetic demands. This discussion focuses on the relationship
between Marlow and Kurtz, and ultimately on their relationship to death
and it is this reliance on death that allows elements of *Aporias* to be
usefully deployed as an intervention into Miller's reading of *Heart of
Darkness*. The something beyond the self that Miller seeks is unnamed but
is, unmistakably, death. It, 'means abandoning the independence of the
ego. Instead of making everything an object for the self, the mind must
efface itself before reality, or plunge into the density of an exterior world,
dispersing itself in a milieu which exceeds it and which it has not made.'[36]
In Conrad's writing, and *Heart of Darkness* in particular, this manifests
itself as darkness. This darkness is the truth behind impressions and
interpretations – it is simultaneously origin and end and, with this in mind,
Miller situates truth in darkness in order to place it in opposition with
the light of civilisation, the redeeming 'idea'. Darkness and light are
incompatible: 'The experience of knowing darkness takes many forms
. . . In any of its forms the darkness causes the collapse of daylight
intentions and ideals.'[37] This construction of truth sets Conrad, and Miller
in his later chapters, an impossible task. Miller suggests that Conrad,
'attempts to rescue man from his alienation. His problem in reaching his
goal is double: to lift the veil of illusion, and to make the truth appear.'[38]
Finding evidence in Conrad's novel to support this claim, Miller draws
attention to his 'impressionistic' technique of deliberately heightened
reality and to Marlow's complaint that 'it seems to me that I am trying to
tell you a dream – making a vain attempt because no relation of a dream
can convey the dream-sensation'.[39] Whilst Miller regards Marlow's
narrative as an attempt to move beyond the subjectivism of nihilism it
would seem more appropriate to read Marlow's struggle as one that brings
him face to face with the impossible demands placed on Being by death:
the demand that Dasein go beyond the empirical evidence of death granted
by the death of the other, instead laying claim to the phrase 'my death'.

Heart of Darkness deliberately and subtly denies any attempts to rescue
man from his alienation: access to truth, figured in the text as access to
death, is denied. The connection between death and truth is made by
Miller: 'The future is death, the return of created things to the night from
which they have sprung. To say that the darkness is the end of all things

is to identify the darkness with death, and to realise that the truth of the universe can only be recognised by those who have entered the realm of death.'[40] What is at stake in the approach to death, in the possibility of the experience denoted by 'my death', is the possibility of accessing, or 'unveiling', truth. For Miller, as for Heidegger, access to meaning or truth is guaranteed by the access to death. Whilst Miller follows Heidegger in the idea that authenticity can only be reached through death he does not find access to death in Being-towards-death but in the relation to the death of the other: 'No man can confront this truth and survive. Death or the horror can only be experienced indirectly, by way of the face and voice of another. The relay of witnesses both reveals death and, luckily, hides it.'[41] It is with this understanding that he reads the death of Kurtz. Death is the moment at which truth is allowed to appear and Kurtz's death is figured as a victory that allows him access to truth. Whilst Kurtz cannot survive this revelation Marlow is able to act as a surrogate and his own apparently unmotivated tale is granted meaning by Kurtz's final utterance: 'The horror! The horror!'[42]

The suggestion that Conrad, at least momentarily, overcomes the nihilism that is so vividly realised in *Heart of Darkness*, runs counter to the claims that Miller set out to make of the novel. The overall argument of *Poets of Reality*, even in the discussion of Conrad, contains the assumption that there is a 'truth' that can be recovered: that if this truth is darkness it can be carried into the light. So whilst he is denying the possibility of accessing truth in Conrad's writing Miller claims more of Conrad than he intends. Kurtz is allowed his 'escape through the darkness': his final cry is regarded as a 'victory' that 'comes at the moment of his death and depends on his proximity to death.'[43] The interpretation of Kurtz's cry 'The horror!', so clearly dependent on his proximity to death, can be restated as the question of the possibility of the experience denoted by 'my death'. Miller concedes that Kurtz cannot survive this revelation, arguing that the narrative of *Heart of Darkness* is structured to allow the return of Marlow who retrieves meaning from Kurtz's last words, 'The horror! The horror!'[44]

Miller's problematic rejection of this relation to non-relation becomes clearer in his later essay 'Heart of Darkness Revisited' (1983) in which he considers the approach to death as the approach to truth in terms of parable and apocalypse. Like the chapter on Conrad in *Poets of Reality*, 'Heart of Darkness Revisited' is possessed of a moment that fractures its overall argument. Miller's thesis is that *Heart of Darkness* is wholly parabolic in that it uses one 'realistic' story, one that is structured according to the everyday conditions of life – in this case Marlow's journey up the Congo – to evoke an otherwise unspeakable truth. A structure which might be likened to Marlow's desire to make his auditors 'see', a seeing which becomes, in true parabolic mode, a seeing through the surface haze to the meaning itself. The novel is, at the same time, only *partly* apocalyptic, a term which Miller uses in the sense of unveiling/ revelation, in that in its approach to death it is unable to reveal anything other than the act of unveiling itself. Miller concludes that *Heart of Darkness* 'fits that strange genre of the apocalyptic text, the sort of text that promises an ultimate revelation without giving it'.[45] Discussing the novel at a structural level that allows him to avoid affixing any meaning to the text Miller argues convincingly that access to meaning is caught up in an endless cycle of deferral: its origin is always already part of a series of relays, here enacted by the complex narrative structure. Miller apparently finds it hard to sustain this argument, falling back onto the desire to overcome what he identified as nihilism in *Poets of Reality*:

> The truth behind the last witness, behind Kurtz for example in *Heart of Darkness*, is, no one can doubt it, death, 'the horror'; or, to put this another way, 'death' is another name for what Kurtz names 'the horror.' No man can confront this truth and survive. Death or the horror can only be experienced indirectly, by way of the face and voice of another. The relay of witnesses both reveals death and, luckily, hides it.[46]

Julian Wolfreys finds in these words 'that absolute certainty of Miller's which apparently brings to a halt the movement of the text, so seemingly focused is it on establishing a determinate value.'[47] Miller's 'absolute certainty' is indeed remarkable in the context of the essay: in this brief passage he fixes the meaning of the text that he has been describing as 'a revelation of the impossibility of revelation.'[48] Despite the clear parallel between this 'revelation of the impossibility of revelation' with Heidegger's 'possibility of impossibility', Kurtz retains his access to death: his cry 'The horror' is identified unequivocally with death. Whilst Wolfreys questions Miller's certainty as to the meaning of 'The horror!' he is in agreement with one aspect of this interpretation: 'Certainly, though, we can agree with Miller when he says that Kurtz's words are apocalyptic inasmuch as they figure for Kurtz a moment of unveiling.'[49] Wolfreys's words institute a question, to Miller's interpretation and to Conrad's text in general: namely, what is being unveiled at this moment? To Kurtz this might be death but it might well be, amongst a number of other possibilities, 'knowledge of the self (as Marlow suggests at one point), of the Other, of the unconscious, of the violence and oppression of colonialism, of the corruption of European civilization, of evil within human nature.'[50] It also becomes necessary to ask: 'what is unveiled to us, to Marlow?'[51] This question becomes one of the transmission of meaning and, if we retain Miller's assertion that 'the horror' refers to death, the possibility of the relation to the death of the other.

Peter Brooks's 'unreadable report': *Heart of Darkness* and 'my death'

The certainty with which Miller and Wolfreys read Kurtz's death as a moment of unveiling is challenged by Brooks in the aptly titled: 'An Unreadable Report: Conrad's *Heart of Darkness*'. Whilst Miller allows Kurtz access to the experience denoted by 'my death' and Marlow access to this as 'truth' experienced through the death of the other, Brooks argues that 'To present "the horror!" as articulation of that wisdom lying in wait at the end of the tale, at journey's end and life's end, is to make a mockery of storytelling and ethics'.[52] Questioning the meaning of 'the horror!' and suggesting that it may not refer to death results in a reading of *Heart of Darkness* that is a radical departure from that given by Miller. Whilst Miller assumes the possibility of Marlow's relation to the 'death of the other', meaning Kurtz, Brooks questions the assumption that Marlow had access to Kurtz at the point of his death. This of course poses a further question: if Kurtz's 'the horror' is not an expression of the wisdom transmitted at the instant of death, then what is unveiled at this final moment?

Brooks's work, whilst offering close readings of a number of literary texts, is primarily concerned with, 'plotting: with the activity of shaping, with the dynamic aspect of narrative – that which makes a plot 'move forward,' and makes us read forward, seeking in the unfolding of the narrative a line of intention and a portent of design that hold the promise of progress toward meaning.'[53] Whilst Brooks devotes much space to the consideration of what he terms the 'textual middle', the main body of the text that is turned into a 'highly charged field of force' by the desire to connect beginnings with endings, his work is ultimately, inevitably, concerned with the endings which generate this force.[54] Noting the circuitous nature of plot, which he discusses in terms of Sigmund Freud's pleasure principle and death instinct, Brooks concludes that the motivation of plot is 'the desire to wrest beginnings and ends from the uninterrupted flow of middles, from temporality itself; the search for that significant closure that would illuminate the sense of an existence, the meaning of life.'[55] This conception of plot, even down to its metaphor of illumination, recalls the reading of *Heart of Darkness* given by Miller: *Heart of Darkness* is literally read as a journey towards illuminating conclusion, a conclusion that is inextricably linked to the question of the human end, of totalitization and death: 'plot is the internal logic of the discourse of mortality': death (for Dasein) like ending (in narrative fiction) is relied upon to determine meaning and significance. [56] In Brooks's work the terms are interchangeable:

> prior events, causes, are so only retrospectively, in a reading back from the end. In this sense, the metaphoric work of eventual totalization determines the meaning and status of the metonymic work of sequence – though it must also be claimed that the metonymies of the middle produced, gave birth to, the final metaphor.[57]

This claim echoes Paul Ricoeur and Frank Kermode's suggestion that meaning is generated by emplotment through an awareness of beginnings and endings, a position that is well expressed by the phrase 'the sense of an ending'. The way in which this idea, which might be described as a phenomenological narratology, parallels Heidegger's phenomenology of Being is readily apparent: 'the paradox of the self becomes explicitly the paradox of narrative plot as the reader consumes it: diminishing as it realizes itself, leading to an end that is the consummation (as well as the consumption) of its sense-making.'[58] Through an argument that draws on elements taken from Freud, Jean-Paul Sartre and Benjamin, Brooks concludes that 'death provides the very "authority" of the tale, since as readers we seek in narrative fictions the knowledge of death which in our own lives is denied to us.'[59] In narrative this end may take many forms but whatever form it takes, be it the solution of mystery, marriage or murder, the authority granted at the end is the authority, and knowledge, granted to life by death.

Having outlined his theory Brooks proceeds to examine it further through a series of close readings of literary texts. Of these texts *Heart of Darkness* provides the most fertile, and arguably the most treacherous, ground. The difficulty in the discussion of *Heart of Darkness* arises because it is in relation to this text that Brooks begins his close reading of death, an argument that becomes increasingly problematic when its logic demands that it contend with the possibility, which relies on impossibility, of attaining the authority denoted by 'my death'.

Brooks emphasizes Marlow's repeated search for meaning, working through the 'various orders of signification and belief – ready made life plots – that the text casts up along the way', thus identifying not only Marlow's story, which includes Kurtz's story, and the telling of his story aboard the *Nellie*, but also the pre-constructed 'ordering systems' that are themselves stories about the world – these include the 'Company', 'the idea . . . the fiction of the mission' (imperialism), the orderings of 'war, camp, enemies', the work ethic exemplified by Towser's book on seamanship, 'maps', Kurtz's 'readable report', and Kurtz himself.[60] Most significant is Marlow's search for Kurtz, in his journey upriver Marlow retraces Kurtz's story motivated by the desire, both his own and that of the Company, to recover the story of the elusive ivory trader of the Inner Station. The retracing of Kurtz's journey makes *Heart of Darkness* well suited to the theory of narrative that Brooks is tracing: 'it engages the very motive of narrative in its tale of a complexly motivated attempt to recover the story of another within one's own'.[61] The text makes the connection between Marlow and Kurtz plain, offering clear parallels between the two characters: Kurtz the 'special being' characterised as 'a voice' is recalled by Marlow who himself 'resembled an idol' and who, sitting in near darkness on the *Nellie*, appears as 'no more . . . than a voice.'[62] In this manner, Marlow retraces the steps of his predecessor Kurtz, and later aboard the *Nellie* he will attempt to recount this journey once again, the river setting recalling the fact that he first heard Kurtz's story on board a boat. Marlow's journey, then, is a quest for meaning that begins, and ends, in the repetition of the story of another. In reading *Heart of Darkness* in this way Brooks makes explicit an understanding that has informed the majority of readings of *Heart of Darkness*, namely that the meaning of Marlow's tale will be contained in the end of Kurtz's story: 'Marlow's own narrative can make sense only when his inquest has reached a "solution" that is not a simple detection but the finding of a message written at and by the death of another.'[63]

It is in the attempt to recover the meaning granted by Kurtz's death that Brooks introduces the possibility that it may not hold the 'meaning' desired by the text. Kurtz's 'The horror!' is read not as a victory but instead as revealing the failure of language at the final moment:

> Kurtz's final words answer so poorly to all of Marlow's insistence on summing-up as a moment of final articulation of wisdom, truth, and sincerity, as affirmation and as moral victory . . . To present 'the horror!' as articulation of that wisdom lying in wait at the end of the tale, at journey's end and life's end, is to make a mockery of storytelling and ethics.[64]

At the moment of his own death, Kurtz is rendered inarticulate: all that he is able to produce is a 'cry' closer to the 'babble' of the natives than it is to civilised language.[65] The consequence of this is the failure of meaning for Marlow: if the 'cry' is denied its status as a meaningful utterance, it becomes instead the failure of language at the moment of death. It is Marlow's description of his own approach to death that casts doubt over Kurtz's final summation – at the last possible moment Marlow finds that, 'probably I would have nothing to say.'[66] This fear, and Marlow's desire to 'think my summing-up would not have been a word of careless contempt. Better his cry – much better', provide the terms for the reassessment of Kurtz's end.[67] These last two sentences work against one another. The first seems so fitting as a description of Kurtz's last words that it is tempting to read it as confirmation that they are words of careless contempt. The second sentence refuses such a reading and points to the meaning intended by Marlow, that Kurtz achieved something more significant and yet here his words are still reduced to a 'cry'. From this Brooks concludes that Kurtz's death fails to adequately answer the call to provide an ending to Marlow's story. This reading of 'The horror' as a meaningless cry is reinforced by an earlier description of Marlow's time with Kurtz: 'the memory of that time itself lingers around me, impalpable, like a dying vibration of one immense jabber, silly, atrocious, sordid, savage, or simply mean, without any kind of sense.'[68]

The similarities between Brooks's reading of Kurtz's end and Derrida's reading of death are clear. The aporia Brooks exposes in *Heart of Darkness* comes in the desire for summation at the moment of death, with what Miller might describe as the attempt to bring darkness into light. It is at the final step that language falters, at the very moment where Marlow hopes to find 'all the wisdom, and all truth, and all sincerity . . . compressed into that inappreciable moment of time in which we step over the threshold of the invisible.'[69] This is a border policed by language, a connection drawn by Marlow who describes Kurtz's situation of 'utter solitude without a policeman – by the way of silence – utter silence'.[70] Kurtz's final cry is the collapse of language at the point of death. There remains no voice for summation and Marlow is left to attempt repeatedly to uncover the meaning of Kurtz's death, and his own story, in language that allows no access to death.

The consequences of this denial of meaning, of the refusal of the tale to grant itself authority, are left unexplored in *Reading for the Plot*. Brooks's discussion does not require that the 'meaning' of the novel be fixed but that the motives for telling, the desire that there should be an end, emerge. Despite this, a hint of inconsistency emerges in this chapter on Conrad: the thesis that Brooks is testing began from the idea of an always already present connection between beginning and end, and in the discussion of *Heart of Darkness* the end seems to be becoming increasingly elusive. Brooks appears to recognize this in his choice of epigraph, which is taken from *Lord Jim*: 'Are not our lives too short for that full utterance which through all our stammerings is of course our only and abiding intention?'[71] The question remains then, how are we to read *Heart of Darkness* with its apparently absent end and its constant return to beginning?

Heart of Darkness, language and absent death

Reading Miller and Brooks against the philosophical horizon of Heidegger and Derrida affords valuable insights into *Heart of Darkness*. Death understood as aporia, as radical impossibility, makes Miller's confident claims that meaning is transmitted at the point of death, with Kurtz's 'The horror!', extremely problematic. Conversely death read as aporia reinforces Brooks's extremely convincing attack on the idea that Kurtz's final words can in any way be seen as a final summation. The question remains, though, how might we read *Heart of Darkness*?

Perhaps a change of emphasis is necessary in this re-evaluation of Conrad's enigmatic text. Critical attention, exemplified here by Brooks and Miller, predominantly focuses on Kurtz's death, to the extent that the other deaths in the text become somewhat obscured. For readings that seek to fix the meaning of *Heart of Darkness* by interpreting Kurtz's dying words this 'overlooking' seems wholly fitting for the text's other deaths are characterised by nothing so much as their absence. A study of the numerous deaths to which we are denied access might answer the demands of a philosophical reading that describes *Heart of Darkness* as a novel whose accepted 'end' refuses to conform to standard interpretative practices. These other 'endings,' the deaths that silently occupy the margins of the Marlow-Kurtz story, offer a possible site at which to consider the novel in terms of the relation to the *non-access* to death – a relation that is necessary when death becomes an aporia.

If Marlow can only relate to the dead Kurtz as the 'something' buried in 'a muddy hole' then this death, now silenced, assumes a new position as the last in a series of absent deaths.[72] For the length of Marlow's journey he is surrounded by the dead and the dying: obscured by darkness on the riverbanks, recalled from the past or expected in the future these are the ubiquitous traces of death that parallel Derrida's concept of the spoken signified which 'is never contemporary, is at best the subtly discrepant inverse or parallel – discrepant by the time of a breath – from the order of the signifier.'[73] In *Heart of Darkness* the signifiers of death that are repeatedly encountered remain markedly distinct from their unknown signified. At the outset of his tale Marlow recalls the Roman invasion, when men were 'dying like flies'.[74] In Marlow's present the invasions continue, this time into Africa, his ship 'landed more soldiers . . . Some, I heard, got drowned in the surf; but whether they did or not, nobody seemed particularly to care.'[75] Later Marlow recalls the surreal scene of a man-of-war off the African coast, 'firing into a continent. Pop, would go one of the six-inch guns; a small flame would dart and vanish, a little white smoke would disappear, a tiny projectile would give a feeble screech

– and nothing happened. Nothing could happen.'[76] Nothing happens. The deaths in the shelled village remain conspicuously absent, marked only by a feeble screech that later will be echoed by Kurtz's final cry, itself 'no more than a breath'.[77] The unseen crew of the man-of-war are reportedly 'dying of fever at the rate of three a-day'.[78] Similarly any deaths caused by the pilgrims during the steamboat attack are carried on in silence: Winchesters are fired 'squirting lead into that bush', again nothing happens and when, at Kurtz's camp, the pilgrims again open fire on the natives Marlow 'could see nothing more for smoke'.[79] The shrunken heads that surround Kurtz's house, the faces of all but one turned away, are a reminder of the deaths that fill the margins of *Heart of Darkness*: they are 'not ornamental but symbolic' – turned away they are a powerful evocation of the impossibility of engaging in a face-to-face encounter with the death of the other.[80]

The literal absence from the text of these and other deaths in *Heart of Darkness* prefigures the impossibility of accessing death that Brooks argues is explicit in Marlow's non-relation to Kurtz's death. Among the many deaths in Marlow's narrative, the death of the steamer's helmsman, 'an athletic black belonging to some coast tribe', most readily invites comparison with that of Kurtz.[81] It is the 'pilgrim in pink pyjamas' who makes this link for us: ' "He is dead," murmured the fellow, immensely impressed . . . "And by the way, I suppose Mr. Kurtz is dead as well by this time." '[82] Both deaths occur on Marlow's steamboat with Marlow in attendance and both demonstrate a concern with deathbed pronouncements. The helmsman, who Marlow dismisses disparagingly as a 'fool', is surprisingly (in the context of *Heart of Darkness*) vocal, 'yelling at the shore' and 'champing his mouth, like a reined-in horse', so much so that Marlow, 'in a fury', demands that he 'keep quiet!'[83] As the helmsman lies dying, the only victim of the attack on the steamboat, 'the two whites stood over him' just as Marlow will later be found 'stood over' a dying Kurtz on the steamer's return journey, and just as Marlow will later find himself 'transfixed' by Kurtz the two men find themselves 'enveloped' by the helmsman's 'lustrous and inquiring glance'.[84] The distinction comes at the moment of death when the helmsman who, rather than being allowed a 'moment of complete knowledge', the moment of summation and judgement afforded to Kurtz, 'looked as though he would presently put to us some question in an understandable language . . . died without uttering a sound.'[85] A reading that rejects Kurtz's 'cry' as a source of wisdom begins to make it impossible to sustain the contrast between these two deaths that the text so clearly suggests. If the significance of Kurtz's death, which Marlow goes to such lengths to privilege over the text's other deaths (most markedly over the deaths of the Africans who silently populate his narrative) rests on the fact that his last words are heard and recorded, then this is a distinction that collapses when his last words are figured as meaningless. Such a reading would suggest that a far more appropriate representation of death as 'the impossibility of possibility' comes in Marlow's account of the 'grove of death' where discarded African slaves lie dying:

> Near the same tree two more bundles of acute angles sat with their legs drawn up. One, with his chin propped on his knees, stared at nothing, in an intolerable and appalling manner: his brother phantom rested its forehead, as if overcome with a great weariness; and all about others were scattered in every pose of contorted collapse, as in some picture of a massacre or a pestilence.[86]

Here death is presented starkly as otherness. All Marlow can find to do is to hand one of his 'good Swede's ship's biscuits' over to the 'black shadows,' a curious silent gesture that emphasises the impossibility of connection.[87] Far more powerfully than Kurtz's 'The Horror!', this scene dramatises the only relation that Derrida allows to the death of the other: access to death as 'properly dying' is not possible in any case and Marlow's attributing of wisdom to Kurtz and to his withholding of that summation from the helmsman becomes entirely inappropriate. If death can only be accessed by the relation to its absence then Marlow's reaction to Kurtz's death, the authority of his own story, can only be misinterpretation. The apparent divide between the treatment of Kurtz's death and of those other silent, silenced, deaths begins to collapse.[88]

If *Heart of Darkness* is to have any significance beyond the senseless vibration of Kurtz's final words then it will be as a novel that is concerned with language and the possibility of the transmission of meaning. For Conrad the relation to death is expressed as the possibility of speaking and hearing death: it becomes the question of language at the point of death. Whilst the natives in the grove of death are conspicuous in their silence and the dying man in the Accountant's office is not only 'too ill to groan' but also 'does not hear', Kurtz is presented in terms of his voice.[89] This is made explicit by Marlow's reaction following the attack on the steamboat: 'I made the strange discovery that I had never imagined him as doing, you know, but as discoursing. I didn't say to myself, "Now I will never see him," or "Now I will never shake him by the hand," but "now I will never hear him." The man presented himself as a voice.'[90] The conception of Kurtz as a voice recalls Heidegger's suggestion that the ability to experience death is somehow connected with language: 'Mortals are they who can experience death as death. Animals cannot do so. But animals cannot speak either. The essential relation between death and language

flashes up before us, but remains still unthought.'[91] Heidegger leaves this
connection unthought, stated obliquely by the juxtaposition of 'Animals
cannot do so', experience death as death, with 'But animals cannot speak
either.' Derrida examines the possible interpretations of this juxtaposition,
concluding that on the one hand there could be no essential link between
the 'as such' of death and language, whilst, on the other hand it could
depend:

> upon an ability to speak and name. But instead of giving us added assurance
> about the experience of death as death, this discourse would lose the *as such*
> in and through the language that would create an illusion, as if *to say death*
> were enough to have access to dying as such – and such would be the illusion
> or the fantasy.[92]

The examination of this second possibility is central to this reading of
Heart of Darkness which concentrates on the possibility of speaking,
or writing, death.

Throughout *Heart of Darkness* Marlow questions the validity of
language. Part way through his tale Marlow interrupts himself,
questioning his listeners' relation to the story:

> Do you see the story? Do you see anything? It seems to me I am trying to tell
> you a dream – making a vain attempt, because no relation of a dream can
> convey the dream-sensation . . .
>
>   No, it is impossible; it is impossible to convey the life-sensation of any
> given epoch of one's existence – that which makes its truth, its meaning – its
> subtle and penetrating essence. It is impossible. We live, as we dream – alone
> . . . .[93]

Doubts are also cast upon the written word, something that is common
in all four Marlow novels, when Marlow finds Towson's *An Inquiry into
Some Points on Seamanship* and mistakes the Russian notes for cipher,
and this uncertainty continues throughout the novel in an overt concern
with language and naming that culminates in Marlow's lie to the Intended:
'The last word he pronounced was – your name.'[94] A lie that reminds the
reader that, of all the living characters that appear in the text, only Marlow
and Kurtz are named at any point.

This mistrust of language appears as a discrepancy between the spoken
and the seen that emerges in what has been described as Conrad's
'impressionistic' style. Conrad's, or Marlow's, attempts to 'make us see',
to articulate perceptions and sensations, have the effect of undermining
the written word by insisting on the distinction between written signs
and their real-world referents.[95] This concern with the relation between
literature and truth is set out in the preface to *The Nigger of the 'Narcissus'*
where Conrad defines art as 'a single-minded attempt to render the highest

kind of justice to the visible universe, by bringing to light the truth . . . All art, therefore, appeals primarily to the senses, and the artistic aim when expressing itself in written words must also make its appeal through the senses'.[96] Conrad's artistic theory, which describes his impressionist techniques well, suggests a project in which 'truth' and representational mimesis will somehow be aligned. It comes as little surprise that his artistic practice poses a challenge to such a simplistic reading: as Andrew Gibson says, whilst *Heart of Darkness* is 'a predominantly representational text' it is also one that 'obstinately insists on the limits of representation and insistently dwells on the significance of those limits.'[97] It is in its exploration of the limits of representation that *Heart of Darkness* exposes the discrepancy between language and reality with which Marlow is so clearly concerned throughout all of his narratives. With this in mind, the unnamed narrator's description of Marlow as storyteller for whom 'the meaning of an episode was not inside like a kernel but outside' opens up the possibility that the 'truth' of *Heart of Darkness* may well be located in the very aspects of the text that question the possibility of mimetic representation, or, more plausibly, in the relation between the novel's mimetic and metalinguistic elements.[98] Accordingly this concern with the limits of representation is enacted on the 'outside' of the story – at the level of its narrative structure. So, just as the frame narrative of 'Youth' is central to reading that story, so too in *Heart of Darkness* where the structural peculiarities of the text play an important role. The structure of the framed narrative underscores the act of narrating which, in the case of Marlow's narrative, is literally the centre of the tale. On a very obvious level the uncertainties thus generated by the placement of Marlow's story within the narrative of another limited, non-omniscient, narrator work to undermine attempts on the part of the reader to 'fix' the meaning of the text, leading instead to a consideration of the ways in which meaning comes to be generated in and by language.

The structural exploration of the limits of representation is echoed by a very deliberate uncertainty of expression in Marlow's narrative. Conrad's repeated use of adjectives such as 'interminable', 'inexpressible' and 'incomprehensible', what F. R. Leavis termed his 'adjectival insistence', frustrates attempts, including those made by Marlow, to close down the possibilities of the text by fixing its meaning.[99] While Leavis would find such 'intrusions' on the part of the author 'little short of disastrous', subsequent critics have made this aspect of the text central to their readings of *Heart of Darkness*.[100] Chinua Achebe's now famous objection to what he describes as 'the dehumanization of Africa and Africans' centres around the very indecipherability of Conrad's African Congo, the 'blank' space on Marlow's map, and the denial of meaningful expression to the Africans – a reading that Marlow's description of Africa as 'that thing that couldn't talk, and perhaps was deaf as well' could be seen to confirm.[101] Similarly Christopher L. Miller identifies the prevalence of adjectives that parade their refusal to affix meaning as a defining feature of an Africanist discourse by which 'Africa is lent the force of myth.'[102] Working with the same aspects of the text, Gibson suggests a way of approaching the novel that responds to, without effacing, these concerns by placing its overt insistence on exploring the limits of representation, what he terms 'Marlovian discourse', against the totalizing ontological discourse, the dominant white male discourse, by which the novel's European powers assert their authority:

> My point is not that what I have called Marlovian discourse somehow 'overcomes' or resists or neutralizes the ontological discourse in Conrad's tale. Rather, it gnaws away at it, like an unease that cannot be stilled. It provides an insistent reminder that ontology itself has a history, that ontology is itself a discursive construction . . . In *Heart of Darkness*, Marlovian discourse might be said to open up an ethical space in which alterity is registered precisely as it persistently and forever exceeds cognition and indicates the limits of ontology.[103]

As Gibson suggests, this ethics of discourse is played out in Marlow's encounter with the Intended in which, having returned to Europe from the 'blank' space of the Congo, that metaphoric site of inexpressibility, he abandons the truths that have played such a significant part in his tale.

Marlow meets Kurtz's fiancée in Brussels in what must be one of the most peculiar episodes in *Heart of Darkness*. In an atmosphere that borders on the gothic, with the dusk breeze whispering Kurtz's last words, it becomes inevitable that Marlow will be asked to repeat them. To his horror Marlow finds himself unable to do so:

> 'I heard his very last words . . .' I stopped in a fright.
> 'Repeat them,' she murmured in a heart-broken tone. 'I want – I want – something – something – to – to live with.'
> I was on the point of crying at her, 'Don't you hear them?' The dusk was repeating them in a persistent whisper all around us, in a whisper that seemed to swell menacingly like the first whisper of a rising wind. 'The horror! The horror!'
> 'His last word – to live with,' she insisted. 'Don't you understand I loved him – I loved him – I loved him!'
> I pulled myself together and spoke slowly.
> 'The last word he pronounced was – your name.'[104]

Whilst Gibson regards this final lie as 'a triumph' for Marlow, other critics have found the scene less convincing.[105] Moser's response to the passage is particularly interesting, he writes: 'Marlow's lie certainly weakens the scene; he has made truth seem too important throughout the novel to persuade the reader now to accept falsehood as salvation.'[106] What Moser remarks upon as a damaging contradiction in *Heart of Darkness* connects truth and lies and identifies this scene as the site at which they are brought into focus. Marlow has indeed insisted on truth but his struggles with its expression have repeatedly emphasized its inaccessibility. Falsehood is not offered as salvation but as the only option: Marlow *cannot* voice the truth of Kurtz's death. However, through Conrad's use of the framed narrative the lie to the Intended is not encountered in its immediacy as a lie, but as the recognition of a lie. Having already mistold Kurtz's story Marlow attempts to tell it truthfully, now with the additional scene of its original mistelling.

When they meet, the Intended insists, very much as Marlow has done, that meaning must be transmissible at the end of life: 'Something must remain. His words, at least, have not died.'[107] Marlow's reply, '[t]he last word he pronounced was – your name' confirms the impression that Kurtz's words are not a fitting conclusion to either a life or a story.[108] In many ways this judgement on Kurtz's last words reflects the ending of the novel: the conclusion of Marlow's story is met by the crew of the *Nellie* with apparent indifference, the Director breaking the silence to remark 'We have lost the first of the ebb'.[109] The unnamed narrator has been listening attentively but refuses to fulfil the traditional role of storyteller, offering no comment on the tale he has just told, leaving the framed narrative without any final sense of closure: an omission that reminds the reader that what was promised all along was an 'inconclusive' tale.[110]

Marlow's lie is significant in that he chooses an act of proper naming, and it is an act of naming that fails to take place. As Nina Pelikan Straus points out, the Intended is 'thrice voided', neither Conrad, nor Marlow, nor Kurtz pronounce her name.[111] The substitution of 'your name' for the nameless, the Intended, suggests the arbitrary nature of language. It does not matter what the Intended is called, that she has any name is sufficient. The absence of the Intended's name recalls Marlow's remarks on Kurtz's name: 'Kurtz – Kurtz – that means short in German – don't it? Well, the name was as true as everything else in his life – and death. He looked at least seven feet long.'[112] Naming becomes not only arbitrary but potentially misleading and words become interchangeable – Kurtz/short, German/English, even here there is ambiguity: while Kurtz the man is half French, his name is a misspelling of the German word 'kurz' meaning 'short', and is very possibly a re-phrasing of 'Klein', the name of a real-life Company agent Georges Antoine Klein who Conrad saw die aboard the *Roi des Belges* in 1890 and whose name in German means 'small'.[113] Language as naming becomes a lie. In this instance it is also incomplete, it is a lie that is not fully told. If 'the horror!' is the realization of the impossibility of summation, of the impossibility of arriving at true names, then Marlow's lie with its refusal to speak the Intended's name, becomes its re-enactment.

This lie, which is the conclusion to Marlow's 'inconclusive tale', recalls his earlier words:

> You know I hate, detest, and can't bear a lie, not because I am straighter than the rest of us, but simply because it appals me. There is a taint of death, a flavour of mortality in lies – which is exactly what I hate and detest in the world – what I want to forget. It makes me miserable and sick, like biting something rotten would do.[114]

This impassioned condemnation of lies offers a useful insight into the lie with which Marlow's story ends. It is not because of any moral 'straightness' that Marlow detests lies, it is because they remind him of his own mortality. It is the 'taint of death' he wishes to forget, not lying. Understanding why Marlow sees mortality in lies provides a way of understanding what *Heart of Darkness* is saying about death. Lying, the point at which language betrays its obligation to truth, reflects the moment at which dying properly becomes perishing. At the end, at the moment of death, when it is demanded that truth be spoken, that meaning be transmitted, language fails. Any attempt at summation must be a lie, the deliberate misuse of language serves as a reminder that language and truth are not the same. When Marlow lies to the Intended he is simply substituting one lie for another. Like death, lies reveal the limit of truth. This reading of death as the limit of truth can be seen clearly in Wolfreys's summation of *Heart of Darkness*: 'we cannot choose but recognise, in Conrad's writing, the written mark as a certain expression of the limit – the limit of what may be known, what may be expressed – and also the undecidability which accompanies the "differential splitting" which occurs as a result of the attempt to narrate.'[115] The horrible fact that Marlow's lie conceals, and simultaneously enacts, is that language has no connection to truth.

This reading of language and lies in *Heart of Darkness* leads back to Kurtz's 'the horror!'. What has emerged is the fact that this last cry does not guarantee access to truth: Kurtz's death, spoken, witnessed, and repeated cannot be distinguished from the mass of silent, absent and ignored deaths that litter the pages of *Heart of Darkness*. 'The horror!' means no more than silence. Marlow's relation to the deaths in *Heart of Darkness* is consistent throughout: the 'ownmost possibility' denoted by 'my death' is also the most readily substitutable. In this novel death is shown to be a word whose referent is unknown and Heidegger's demise, perishing and properly dying all name the same thing in what is a meaningless, but necessary, linguistic distinction. Paradoxically, in its very failure to pronounce 'my death', in Marlow's lie to the Intended, *Heart of Darkness* suggests a relation between language and death, more specifically it suggests a connection between literary language and death, an idea that is taken up in Maurice Blanchot's writings and which will form the basis of the next chapter.

Notes

1 Joseph Conrad, *Youth, Heart of Darkness, The End of the Tether* (London: J. M. Dent and Sons Ltd, 1946), pp. 53, 66, 69, 71, 110, 150.
2 Albert J. Guerard, *Conrad the Novelist* (Cambridge, MA: Harvard University Press, 1958), p. 35; Peter J. Glassman, *Language and Being: Joseph Conrad and the Literature of Personality* (New York: Columbia University Press, 1976), p. 198.
3 Thomas Moser, *Joseph Conrad: Achievement and Decline* (Cambridge, MA: Harvard University Press, 1957), p. 24.
4 J. Hillis Miller, *Poets of Reality: Six Twentieth Century Writers* (Cambridge, MA: The Belknap Press of Harvard University Press, 1966), p. 31.
5 Peter Brooks, *Reading for the Plot: Design and Intention in Narrative* (Oxford: Clarendon, 1984), p. 246.
6 Walter Benjamin, *Selected Writings: Volume Three: 1935–1938*, trans. Edmund Jephcott, Howard Eiland *et al.*, ed. Howard Eiland and Michael W. Jennings (Cambridge, MA: The Belknap Press of Harvard University Press, 2002), p. 151.
7 Jacques Derrida, *Aporias*, trans. T. Dutoit (Stanford, CA: Stanford University Press, 1993), p. 25. See also, Philippe Ariès, *Western Attitudes Towards Death: From the Middle Ages to the Present*, trans. Patricia M. Ranum (London: Marion Boyars Publishers, 1994).
8 Brooks, *Reading for the Plot*, p. 95.
9 Brooks, *Reading for the Plot*, p. xi.
10 Martin Heidegger, *Being and Time*, trans. J. Macquarrie and E. Robinson (Oxford: Blackwell, 1962), p. 33.
11 Derrida, *Aporias*, pp. 43–4.
12 Heidegger, *Being and Time*, p. 280.
13 Heidegger, *Being and Time*, p. 288.
14 Heidegger, *Being and Time*, p. 303.
15 Derrida, *Aporias*, p. 22.
16 Heidegger, *Being and Time*, p. 294.
17 Heidegger, *Being and Time*, p. 303.
18 Joshua Schuster, 'Death Reckoning in the Thinking of Heidegger, Foucault, and Derrida', *Other Voices* (1997). 14 Dec.1999 <*http://dept.english.upenn.edu/~ov/jnschust/death.html*>.
19 Heidegger, *Being and Time*, p. 284.

20 Heidegger, *Being and Time*, p. 284.
21 Heidegger, *Being and Time*, p. 301.
22 Derrida, *Aporias*, p. 30.
23 Derrida, *Aporias*, p. 5.
24 Derrida, *Aporias*, pp. 35–6.
25 Derrida, *Aporias*, p. 63.
26 See Derrida, *Aporias*, pp. 63, 76–7.
27 Heidegger, *Being and Time*, p. 294.
28 Derrida, *Aporias*, p. 71.
29 Derrida, *Aporias*, p. 75.
30 Derrida, *Aporias*, p. 75.
31 Derrida, *Aporias*, p. 76.
32 Miller, *Poets of Reality*, pp. 3–4.
33 Miller, *Poets of Reality*, p. 3.
34 Simon Critchley, *Very Little ... Almost Nothing: Death, Philosophy, Literature* (London: Routledge, 1997), p. 2.
35 Miller, *Poets of Reality*, pp. 7, 9.
36 Miller, *Poets of Reality*, pp. 7–8.
37 Miller, *Poets of Reality*, p. 29.
38 Miller, *Poets of Reality*, p. 19.
39 Conrad, *Youth, Heart of Darkness, The End of the Tether*, p. 82.
40 Miller, *Poets of Reality*, p. 31.
41 J. Hillis Miller, 'Heart of Darkness Revisited', *Conrad Revisited: Essays For the Eighties*, ed. Ross Murfin (Alabama: University of Alabama Press, 1985), pp. 31–50, p. 43.
42 Conrad, *Youth, Heart of Darkness, The End of the Tether*, p. 149.
43 Miller, *Poets of Reality*, pp. 7, 31.
44 Conrad, *Youth, Heart of Darkness, The End of the Tether*, p. 149.
45 Miller, 'Heart of Darkness Revisited', p. 48.
46 Miller, 'Heart of Darkness Revisited', p. 43.
47 Julian Wolfreys, *Deconstruction: Derrida* (Houndmills: Macmillan, 1998), p.169.
48 Miller, 'Heart of Darkness Revisited', p. 39.
49 Wolfreys, *Deconstruction: Derrida*, p. 170.
50 Andrew Michael Roberts, *Conrad and Masculinity* (London: Macmillan, 2000), p. 126.
51 Wolfreys, *Deconstruction: Derrida*, p. 170.
52 Brooks, *Reading for the Plot*, p. 250.
53 Brooks, *Reading for the Plot*, p. xiii.
54 Brooks, *Reading for the Plot*, p. xiii.
55 Brooks, *Reading for the Plot*, p. 140.
56 Brooks, *Reading for the Plot*, p. 22.
57 Brooks, *Reading for the Plot*, p. 29.
58 Brooks, *Reading for the Plot*, pp. 51–2.
59 Brooks, *Reading for the Plot*, p. 95.

60 Brooks, *Reading for the Plot*, pp. 239–43.

61 Brooks, *Reading for the Plot*, p. 238.

62 Conrad, *Youth, Heart of Darkness, The End of the Tether*, pp. 79, 147, 46, 83.

63 Brooks, *Reading for the Plot*, p. 247.

64 Brooks, *Reading for the Plot*, pp. 249–50.

65 Conrad, *Youth, Heart of Darkness, The End of the Tether*, pp. 151, 69.

66 Conrad, *Youth, Heart of Darkness, The End of the Tether*, p. 151.

67 Conrad, *Youth, Heart of Darkness, The End of the Tether*, p. 151.

68 Conrad, *Youth, Heart of Darkness, The End of the Tether*, p. 115.

69 Conrad, *Youth, Heart of Darkness, The End of the Tether*, p. 151.

70 Conrad, *Youth, Heart of Darkness, The End of the Tether*, p. 116.

71 Joseph Conrad, *Lord Jim* (London: J. M. Dent and Sons Ltd, 1946), p. 225.

72 Conrad, *Youth, Heart of Darkness, The End of the Tether*, p. 150.

73 Jacques Derrida, *Of Grammatology*, trans. Gayatri Chakravorty Spivak (Baltimore: The Johns Hopkins University Press, 1976), p. 18.

74 Conrad, *Youth, Heart of Darkness, The End of the Tether*, p. 49.

75 Conrad, *Youth, Heart of Darkness, The End of the Tether*, pp. 60–1.

76 Conrad, *Youth, Heart of Darkness, The End of the Tether*, p. 62.

77 Conrad, *Youth, Heart of Darkness, The End of the Tether*, p. 149.

78 Conrad, *Youth, Heart of Darkness, The End of the Tether*, p. 62.

79 Conrad, *Youth, Heart of Darkness, The End of the Tether*, pp. 110, 147.

80 Conrad, *Youth, Heart of Darkness, The End of the Tether*, p. 130.

81 Conrad, *Youth, Heart of Darkness, The End of the Tether*, p. 109.

82 Conrad, *Youth, Heart of Darkness, The End of the Tether*, p. 113.

83 Conrad, *Youth, Heart of Darkness, The End of the Tether*, pp. 111, 110.

84 Conrad, *Youth, Heart of Darkness, The End of the Tether*, pp. 112, 149, 112.

85 Conrad, *Youth, Heart of Darkness, The End of the Tether*, pp. 149, 112.

86 Conrad, *Youth, Heart of Darkness, The End of the Tether*, p. 67.

87 Conrad, *Youth, Heart of Darkness, The End of the Tether*, pp. 67, 66.

88 The collapse of the distinction between Kurtz's death and the other deaths in *Heart of Darkness*, a collapse that is brought about through the possibility of language at the point of death, might go some way to responding to very persuasive readings of the novel that emphasize the racism inherent in its denial of language to the Africans who, as a consequence, appear as an almost silent backdrop to the stories of Conrad's European characters. For a further discussion of this area of debate see Robert Hampson's essay ' "Heart of Darkness" and "The Speech that Cannot be Silenced" ', *English*, 39:163 (Spring 1990), pp. 15–32. This connection of Being to language would, if it were sustained (and my argument here, following Derrida, is that it is not) lend great weight to Chinua Achebe's attack on Conrad as racist – an attack that is largely based on Conrad's denial of language to the Africans in his novel. See Chinua Achebe, 'An Image of Africa: Racism in Conrad's *Heart of Darkness*', in Chinua Achebe, *Hopes and Impediments: Selected Essays* (London: Heinemann, 1988), pp. 1–20.

89 Conrad, *Youth, Heart of Darkness, The End of the Tether*, p. 69.

90 Conrad, *Youth, Heart of Darkness, The End of the Tether*, p. 113.

91 Martin Heidegger, *On The Way to Language*, trans. Peter D. Hertz (New York: Harper, 1971), p. 107. Quoted in slightly different form in Derrida, *Aporias*, p. 35.

92 Derrida, *Aporias*, pp. 36–7.

93 Conrad, *Youth, Heart of Darkness, The End of the Tether*, p. 82.

94 Conrad, *Youth, Heart of Darkness, The End of the Tether*, p. 161.

95 Ian Watt, *Conrad in the Nineteenth Century* (London: Chatto & Windus, 1980), pp. 175–9. See also Bruce Johnson, 'Conrad's Impressionism and Watts "Delayed Decoding"', *Conrad Revisited: Essays for the Eighties*, ed. Ross C. Murfin (Alabama: Alabama University Press, 1985), pp. 51–70.

96 Joseph Conrad, *The Nigger of the 'Narcissus'* (London: J. M. Dent and Sons Ltd, 1950), pp. vii–ix.

97 Andrew Gibson, 'Ethics and Unrepresentability in *Heart of Darkness*', *The Conradian*, 22:1/2 (1997), pp. 113–37, p. 114.

98 Conrad, *Youth, Heart of Darkness, The End of the Tether*, p. 48.

99 F. R. Leavis, *The Great Tradition* (London: Chatto and Windus, 1962), p. 177.

100 Leavis, *The Great Tradition*, p. 179.

101 *Conrad, Youth, Heart of Darkness, The End of the Tether*, p. 52; Achebe, Hopes and Impediments, p. 12; Conrad, *Youth, Heart of Darkness, The End of the Tether*, p. 81.

102 Christopher L. Miller, 'The Discoursing Heart: Conrad's *Heart of Darkness*', *Joseph Conrad: Contemporary Critical Essays*, ed. Elaine Jordan (Houndmills: Macmillan, 1996), pp. 87–102, p. 99.

103 Gibson, 'Ethics and Unrepresentability in *Heart of Darkness*' p. 131.

104 Conrad, *Youth, Heart of Darkness, The End of the Tether*, p. 161.

105 Gibson, 'Ethics and Unrepresentability in *Heart of Darkness*' p. 135. The passage has been regarded by many critics including, Cedric Watts, F. R. Leavis, Raymond Williams and Thomas Moser, as the novel's least satisfactory scene. Leavis describes the scene with the Intended as 'another bad patch' complaining again of Conrad's 'adjectival insistence' (Leavis *The Great Tradition*, pp. 181, 177). More recent feminist criticism has made interesting use of the scene with the Intended, see Nina Pelikan Straus, 'The Exclusion of the Intended from Secret Sharing', *Joseph Conrad: Contemporary Critical Essays*, ed. Elaine Jordan (Houndmills: Macmillan, 1996), pp. 48–66.

106 Moser, *Joseph Conrad*, p. 79.

107 Conrad, *Youth, Heart of Darkness, The End of the Tether*, p. 160.

108 Conrad, *Youth, Heart of Darkness, The End of the Tether*, p. 161.

109 Conrad, *Youth, Heart of Darkness, The End of the Tether*, p. 162.

110 Conrad, *Youth, Heart of Darkness, The End of the Tether*, p. 51.

111 Nina Pelikan Straus, 'The Exclusion of the Intended from Secret Sharing', *Joseph Conrad: Contemporary Critical Essays*, ed. Elaine Jordan (Houndmills: Macmillan, 1996), pp. 48–66, p. 63.

112 Conrad, *Youth, Heart of Darkness, The End of the Tether*, p. 134.

113 Zdzisław Najder describes Conrad's encounter with Klein: 'The steamer took aboard Georges Antoine Klein, a twenty-seven-year-old Frenchman suffering from dysentery, who had recently been appointed the Company's commercial agent at Stanley Falls. Klein died during the journey, on 21 September [1890], and was buried at Tchumbiri. His name, later changed to Kurtz, may be found in the manuscript of "Heart of Darkness". Apart from Klein's presence on board, and his death, there seems to be no reason to suppose that he had much in common with the demonic character in the novel.' [Zdzisław Najder, *Joseph Conrad: A Chronicle*, trans. Halina Carroll-Najder (Cambridge: Cambridge University Press, 1983), p. 136.] On reflection, having listed several other candidates that have been proposed as models for Kurtz, Najder concludes that 'in the end, as a character with his own specific life history, Kurtz is the author's own creation.' (526n).

114 Conrad, *Youth, Heart of Darkness, The End of the Tether*, p. 82.

115 Wolfreys, *Deconstruction: Derrida*, p. 176.

3

Lord Jim and the structures of suicide

To be busy with material affairs is the best preservative against reflection, fears, doubts – all these things which stand in the way of achievement. I suppose a fellow proposing to cut his throat would experience a sort of relief while occupied in stropping his razor carefully. (Joseph Conrad, *Chance*)

Suicide in Conrad's novels

In *Writing as Rescue* Jeffrey Berman makes the claim that 'a higher suicide rate inheres within Conrad's world than within that of any other major novelist writing in English', a bold statement that Todd G. Willy echoes, identifying a 'chronic epidemic of suicides that broke out in the late Victorian fiction of Joseph Conrad', whilst Ian Watt notes that 'the role of suicide in Conrad's fiction is certainly of exceptional importance.'[1] Certainly there is a prodigious suicide rate among Conrad's characters. Jocelyn Baines counts nine 'leading' characters who commit suicide in *Joseph Conrad: A Critical Biography*, C. B. Cox lists fifteen in *Joseph Conrad: The Modern Imagination*, and Bernard C. Meyer seventeen in his *Joseph Conrad: A Psychoanalytic Biography*.[2] The tally that is offered here, which numbers seventeen, is at variance with all three accounts for reasons that are more to do with the definition of suicide that I am applying, the significance of which will emerge shortly, than with any discrepancies of counting.

My list of suicides in Conrad's fiction would therefore include, in chronological order, the following characters, some major and some minor. Kayerts who, in 'An Outpost of Progress' (1897), hangs himself from the cross that marks the grave of his assistant Carlier. *Lord Jim* (1900) sees the enigmatic suicide of Captain Brierly who drowns himself at sea and later Jim's 'suicide' when he dies at the hands of Doramin. The ageing Captain Whalley drowns himself in 'The End of the Tether' (1902). In *Heart of Darkness* (1902) there is the suicide of an unnamed Swede who hangs himself. In *Nostromo* (1904) the dilettante Martin Decoud drowns himself. Sevrin drinks poison in 'The Informer' (1906) when he is uncovered as the informant of the title. In *The Secret Agent* (1907) Winnie Verloc drowns herself, and in the same text there is an important reflection on suicide in the character of the 'Professor' who, armed as he is with a powerful bomb, is always moments away from a violently destructive suicide. In 'Gaspar Ruiz' (1908) Erminia throws herself to her death into a chasm following the death of her husband. *Under Western Eyes* (1910) sees the suicide of the driver Ziemianitch. Flora de Barral considers suicide in the early chapters of *Chance* (1914) and later her father poisons himself. In *Victory* (1915) Axel Heyst burns to death in the fires that consume Lena's body. In 'The Planter of Malata' (1915) Geoffrey Renouard recalls a beautiful waterfall and the 'legend of a governor-general of the Dutch East Indies, on official tour, committing suicide on that spot by leaping into the chasm. It was supposed that a painful disease had made him weary of life' and later commits suicide himself, setting out 'calmly to swim beyond the confines of life – with a steady stroke – his eyes fixed on a star!'[3] In 'The Warrior's Soul' (1915) the French officer de Castel is killed after he begs his captor Tomassov to shoot him. In *The Rescue* (1920) Jörgenson kills himself and all aboard the *Emma* by jumping into a hold full of explosives with a lighted cigar. Finally, Jean Peyrol's death in *The Rover* (1923) might be considered a suicide, in a manner similar to that of Jim, as he sacrifices himself for his country. So this list includes seventeen characters whose deaths I am counting as suicide (Kayerts, Captain Brierly, Jim, Captain Whalley, the 'unnamed Swede', Martin Decoud, Sevrin, Winnie Verloc, Erminia, Ziemianitch, Mr de Barral, Axel Heyst, the 'governor general', Geoffrey Renouard, de Castel, Jörgenson and Jean Peyrol) and a further two characters for whom suicide is central (Flora de Barral and the Professor). To this latter pair might be added, as Baines, Cox and Willy variously suggest, Kurtz (*Heart of Darkness*), Lena (*Victory*) and Susan ('The Idiots').

Whilst cataloguing the suicides within Conrad's world in this way is useful in the respect that it confirms the high suicide rate identified by Willy and Berman, the true utility of such a survey arises in the specifics of these suicides which in their differences suggest that there might be more than one way of defining suicide. This is readily apparent in the inclusion of Jim, Heyst and Peyrol whose deaths are not suicides in the most commonly understood usage of the term in that the protagonists do not, strictly speaking, take their own lives. To classify these deaths as suicide is to follow Émile Durkheim's influential definition of suicide as an act with both active and passive forms: 'suicide is commonly conceived as a positive, violent action involving some muscular energy, it may happen that a purely negative attitude or mere abstention will have the same consequence.'[4]

Suicide, then, is allowed these two aspects: the active and the passive. With this in mind, Willy suggests that Kurtz should be numbered amongst Conrad's suicides, arguing that 'Kurtz did in fact commit suicide, a suicide that falls well within the definition insisted upon by Durkheim'.[5] Willy supports his claim by arguing that 'Kurtz was safely on his way downriver to the security of the "Central Station" when suddenly he decided to break off his retreat and to return to an "Inner Station" which he knew full well was "by that time bare of goods and stores" (*HD*, 90). It is that lack of necessary supplies that will surely – albeit indirectly – kill him.'[6] While all of this may be true Willy's reading stems from a reading of Durkheim that neglects the element of desire that underlies both forms of suicide. Rather than indicating a wilful intention on Kurtz's part to let himself die, the text of *Heart of Darkness* seems instead to support the view that he actually wishes to cling to his life in the jungle. In contrast to this, the suggestion that Jim's surrender to Doramin should be read as a form of suicide is clearly supported by the text of *Lord Jim*. It is, says Jim as he sets out to face Doramin, the father of Dain Waris whose death is the result of his actions, 'Time to finish this.'[7] His arrival at Doramin's campong confirms the interpretation of this as a deliberate act: ' "He hath taken it upon his own head," a voice said aloud. He heard this and turned to the crowd. "Yes. Upon my head." '[8] Clearly while Jim does not pull the trigger himself he is, unlike Kurtz, the agent of his own death.

This reading of Jim's death as suicide is strengthened when it is placed alongside the suicide of Captain Montague Brierly, the commander of the *Ossa* and one of two nautical assessors assigned to the *Patna* inquiry. 'Big Brierly,' a man who 'had never in his life made a mistake, never had an accident, never a mishap, never a check in his steady rise,' and who 'seemed to be one of those lucky fellows who know nothing of indecision, much less of self-mistrust', apparently with a good deal of deliberation, 'jumped overboard at sea barely a week after the end of the inquiry'.[9] As Anthony Winner says, 'Brierly's sudden intuition of kinship with Jim can be understood as a subjective explanation of his offer to pay Jim to disappear, and a further empathic identification with Jim's untested faith and its result helps explain the suicide.'[10] The text invites its readers to interpret Jim's actions in terms of Brierly's death by mirroring the discovery of this 'kinship' between Brierly and Jim with the equally unsettling kinship that Jim recognizes between himself and Brown. In the first of these pairs Jim acts as a catalyst to action: Brierly commits suicide by drowning himself at sea when he finds his own honour, and by

extension the foundation of his identity, questioned by Jim's dishon-
ourable act to which, to his horror, he finds he is able to relate – Jim is,
after all, 'one of us' and his membership of that 'body of men' calls its very
identity into question.[11] It would seem that *Lord Jim*, the text and the
man, has a tendency to undermine certainties – as Brierly says, 'Such an
affair destroys one's confidence.'[12] In the second pairing it is Gentleman
Brown, the 'latter-day buccaneer', that prompts action. Brown is, as John
Batchelor puts it, 'Jim's "double". The Döppelganger of romantic fiction
is both the *opposite* of the protagonist . . . and his *mirror-image*.'[13]
Stephen K. Land, who talks of Brown as Jim's '*Alter-ego*' concurs:

> Brown comes from the white world which the hero has abandoned,
> challenges the hero's achievement by confronting him with his past failures,
> and effectively ends his career. Brown, however, opposes the hero not from
> a contrasting position of orthodoxy, as do his predecessors, but as himself
> a case of failure and dereliction of the hero's own type.[14]

Brown himself plays on this connection, asking Jim 'whether he had
nothing fishy in his life to remember that he was so damnedly hard upon
a man trying to get out of a deadly hole.'[15] Ultimately it is Jim's recognition
of himself in Brown, which recalls his early stuttered insistence 'I am – I
am – a *gentleman*, too . . .' [my emphasis], that undermines the status
to which he has risen in Patusan, and his attendant self-esteem, leading to
his decision to seek out death at Doramin's hands.[16] Thus Jim's surrender
to Doramin, 'a mighty deliberate force', seems little different to Brierly's
surrender to the ocean, an act which the text presents very clearly as
suicide.[17]

A consideration of the suicides in Conrad's work suggests a way
of categorising suicide that diverges from, without contradicting,
Durkheim's 'active/passive' pairing. Whilst Durkheim's concern is with
defining the means of death in terms of either personal individual agency
(active) or external factors (passive) it is possible to rethink those suicides
in a way that responds to the demands that suicide makes of death and
which returns us, through the work of Maurice Blanchot, to Martin
Heidegger's phenomenological account of death as the 'possibility of
impossibility'.

Blanchot's work sees a certain doubling of death that becomes most
evident in the discussion of suicide. The first form of suicide is chosen by
Brierly, Jim, Decoud, Peyrol, Jörgenson and the Professor: it is a form of
suicide that has everything to do with living. As Cox suggests, Brierly and
Decoud, 'appear to choose suicide deliberately and consciously as a proper
response to the meaninglessness of their lives.'[18] This intended connection

between suicide and life is the key to this first, active, form of suicide which is linked to hope and which attempts to make death somehow answer the demands of life. This is the suicide that is implied by Conrad's 'act of savage energy' and is witnessed in Jim's attempt to regain what he perceives as his lost honour by dying well. These characters actively seek out death, attempting to achieve mastery both of and through it. Theirs are deliberate and often violent deaths: Brierly and Decoud drown, Jim and Peyrol are shot, Jörgenson blows himself up, and the Professor plans to do the same. This attempt to master death finds its clearest expression in the anarchist nicknamed the 'Professor' who is never more than twenty seconds from his death; in a 'thick glass flask' he carries 'enough stuff . . . to blow [himself] . . . and everything within sixty yards of [him] . . . to pieces.'[19] The possibility of his suicide acts as a constant deterrent to the authorities who would otherwise have him arrested and so his potential death becomes a mechanism through which he orders his life. The Professor's constant search for the 'perfect detonator' illustrates the desire to control death by choosing the instant of its arrival. His need is to eliminate the twenty second delay of his current detonator: 'it's the weak point of this special system, which is only for my own use . . . I am trying to invent a detonator that would adjust itself to all conditions of action, and even to unexpected changes of conditions. A variable and yet perfectly precise mechanism.'[20] His strength comes from this use of death's threat: 'In the last instance it is character alone that makes for one's safety . . . I depend on death, which knows no restraint and cannot be attacked.'[21] The Professor relies completely, and very effectively, on a notion of death that is figured as a part of his life and in this version of suicide it would be inappropriate to describe the Professor as a 'victim'.

For Blanchot this first form of suicide, which attempts to make death a part of life, misrecognizes the very nature of death:

> The weakness of suicide lies in the fact that whoever commits it is still too strong. He is demonstrating a strength suitable only for a citizen of the world. Whoever kills himself could, then, go on living: whoever kills himself is linked to hope, the hope of finishing it all, and hope reveals his desire to begin, to find the beginning again in the end, to inaugurate in that ending a meaning which, however, he means to challenge by dying.[22]

The alternative is the more obviously passive death: the suicides that Marlow describes in *Chance* when he remarks, '[s]uicide, I suspect, is very often the outcome of mere mental weariness . . . the final symptom of complete collapse.'[23] The suicides of Kayerts, Erminia, Captain Whalley, Winnie Verloc, Mr de Barral, the Governor-general and Renouard belong to this group.

Blanchot: suicide and the 'double death'

Blanchot's reading of death, which comes through Heidegger from Hegel, is similar to Derrida's and his consequent discussion of suicide takes into account the impossibility of the formulation 'my death'. Blanchot approaches Heidegger's 'possibility of impossibility', the sentence which for Derrida led to the characterisation of death as an aporia, through a consideration of suicide. In light of a philosophy that regards death as the guarantor of Being, suicide is an attempt to control death: '[s]uicide is the fantasy of total affirmation', it is an attempt to realise death as an action of an 'I' in an instant that cannot pass or be surpassed.[24] In other words suicide is the attempt to remain oneself, as an active agent, even at the instant of death and is thus a denial of the passivity of death. Blanchot makes the mechanics of this fantasy clear: 'To take one's own life: is this not the shortest road from man to himself, from animal to man and . . . from man to God?'[25] When death is regarded as the most proper possibility, voluntary death is the mistaken attempt to bring this possibility within reach. This is the *attempt* made by suicide, and in Blanchot's analysis it is the final act of inauthentic bad faith. It is the attempt to make death a part of life, to make it an act of will and to become the creator of one's own nothingness. In this sense, suicide, understood as an attempt to make of the absence a presence, might be said to be an impossibility, impossible for the very reasons outlined by Derrida in *Aporias*, namely that at the point at which death appears to be claimed as this possibility the subject, its claimant, is no longer present. Blanchot regards suicide as an attempt to interpret Heidegger's 'possibility of impossibility' in a way that retains access to death, that allows the suicide to achieve completion by laying claim to his or her own death. Understood in this Heideggerian context the desire evinced by suicide is to be 'conscious of disappearing and not consciousness disappearing'.[26] The desire to be 'conscious of disappearing' is, simply put, the desire for there to remain an 'I' to witness its own disappearance. This wish to be present at the instant of death can be interpreted both temporally and spatially. The suicide's wish is for *presence* at the point of death and to constrain death's arrival to the *present* moment in time. Suicide is this attempt to constrain death to a particular moment in time, demanding that the possibility of death be made present in an absolute instant.

Blanchot points out the logical contradiction in this demand: suicide is the wish to be able to say 'I die' at exactly the instant when the 'I' disappears. Such a relation to death can only be a misrecognition: 'death's rightful quality is impropriety, inaccuracy . . . It is the abyss of present time, the reign of time without a present'.[27] For the suicide death will always come too late because at the instant of death the concept of time becomes inapplicable. In positing a relation between the witnessing suicidal 'I' and time, Blanchot is following Heidegger for whom, 'Being cannot be grasped except by taking time into consideration'.[28] For Heidegger this is true because Dasein exists historically in terms of the past actions of both itself and others, and the possibility of its own future actions. Heidegger makes this connection between Dasein and time clear: 'The ecstatical character of the primordial future lies precisely in the fact that the future closes one's potentiality-for-Being; that is to say, the future itself is closed to one'.[29] This 'primordial future' distinguishes between the future that will continue after the death of the individual Dasein and the future of that individual Dasein whose future is 'primordial' precisely because it is finite. This 'closed' future is what makes it possible to understand authentically one's ownmost possibility. What is crucial to Dasein's relation to this 'primordial future' is the fact that it includes the closure of Being: essentially Being-towards invokes the right to a future that promises the end of Being. It is the individual Dasein that ends and not time. In this sense time does not end with death, but becomes inapplicable to the 'I' that hopes to die. This recalls Blanchot's description of death as the reign of time without a present where 'present' denotes not only the absent 'now' but also the absent 'being (t)here'. Blanchot's formulation of death as impropriety means that suicide can only have possibility within the time that Heidegger designates as 'primordial' and that is precisely the reason for its impossibility: death is the limit, or perhaps more accurately the horizon, of the primordial. Death, as the condition of possibility is necessarily the other as such: that which the primordial cannot access as its other. It is this quality of death that leads Derrida to characterise Dasein's relation to the death of the other as 'the other, who is not the other'.[30] Blanchot further illustrates this non-relation to death by refusing the idea of a natural link to death, claiming that it is not possible to say, 'I produce my death as the body produces cancer', rather 'One never dies simply of an illness, but of one's death.'[31] Unlike death, illness as an experience of the living which is linked to time and can get better or worse. It is something which it is possible to own, of which can be said 'my illness' and therefore belongs to life in a way that cannot be said of death.

To answer the contradictory demands thus made on death Blanchot constructs his notion of the 'double death' around the fact that the first, false, death is accessible whilst the second death exists outside of time and allows no access except as its misrecognition as the first death:

> Death is somehow doubled: there is one death which circulates in the
> language of possibility, of liberty, which has for its furthest horizon the

freedom to die and the capacity to take mortal risks; and there is its double, which is ungraspable. It is what I cannot grasp, what is not linked to *me* by any relation of any sort. It is that which never comes and toward which I do not direct myself.[32]

This is clarified further in 'Literature and the Right to Death':

> Death works with us in the world; it is a power that humanizes nature, that raises existence to being, and it is within each one of us as our most human quality; it is death only in the world – man only knows death because he is man, and he is only man because he is death in the process of becoming. But to die is to shatter the world; it is the loss of the person, the annihilation of the being; and so it is also the loss of death, the loss of what in it and for me made it death.[33]

The death that 'works with us in the world' is the first death, that which Heidegger situates Dasein as Being-towards, or in Blanchot's words, the individual as 'death in the process of becoming'. This is the death of which it would be possible to say 'my death', it is what 'names the very irreplaceability of absolute singularity (no one can die in my place or in the place of the other)' and makes possible access to truth and knowledge.[34] The second death 'shatters the world,' reversing this idea of death as activity, transforming it into the passivity of dying where, 'we leave behind not only the world but also death.'[35] Blanchot describes this as the paradox of death, that our relationship to the first death raises existence into Being, as our ownmost possibility, but to die, the second death, is the loss of this relation. The double logic of the phrase 'my death' is at the centre of this double death. As Derrida puts it, ' "My death" in quotation marks is not necessarily mine; it is an expression that anyone can appropriate; it can circulate from one example to another.'[36] This second death, in direct contrast to the ownmost possibility that is the first death, is the 'impossibility of every possibility', the point at which it is no longer possible to say 'I die' but only 'one dies'. That this is the case is emphasized by Blanchot's insertion of the word 'every' into his rewriting of Heidegger's sentence: this is not simply the 'impossibility of possibility', where possibility might still belong to an individual 'I', 'my possibility', but the impossibility of 'every(one's) possibility'. This possibility of infinite substitution is what leads Blanchot to regard death as the annihilation of Being. In direct contrast to the individualising 'I die', 'one dies' merges the self with the other in an instant that forces the individual to take its place amongst that which is outside the self.

To fully grasp this aspect of Blanchot's writing on death and literature it is important to grasp the significance of Heidegger's phrase, 'the possibility of impossibility'. It is not sufficient to regard it as an aporia where the impossible becomes possible – simultaneously appearing and collapsing by the force of its own logic. It is not simply the moment of death where Dasein experiences that which is denied to experience: the 'I' disappearing at the moment when that same 'I' would experience the impossible, the very experience of its own disappearance constituting the aporia. To read Heidegger's phrase in this way is to simplify and rewrite the sentence as, 'the making possible of the impossible'. To this understanding must be added another reading of the sentence, one which doesn't necessarily contradict this earlier idea but that has far greater significance, in which the 'of' of 'possibility of impossibility' should be read as 'belonging to/coming from'. Thus the sentence could be rewritten 'impossibility's possibility' – that is, the possibility created, generated and guaranteed by impossibility. Hence the impossibility of the phrase 'my death' is significant not so much in the inability of the individual to experience her or his death but in the possibility that such an impossibility generates. This is the possibility of authentic action undertaken with the awareness of the responsibility that 'my death' confers. This understanding of the phrase fully takes into account Heidegger's notion of Being-towards and the existential self-determination that that implies.

For Blanchot, the 'impossibility of every possibility', read as 'every possibility's impossibility', is the second death; that is, the impossibility generated by the possibility of death. The possibility of death here, where death is read as possibility, the point at which the 'I' dissolves in the move from 'I die' to 'one dies', guarantees the opposite of Heidegger's death: it is the guarantee of inauthenticity. Blanchot suggests that the suicide mistakes this second death for the first death. The first death makes possible the desire of the suicide who in attempting to claim the mastery of Being achieves instead the second death. Suicide is thus linked to life: paradoxically the suicide desires death to gain the power necessary to live. In striving to master death, in invoking the right to death, the suicide,

> comes up against death as that which doesn't happen or as that which reverses itself (betraying, as though demented, the mendacity of the dialectic by bringing it to its conclusion) – reverses the possibility of impossibility into *the impossibility of every possibility*.
>
> Suicide is in a sense a demonstration (whence its arrogant, hurtful, indiscreet character), and what it demonstrates is the undemonstratable: that in death nothing comes to pass and that death itself does not pass.[37]

Voluntary death takes as its goal a self-completion that necessarily seeks to include death, as the possibility of impossibility, in its definition of Being. As an attempt to control death suicide works as a 'demonstration' of what is at stake in dying: the suicide's intention is that death should be constrained to arrive at a certain time and as the result of a certain sequence of events. According to Blanchot this is impossible: the suicide can only know the first death, the second death allows no access. Thus Blanchot says, 'I cannot conceive of the end as an end in itself'; it is only possible to make an end of the first death, it is not possible to conceive of the second death as an end as this second death has no relation to the living.[38] The reversal of the possibility of impossibility into the impossibility of every possibility denies the experience of death to Being. The paradox of the first death, read as the possibility generated by impossibility is that such a reading, necessary for Heidegger, can only function in conjunction with this second death. That is as much as to say that in order to guarantee possibility for Dasein impossibility, death, must be such that refuses possibility. It is this misrecognition that Blanchot explores when he gives suicide such a central position in the attempt to comprehend what is at stake at the point of death, and more specifically for 'my death'.

Death and art

As Blanchot argues in 'Literature and the Right to Death', literary language poses questions that are central to the philosophy of Being, questions that are firmly rooted in the (im)possibility of death. What Blanchot calls 'the "question" that seeks to pose itself in literature' reverses the expected movement in which philosophy is applied to literature.[39] In Blanchot's hands this question becomes an interrogation of philosophy *by* literature.

Blanchot, who follows Hegel in regarding negativity as the essence of language, sees naming as a 'deferred assassination' in that names function to negate the reality of objects. In a deliberate refiguring of Hegel, Blanchot remarks that 'For me to be able to say, "This woman" I must somehow take her flesh and blood reality away from her, cause her to be absent, annihilate her. The word gives me the being, but it gives it to me deprived of being.'[40] The negativity inherent in naming is, according to Hegel's analysis, derived from the nature of the claims required by the statement 'This'. Specifically Hegel points to the 'twofold shape' of the 'This' which encompasses both 'now' and 'here'. It is the specific nature of this twofold 'sensuous This' that means that it *'cannot be reached* by language, which belongs to consciousness, i.e. to that which is inherently universal'.[41] Blanchot pursues the implications of the negation of the 'This' replacing Hegel's example of 'This Tree/Night' with the more emotive 'This woman' – a substitution that moves the discussion from language to death. Of course language does not kill anyone in this direct sense, but it does announce real death. The woman of the example above is not killed by words, but the act of naming her 'this woman' announces that she can be detached from herself, from her actual existence, and 'plunged', to use Blanchot's term, 'into a nothingness in which there is no existence or presence; my language essentially signifies the possibility of this destruction . . . if this woman were not really capable of dying . . . I would not be able to carry out that ideal negation.'[42]

The mechanics of this negation by language are made clear in 'Two Versions of the Imaginary' an essay that begins from the straightforward position that the image and the thing that image represents are not the same, and that the thing that is represented necessarily precedes the image. Blanchot writes: 'The image, according to the ordinary analysis, is secondary to the object. It is what follows. We see, then we imagine. After the object comes the image.'[43] Blanchot begins his analysis of the statement by arguing that, ' "After" means that the thing must first take itself off a ways in order to be grasped.'[44] It is the nature of this (re)movement that becomes the focus of Blanchot's examination of the image: 'But this remove is not the simple displacement of a moveable object which would nevertheless remain the same. Here the distance is in the heart of the thing.'[45] The suggestion that 'the distance is in the heart of the thing' is crucial. The distance that the process of language institutes between object and image can be usefully discussed in terms of mimesis, understood not as Plato used the term as resemblance (this would be 'the simple displacement of a moveable object which would nevertheless remain the same') but in the narrower Aristotelian sense in which mimesis involves the *making* of likeness. Leslie Hill uncovers the paradox of Aristotelian mimesis as making in Blanchot's *Thomas the Obscure*:

> Before any object may be perceived as an exact, mimetic copy of another, a margin of alterity must first have differentiated object from copy in order that the relation of resemblance between the two may be instituted at all. But in so far as resemblance is founded in differentiation, mimesis in the true sense proves to be an impossibility.[46]

Hill's 'margin of alterity' equates to Blanchot's 'distance': in other words, the object and its image are not only not the same thing but the process of naming removes the possibility of locating the original. The necessity of this distancing, necessary in order to institute any notion of resemblance, reveals the impossibility of a mimesis that is founded on the notion of differentiation. Blanchot continues his analysis of the double image:

> The thing was there; we grasped it in the vital movement of a comprehensive action – and lo, having become image, instantly it has become that which no one can grasp, the unreal, the impossible. It is not the same thing at a

distance but the thing as distance, present in its absence, graspable because ungraspable, appearing as disappeared.[47]

In the mimetic image the absent presence of the original thing remains, that is as much as to say that the mimetic process itself remains.

With his Hegelian concept of language as negativity established Blanchot pursues his philosophy of literature which is, and always was, inextricable from a philosophy of Being that starts from death. Blanchot sees language, like death, as doubled, divided into 'two slopes': everyday language and literary language. The first 'slope', that of meaningful prose, is that as set out by Heidegger which reduces death to its positive side, the side of activity where death is regarded as an affirmation of Dasein, where death is written as the 'possibility of impossibility'.

Despite the negation that makes language possible, and the appearance of language as both negation *and* the appearance of this negation as a distance between object and name, Blanchot makes it clear that the absence at the heart of language is masked in 'everyday', non-literary, language. In everyday language the appearance of the concept masks the absence of the object. This side of language 'is turned toward the movement of negation by which things are separated from themselves and destroyed in order to be known, subjugated, communicated'.[48] Put in simple terms, 'The first slope is meaningful prose . . . ordinary language limits equivocation. It solidly encloses the absence in a presence'.[49] If negation is the true origin of language in general then literature, Blanchot argues, reveals this essential quality. Ullrich Haase and William Large summarise: 'If language is negation, then it is literature that truly embodies its strange power, for it negates both the reality of the thing and the presence of the idea. It is a double absence.'[50] The second slope, that side of language that Blanchot identifies as literary, takes as its aim to make the absence its centre: 'the truth of the work' occurs when '[t]he work disappears, but the fact of disappearing remains and appears as the essential thing'.[51] In literary use, language is a site of a double absence, referring to neither object nor concept. The literary word refers to nothing other than itself and its position in relation to other words. This second slope reveals the absence that was masked by the first, it is here that death must be written as the 'impossibility of every possibility'.

The inversion of Heidegger's 'possibility of impossibility' to become the 'impossibility of every possibility' begins to answer the question that Blanchot poses so often: what is literature? Blanchot approaches this question through another question: why write? Or, more significantly, how is it possible to write? Blanchot's claim is that the demand of writing, the demand that compels the artist to write, emerges from the dread that is first experienced in relation to death as the realisation of the nullity that is at the heart of existence. It is the writer's attempt to overcome this nullity that leads to the comparison of the impulses of the artist with those of the suicide, 'Not that the artist makes death his work of art, but it can be said that he is linked to the work in the same strange way in which the man who takes death for a goal is linked to death.'[52] The misrecognition inherent in the notion of the 'double death', by which the suicide mistakes one form of death for another, and which was discussed at length above, is repeated by the writer who in attempting to write the 'work' can only produce the 'book'.

These two terms, 'work' and 'book', are introduced to discuss the 'strange way' in which the artist is linked to the work, locating literature in relation to the first and second deaths. The work is an attempt to make language, that which is never the property of the 'I' but which always already belongs to the other, an expression of the individual, affirming Being. Perversely, at the moment in which the work would be completed, when it is rendered into language, it becomes a book. The unknowable nature of the work is emphasized throughout *The Space of Literature*, and is perhaps best described when Blanchot writes, '[the writer] exists only in his work, but the work exists only when it has been made this public, alien reality, made and unmade by colliding with other realities. So he really is inside the work, but the work itself is disappearing.'[53] At work in literature is the reversal of Heidegger's ownmost possibility: at the moment of writing, just as at the point of death, it is no longer possible to speak in the voice of the 'I', only in the shared language of the 'one'. As Blanchot shows with his example of the annihilated 'woman', the artist is bound to repeat the mistake of the suicide who mistakes one death for the other, the 'work' for the 'book'. The misrecognition of the first for the second death is what motivates writing and guarantees its failure.

Despite this strange, impossible relationship between the artist and the work, the writer continues to write. Blanchot identifies a vicious circle enacted between author and work and asks, how is it possible to write? To this question there can be no answer that is not the appearance of an aporia. Blanchot considers the relation between Kafka and a single sentence he has written: 'he was looking out the window'.[54] He concludes: 'The point is that he is the author of it – or rather that because of it, he is an author: it is the source of his existence.'[55] The analysis of this claim illustrates the complexity of the author-work relationship. Up to the colon the sentence states the aporetic circle author-work. A writer is not a writer until the sentence is written. After the colon this is clarified further: the written sentence makes him a writer. But, and this is essential, the sentence that is the source of existence for the writer is a 'universal sentence', it is a sentence that belongs to other people because language is universal. In this way existence, which begins through language, negates Being. The question that literature poses both to itself and to Being is how life can both endure death and maintain itself in death in order to gain from death the possibility of speaking truthfully? This question is not a question as such, it is the aporia that literature presents and sustains. Literature's essence, its truth, can be found in the simultaneous existence of its two slopes – it is both made possible and, *at the same time*, made impossible by the negative function of language. This is what, for Blanchot, makes literature literature. As he says, 'literature's ideal has been the following: to say nothing: to speak in order to say nothing.'[56] It is literature as the site of this aporia that allows Blanchot to rephrase the question literature poses to itself as the question posed by literature to Being.

As the title of his collection of essays suggests, Blanchot's intention is to find a space for literature within a reading of death that renders narrative, understood as a movement towards ending, extremely problematic. Accordingly, whilst Blanchot figures death as the 'impossiblity of every possibility' he also retains Heidegger's 'possibility of impossibility' in its original form and the two phrases form the basis of his idea of the double death. The first, 'the possibility of impossibility', then, is what makes narrative possible. Accordingly, the first death might be phrased as a reading of Frank Kermode's 'the sense of an ending' in which it is the assumption of the 'sense making' of the ending that legitimises narrative. In such a reading, ending is understood to be necessary for the possibility of narrative in the same way that the possibility of death is the guarantee of all possibility. The second death reads the same sentence in a different way. Here the word 'sense' institutes a distancing from ending where this distancing is also the mark of misrecognition, it is not the ending itself, 'it is not the same thing at a distance but the thing as distance, present in its absence, graspable because ungraspable, appearing as disappeared.'[57]

The second death, the double absence, leaves only the narrative act as a relation between its own elements:

> When literature refuses to name anything, when it turns a name into something obscure and meaningless, witness to the primordial obscurity, what has disappeared in this case – the meaning of the name – is really destroyed, but signification in general has appeared in its place, the meaning of the meaninglessness embedded in the word as expression of the obscurity of existence, so that although the precise meaning of the terms has faded, what asserts itself now is the very possibility of signifying, the empty power of bestowing meaning – a strange impersonal light.[58]

When one has access to neither image nor object what remains is signification, or in the terms used here, narrative. Put another way, narrative requires the first death in order to exist at all as a meaningful construction, but it will also always reveal the second death in its lack of ending, in the double absence of the thing. This recalls Kermode's claim that 'Novels, then, have beginnings, ends, and potentiality, even if the world has not': the relation that Kermode posits between novels and the world is close to that which Blanchot sets up between the first and second deaths: one is a *necessary* misrecognition of the other.[59] The word 'necessary' is crucial here because without this misrecognition the attempt to create the work would be meaningless. Blanchot's ideas about literature can be linked to Kermode's in the suggestion that literature derives its possibility from the consonance granted by the first death. However, Blanchot goes on to suggest that literature's mechanisms will always expose the second death, as narrative. This diverges from Kermode's 'world-fiction' relation in that it is fiction that reveals the lack of potential for ending that exists in the world. In fact this divergence might be better characterised as a reversal. Paradoxically literary narrative is the site at which consonance, the potential for ends that Kermode suggests may not exist in the contingent 'real world', that potential promised by the first death, is always already revealed to collapse into the impossibility of the second death. What emerges from this discussion is the notion that narrative ending becomes impossible and yet that it is because of the sense of the ending that writers are compelled to write. The sense of the ending is possible only as a misrecognition and it is this that allows narrative to emerge.

Conrad, suicide and the structure of biography

Whilst suicide is a regular feature in Conrad's fiction, reference to the fact that he attempted to take his own life is almost, if not entirely, absent from both his correspondence and his more 'autobiographical' writings. This absence was continued in the work of his early biographers, including Gérard Jean-Aubry's 'official' 'definitive biography' *The Sea Dreamer* which makes no mention of the event, a silence that Zdzisław Nadjer attributes to 'a peculiar collaboration of excessive good will on the part of biographers – and Conrad's flights of retrospective imagination' which, in *The Mirror of the Sea* (1906), *A Personal Record* (1912), and *The Arrow of Gold* (1919), obscure the events of the 'Marseilles period' with semi-autobiographical, and occasionally contradictory, tales of gun-running, romance and, most significantly, a duel.[60] 'Conrad', writes Najder,

> ... altered facts, confused dates, and changed effects into causes, even in
> his private correspondence. Although scholars have shown beyond doubt
> that his literary works are mostly based on material drawn from real life or
> from reading, with his imagination playing a lesser part, we should not

conclude that whatever we find in those works is a faithful rendering of fact. Conrad's tendency to color and turn into a myth his own past is most apparent in his 'autobiographical' works.[61]

As a result of this 'self-mythologising' the facts of Conrad's suicide attempt were obscured during his lifetime and the physical scars it left on his body were attributed to a duel – an event recounted in *The Arrow of Gold*:

> What happened was this. Monsieur George fired on the word and, whether luck or skill, managed to hit Captain Blunt in the upper part of the arm which was holding the pistol. That gentleman's arm dropped powerless by his side. But he did not drop his weapon. There was nothing equivocal about his determination. With the greatest deliberation he reached with his left hand for his pistol and taking careful aim shot Monsieur George through the left side of his breast. One may imagine the consternation of the four seconds and the activity of the two surgeons in the confined, drowsy heat of that walled garden.[62]

Despite this misdirection on Conrad's part, details of the events of early 1878 would later emerge in a letter from Thaddeus Bobrowski, Conrad's uncle, to Stefan Buszcyński (12/24 March 1879). Bobrowski writes:

> he [Conrad] borrows 800 fr. from his friend Mr. Fecht and sets off for Villa-Franca [Villefranche] where an American squadron was anchored, with the intention of joining the American service. He achieves nothing there and, wishing to improve his finances, tries his luck in Monte Carlo and loses the 800 fr. he had borrowed. Having managed his affairs so excellently he returns to Marseilles and one fine evening invites his friend the creditor to tea, and before his arrival attempts to kill himself with a revolver. (Let this detail remain between us, as I have been telling everyone that he was wounded in a duel. From you I neither wish to nor should keep it a secret). The bullet goes durch und durch [through and through] near his heart, without damaging any vital organ. Luckily, all of his addresses were left on top of his things so that this worthy Mr. Fecht could instantly let me know, and even my brother, who in his turn bombarded me. Well, that is the whole story![63]

This letter, aside from some rather oblique references in his fiction and letters, remains the key piece of documentary evidence concerning the specifics of Conrad's suicide attempt. Like Jim, who in the final 'Patusan episode' of *Lord Jim*, effectively drops off Marlow's map, Conrad proves particularly elusive during his time in Marseilles, what both Baines and Karl term tellingly as the 'French Interlude' (1874–1878), and there is little to aid his biographers in the interpretation of the event. As Nadjer says of this period, 'it is best to believe only the documents' and the unsurprising consequence of the paucity of source material is that Conrad's biographers offer cautious, and necessarily brief, discussions of the event.[64] In his *Joseph*

Conrad: A Chronicle (1983) Najder gives what he calls 'the truly legendary period of his [Conrad's] life' eight pages, whilst John Batchelor's *The Life of Joseph Conrad* (1994) covers it in four, Frederick R. Karl's extensive *Joseph Conrad: Three Lives* (1979) gives it around three, and Jeffrey Meyers's *Joseph Conrad: A Biography* (1991) just two.[65] Jocelyn Baines, who is generally credited with uncovering the suicide attempt, offers a more extensive discussion of the events of 1878 in his *Joseph Conrad: A Critical Biography* (1960), however, the majority of the thirteen pages given over to the matter are concerned with verifying the event and debating a number of competing theories – a move that largely obscures the lack of detail available about the suicide itself.

Of the numerous accounts available, Najder's is one of the most comprehensive. In contrast to the self-mythologising tendencies that he finds in his subject, Najder's discussion of Conrad's life in Marseilles, based 'only on the documents', is impressive for both its circumspection and its detailed conclusions.[66] Making admirable use of the available evidence, he offers the following summary:

> Apparently financial setbacks [when Bobrowski arrived in Marseilles in March 11th 1878 he paid of debts amounting to three-thousand Francs], sudden and insurmountable difficulties in his professional life [his nationality was proving a barrier to his maritime career], and perhaps an unhappy love life [a number of romantic hypotheses have been offered concerning the real-life identity of Doña Rita of *The Arrow of Gold*] fell upon a young man susceptible to youthful depression, thereby producing an acute crisis in self-confidence and plunging him into utter despair . . . It has also been established that suicide, or attempted suicide is often the first sign of depression . . . .
>
> The fact that when Bobrowski came to Marseilles, not more than ten days after the accident, he found his nephew out of bed excludes the possibility of Korzeniowski [Conrad] having shot right through his chest, since this would have entailed many weeks of lying down . . . Either Korzeniowski placed the revolver badly and the bullet went almost parallel to his body, or the suicide was simulated and he never intended to take his own life. The careful preparation preceding the act – the invitation of Fecht and leaving out the list of addresses [As Bobrowski informs us, Fecht found a list of addresses on top of Conrad's belongings] points towards the latter possibility . . . Even Konrad Korzeniowski himself may not have known the whole truth of his action.[67]

Beyond establishing a plausible account of Conrad's time in Marseilles, Najder's account, which distinguishes between documented fact (the known extent of Conrad's allowance from Bobrowski for example) and informed interpretation with consummate subtlety, allows insight into the biographer's art. The biographer's role involves both the marshalling and the interpreting of facts. As Karl says in his well-known essay 'Three Problematical Areas of Conrad Biography,' the biographer 'must create not only a life – although he must do that as accurately as possible – but also an understanding of it.'[68] Accordingly, in Najder's work we see a careful framing of the material in which the status of any necessary speculation is clearly indicated: note the tags that mark the status of his narrative in the above passage – 'apparently', 'perhaps,' 'the fact' and 'either . . . or'. So, the lack of evidence, and perhaps the nature of the event itself, leaves Conrad's suicide attempt as something of a lacunae in his biography which interrupts the biographical project as it gestures, always aware of its limitations, towards a sense of conclusion.

The sense of these events as an 'unfillable gap' is more acute in the work of Baines and Karl who both reflect on the difficulties specific to the interpretation of Conrad's suicide attempt, and in doing so offer a consideration of suicide in a broader sense. Like Najder, Baines makes little attempt to ascribe any motive to the suicide beyond recalling the assumption that it was due to gambling debts and proposing the largely unsubstantiated idea that Conrad may have been distressed by the collapse of some love affair, presumably with the real-life figure who appears as Doña Rita in *The Arrow of Gold*. It is in his reflection on the nature of suicide that Baines moves beyond the specifics of Conrad's life to offer comment on suicide in a more abstract sense:

> This was one of those events in a person's life whose importance must be asserted but cannot be demonstrated; of no specific occasion is it possible to say that Conrad would have acted or expressed himself differently had he not tried to kill himself, and yet his action inevitably exerted an influence throughout the rest of his life. It is only necessary to recall how often suicide crops up in his work to realise how profoundly he must have been affected.[69]

Karl, who offers the suggestion that Conrad's suicide attempt was a necessary reaction to Bobrowski's constant admonitions, regarding it as the final action in Conrad's attempt to distance himself from his Polish heritage, makes a similar comment:

> A serious suicide attempt is so complicated that no explanation can suffice, but for the person who survives it, it becomes a form of rebirth. In Conrad's case, the attempt was a real display of independence – however self-destructive – and it was one way of exorcising his uncle directly, and Poland indirectly, from his past.[70]

What is significant in these two quotations is the shared belief that 'no explanation can suffice', that the significance 'must be asserted but cannot be demonstrated'. What is revealed by the impossibility of adequately answering the demands of Conrad's suicide in his biography, which appears in the work of Baines and Karl as an undemonstrable assertion, is embedded in the structure of biographical writing. The relation to the subject is revealed to be a project that necessarily holds that subject at a distance.

It is on this structural level that similarities between Conrad's biographers and Conrad's own techniques as a novelist emerge. The interpretive structure of biography, in which the biographer is recognized as a creator of narrative, parallels Conrad's use of Marlow who himself is consistently placed in the position of biographer. In a contrast that is perhaps more a matter of degree than of difference, Marlow's biographical narratives are simultaneously autobiographies in which he is the central figure: just as biographers necessarily figure as interpreters, and not as omniscient narrators, within their own texts. The similarity becomes clear when the structures of biography are set alongside those of *Lord Jim*. Here Karl's self-reflexive discussion is taken as an example with each level of narration bracketed off, creating a nested structure at the centre of which is the event of Conrad's suicide attempt:

> First person narration (Karl) [Factual biographer and implied reader [Other Biographers (Notably Baines) [Bobrowski's letter to Buszcyński [Richard Fecht's telegram to Bobrowski [Conrad's suicide attempt.

At the outer extreme of the diagram is Karl as he appears in the foreword, introduction, and footnotes which are written predominantly in the first person and comment directly on 'the biographer's' work. This narrator is consciously not omniscient and is aware of the limitations of what follows. Inside the next bracket is the narrator of the bulk of the work, a 'we' that implicates the reader in the creation of the facts of Conrad's biography. With the next bracket the limitations of the diagrammatic form become more obvious as Karl draws on primary evidence (letters and fiction) much of which has been interpreted by earlier critics and biographers: in the case of Conrad's suicide Baines is credited as being the first biographer to draw attention to the letter although Karl points out that it has a long publishing history.[71] Recognizing the accretion of an almost mythic meaning around Conrad's life and works, Karl, and here he and Najder concur, finds there 'a mélange of fact and fiction, real events intermixed with romance and fantasy.'[72] At the next level is the letter from Bobrowski to Buszcyński that Baines took as his primary source. Conrad's suicide attempt is then displaced a further level, reported to Bobrowski by Fecht in a telegram that is not included in the text (it was presumably destroyed, if indeed it had been preserved, in 1917 when Kazimierówka Manor, Bobrowski's estate, was burnt down) nor does he produce evidence to support his claim that 'Conrad himself had told Bobrowski' about the attempted suicide.[73] Taking this into account, access to the suicide attempt is complicated not only by the chain of interpretation, but also by the absence of elements of that chain. At the end of the scale is Conrad whose name might be better written under erasure as it is at this point that it is absent: undemonstrable except as part of a continued sequence of interpretation.

This complex double structure of biography-autobiography can be traced through the Marlow texts in the use Conrad makes of framed narratives at the extremes of which he places unnamed, but not omniscient, narrators whose words introduce Marlow first as a character and second as a narrator. By the end of *Lord Jim* Marlow has lost sight of Jim and must continue his narrative through the words of others. Again the structure can be illustrated in diagrammatic form:

First Narrator [Marlow's written narrative [Stein and Brown's narrative [Jim's death.

The similarities between this diagram and the earlier diagram of Karl's biography are clear: at the centre of both is what I shall argue is an absent suicide. The attempt to narrate the moment of death enters into the same contradiction that for Blanchot characterises voluntary death: 'he who espouses negation cannot allow it to be incarnated in a final decision which would be exempt from that negation.'[74] Consequently the only possible relation to death is in the *approach* to death, what is replayed in the narrative of biography and fiction by the act of narration itself. This is what Blanchot suggests when he writes about the paradox of death, and is the necessary result of the institution of the double death. The circularity of a narrative structure that must end before it can begin is reflected in Blanchot's impossible claim that the writer 'has no talent until he has written, but he needs talent in order to write'.[75] With this idea in mind I turn now to Conrad's structuring of *Lord Jim* and its relation to death and narrative ending.

The structure of *Lord Jim*

Lord Jim is perhaps the slipperiest of all Conrad's narratives, so much so that Cedric Watts's initial reaction to the text, recounted in his introduction to the Penguin edition, was to find both Jim, as a character, and Conrad as a writer, equally 'infuriating'.[76] Once again Conrad employs a framed narrative, the effect of which is heightened by an increased tension between the intended subject as proclaimed by both Marlow and its title, the life of a young water clerk named Jim, and a structure that allows Marlow to cross back and forth between the roles of narrator and principle character, confusing any sense that the narrator and his narrative can be clearly delineated. Locating Marlow as both narrator and character creates a double emphasis in the novel: at one level there is Jim's story, that which Marlow believes is the true focus of his tale, and at another there is Marlow's story which recounts the telling of Jim's story. The narrator's attempt to retell Marlow's story whilst including the scene of its original telling is of crucial interest to readings of *Lord Jim*, a claim borne out by the fact that with the conclusion of Marlow's oral narrative we are left with the altogether less engaging 'Patusan' section that deals more directly with Jim's adventures.

There are many similarities between *Lord Jim* and *Heart of Darkness*, similarities that go beyond their contemporaneity, their common narrator and sailing themes. Structurally they are remarkably alike: both are framed narratives in which an unnamed narrator introduces the oral narrative of Marlow who, in turn, is telling the story of a third party. This similarity can be readily observed when the structures of the texts are diagrammed. Brooks provides just such a structural map for *Heart of Darkness*:

> First Narrator [Marlow [Kurtz [ ] K's death] end M's narrative] First
> Narrator final paragraph.[77]

Whilst the narrative of *Heart of Darkness* makes such a diagram highly problematic, *Lord Jim* is even more resistant to such an approach, requiring two separate diagrams, the first for the tale Marlow tells his assembled listeners, the second as related by letter to a single 'privileged' listener, presumably a member of the first group. It might be diagrammed in the following way. Part one (chapters 1–35):

> First Narrator [Marlow's oral narrative [Jim [ ] Jim to Patusan] end
> Marlow's oral narrative]

Part two (chapters 36–45) is more complex still:

> First Narrator [Marlow's written narrative [letters from Jim and his father
> [Stein and Brown's narrative [Jim's death] end Stein and Brown's narrative]
> end Marlow's written narrative.

In terms of its framing technique *Lord Jim* presents a number of problems. Alongside the fact that the text contains two stories which, through the fact of their very relation call into question notions of beginnings and endings, the novel's structure complicates attempts to identify a stable voice or source. Watts brings out the polyphonic aspect of the text nicely:

> The 'privileged listener' was, we are told, one of the group of Marlow's
> auditors, one of those who had heard the tale of Jim (the narrative of
> chapters 5–35 inclusive). He is the 'only . . . man of all these listeners who

was ever to hear the last word of the story'. But who is telling us this? An anonymous narrator has been present from the start and is now telling us of the unique status of the privileged man. But if the privileged man is the only person who ever hears the end of the story, it follows that the anonymous narrator is not a character but a disembodied commenting self, rather like a traditional omniscient narrator – except that this person is particularly self-effacing. He grants the concluding chapters, after the first four paragraphs of chapter 36, entirely to Marlow, and, as we have seen, makes no comment when Marlow's narrative is complete. Where a more conventional novelist would have let the disembodied narrator sum matters up, Conrad here denies him that role.[78]

This unconventional breaking of the frame demands that the reader, who in a sense assumes the position of the absent narrator, should attempt to discover some form of closure for the novel. In attempting to interpret the absence of the frame narrator at this final point it is useful to recall his summation of the first section. At the conclusion of Marlow's oral story, which stops short of the end of the book, the reaction of his patient listeners is as non-committal as that of those men who hear the story of Mr. Kurtz aboard the *Nellie*: 'Men drifted off the verandah in pairs or alone without loss of time, without offering a remark, as if the last image of that incomplete story, its incompleteness itself, and the very tone of the speaker, had made discussion vain and comment impossible.'[79] A lack of reaction that might be read as the only possible reaction to the absence of an ending.

Referring to *Heart of Darkness*, Brooks writes: 'In the lack of finality of the promised end, Marlow must continue to attach his story to Kurtz's, since to detach it would be to admit that his narrative on board the *Nellie* is radically unmotivated, arbitrary, perhaps meaningless.'[80] The same relation exists between Marlow and Jim. At the end of the oral narrative, the story Marlow has told is firmly attached to Jim but at this point Jim's story is incomplete and Marlow's narrative trails off unfinished, marked by an ellipsis. What is absent from the story is a proper ending, and that is what Marlow will attempt to provide to the one 'privileged' listener two years later in what is commonly referred to as the 'Patusan' episode. This section led F. R. Leavis to describe the novel as one of Conrad's lesser works: 'the romance that follows, though plausibly offered as a continued exhibition of Jim's case, has no inevitability as that; nor does it develop or enrich the central interest, which consequently, eked out to provide the substance of a novel, comes to seem decidedly thin.'[81] In its rather dramatic shift of register the Patusan section that follows challenges the notion of narrative wholeness implied by Leavis's 'inevitability'. As Bruce Henricksen summarises,

Many readers have felt the novel . . . shifts from the mode of psychological
realism into the mode of romance and adventure literature in the Patusan
story. Further, the novel's criticism of the romantic imperialist and of
adventure literature's collusion with imperialism that is implied in the
opening depiction of Jim and his self-concept derived from 'holiday
literature' may be undermined when the second half of the novel itself
becomes an imperialistic adventure story.[82]

Whilst Leavis regards this as a weakness of the novel, for Henricksen,
whose reading of the novel might usefully be studied alongside the work
of Linda Dryden, Robert Hampson, and Andrea White, the double
structure is typical of the novel's dialogism that allows the Pastusan
episode to exist both as 'an evocation and a critique of the romantic, self-
congratulatory myths produced by an early capitalism in its narrating of
its encounter with other cultures'.[83] In this, the ending of Jim's tale, rather
than concluding *Lord Jim*, opens the text up to further 'writerly' readings.

Death and absence in *Lord Jim*

Lord Jim is a retelling of a story told by Marlow to a group of his friends
with the addition of a final section intended to allay the disappointment
of the tale's original recipients. A disappointment that results from the
unsatisfactory and incomplete conclusion to the first story which tails off
into embarrassed silence, 'And, suddenly, I lost him . . . .'[84] The ellipsis
with which Marlow's evening of storytelling ends makes it clear that it
has not reached its conclusion and the party of listeners breaks up with
the feeling that the very incompleteness of the story makes 'discussion
vain and comment impossible'.[85] What is remarkable is the way in which
the first section of the novel has been structured towards this denial of
any final meaning, what might be termed a non-ending. *Lord Jim* is a
text that goes to great lengths to reveal its absences whilst demanding
that they carry the weight of the entire plot, and in this way the novel
is a prime example of the manifestation of the double death within
narrative, revealing narrative as the site of absence that emerges from a
misrecognition of the nature of ending as possibility.

In this *Lord Jim* is close to *Heart of Darkness* in which the shadowy
figure of Kurtz, the name of the Intended, women, the Africans, Africa,
and death are all present only as absences and where the ending of
the novel is the presentation of a lie. A refusal of stable meaning can be
found in the very title '*Heart of Darkness*' and critics, particularly those
interested in deconstruction, have pointed to the title's ambiguity, asking:
is 'darkness' a property of the heart, or is the 'heart' to be applied spatially
to the darkness, or indeed, can darkness have a heart? Julian Wolfreys

gives one such reading in '*Heart? of Darkness?* Reading in the Dark with J. Hillis Miller and Joseph Conrad', in which he moves from a close examination of the problematic nature of the title to a reading that focuses on the undecidable nature of the text.[86] Wolfreys's conclusion situates *Heart of Darkness* as a narrative that denies itself any fixed meaning and which is always in a process of deconstructing its own text. This refusal to settle on a single meaning is a rejection of the authority that Walter Benjamin suggests is granted to the text by death, or rather it is the acceptance of Benjamin's formulation and the expression of the impossibility of gaining access to this possibility.

The idea of the absence at the heart of the text is very clear in *Lord Jim*. The Official Inquiry into the *Patna* case demands, and receives, a factual account of events:

> They wanted facts. Facts! They demanded facts from him, as if facts could explain anything! . . .
> The facts those men were so eager to know had been visible, tangible, open to the senses, occupying their place in space and time, requiring for their existence a fourteen-hundred-ton steamer and twenty-seven minutes by the watch . . . [87]

But, as Marlow infers, despite the presence of this factual account *Lord Jim* has at its centre an absent event that will return throughout the narrative, controlling the story. This absence is Jim's terrible secret, his leap from the stricken *Patna*, and what amounts to his refusal to acknowledge the significance of this event. 'The crucial action itself, Jim's jump,' writes Jocelyn Baines, 'is presented with consummate subtlety.'[88] Although the actuality of the jump, upon which the plot rests, is not in question the subtlety that Baines notes comes from nothing so much as the fact that the 'crucial action' is absent from the book. This one action which sets in motion the events of the entire book evades narration. Neither Jim nor Marlow seem inclined to relate the moment of the jump, and after one hundred and twenty five pages of anticipation Jim's account of the event to the Court of Inquiry manages to negate the moment of the jump itself. The significance of this omission should not be neglected: as Jim's jump goes on to inform his entire life story the omission of the event in its narrative, or, more properly, the *inclusion* of that omission in its narrative, becomes central to reading *Lord Jim*.

Jim recounts his actions, the actions at which the first narrator stopped short, when he meets Marlow at Malabar House:

> 'With the first hiss of rain, and the first gust of wind, they screamed, 'Jump, George! We'll catch you! Jump!' The ship began a slow plunge; the rain swept over her like a broken sea; my cap flew off my head; my breath was

driven back into my throat. I heard as if I had been on the top of a tower another wild screech, 'Geo-o-o-orge! Oh, jump!' She was going down, down, head first under me. . . . '

He raised his hand deliberately to his face, and made picking motions with his fingers as though he had been bothered with cobwebs, and afterwards he looked into the open palm for quite half a second before he blurted out – 'I had jumped . . .' He checked himself, averted his gaze. . . . 'It seems,' he added.[89]

Marlow responds humourlessly,

'Looks like it,' I muttered.
    'I knew nothing about it till I looked up,' he explained, hastily. And that's possible, too. You had to listen to him as you would to a small boy in trouble. He didn't know. It had happened somehow. It would never happen again.[90]

There is a subtle change of tense in Jim's description that enacts a refusal to recreate the actual moment: one moment Jim is about to leap and at that point his narrative pauses as he fidgets with his face. When the story resumes Jim has already leapt. As with the rest of the novel, the story Jim tells Marlow is in the preterit tense: a conventional form that presents past action in a way that it can be read to unfold chronologically towards an end which has already happened. Jim recounts the events onboard the *Patna* as an unfolding story; 'they screamed', 'I heard'. After his pause the tense is deliberately changed to the less commonly used pluperfect; 'I *had* jumped' [my emphasis].[91] The addition of the auxiliary verb 'had' to a sentence which would otherwise read 'I jumped' disrupts the continuity of Jim's narrative and situates the jump in a way that suggests that it is somehow exterior to the narrative.[92] This complex use of tenses continues in the darkness of the lifeboat as Jim's companions mistake him for George the third engineer. Even in the midst of this mistake their words point to the jump as an absence, 'What kept you from jumping, you lunatic?'[93] 'Jumping', as an action of the present, as in he is jumping *now*, does not occur. When their mistake is revealed the disbelief continues, ' "Why, it's that blasted mate!" "What!" howls the skipper from the other end of the boat. "No!" shrieks the chief. And he too stooped to look at my face.'[94] Like the reader they miss the moment of Jim's leap and, as Marlow says, it will never happen again, it will not find expression in the narrative but remain permanently as an absence.

Conrad's presentation of Jim's leap, with its remarkably circuitous nature, has been the subject of a great deal of critical work. H. M. Daleski gives a highly attentive reading of *Lord Jim* in *Joseph Conrad: The Way of Dispossession*, where he rightly identifies the numerous allusions to events that are central to Jim's story but of which the reader remains unaware for over one hundred pages. [95] The import of the 'mysterious cable message' from Aden and the thirty or so other references that Daleski counts remain obscure until the French Lieutenant's narrative finally completes the story in chapter eleven.[96] Daleski gives the following verdict on the novel's construction:

> It is doubtless true that Marlow's procedure effectively engenders an air of mystery and so makes for narrative interest, but such an achievement would hardly be worth the bewilderment caused the reader. Marlow's narrative seems designed, rather, to draw our attention repeatedly to the existence of hidden fact.[97]

The assumption here is that narrative interest is a function of the untangling of the facts behind the presentation, in recovering what Genette terms story, 'the actual events', or what Daleski calls 'hidden facts', from the narrative which is the way in which these events are ordered in the text. Daleski's second sentence suggests that the story itself contains 'hidden fact' – what, for want of a better term, might be called its 'moral'. Daleski pursues the argument that this 'hidden fact' is universal human weakness and by so doing effectively fills in the space he has located in the text. Berman, like Daleski, succumbs to an impulse to retrieve the meaning of these omissions, and pursues a Freudian reading of Jim's actions as a failure to sublimate his sexual desires: regarding the frequent ellipses that disrupt the narrative of Jim's jump as 'a form of intellectual impotence, a stuttering of his mental facilities as he tries to perceive the sinister inner forces which have defeated his will'.[98] In their readings both Berman and Daleski attempt to recover what they regard as hidden meaning from the 'omissions' of the text.

As more recent readings of *Lord Jim* demonstrate, Conrad's text resists attempts to uncover some final meaning – if indeed the notion of there being some 'hidden' meaning were to be accepted at all. Allan H. Simmons, who argues that the text is 'composed of frustrated anticipatory gestures that predict the tale and are then confounded' suggests that 'delay and deferral ensure that final meaning is suspended indefinitely' whilst Gail Fincham, who describes *Lord Jim* as 'self-parodic', and Watts both evoke Mikhail Bakhtin, albeit from rather different angles, to characterise the novel as a site of competing voices and values.[99] As Henricksen affirms, 'Conrad's texts . . . are nothing if not dialogic.'[100] Such readings contrast with attempts to 'complete' Marlow's narrative by making it possible to read the text in a manner that makes its absences integral to the way in which it is understood.

The inability of Jim's narrative to properly speak of his jump from the *Patna* demonstrates what Blanchot would call the 'double absence' of literary language. Jim's reluctant attempts to speak the event leads to its eventual disappearance, or, more properly, to the appearance of that disappearance, in a language that reveals its dislocation from the objects that it describes. As Blanchot puts it, 'having become image, instantly it has become that which no-one can grasp . . . present in its absence'.[101] By drawing attention to the absence at its centre, the text evinces a concern with questions of representation and discourse that, rather than denying the possibility of textual meaning, make questions of language and power central to reading the text. Accordingly, fictionality becomes a key issue in the text, not only is its central character a reader of 'holiday literature' and its narrator an inveterate teller of tales, but the tales that Marlow relates include a number of acknowledged fictions that recall his, similarly acknowledged, lie to the Intended. The fate of the *Patna* is one such example.

The fact that the *Patna* does not sink is as central to the novel as the fact that Jim does indeed jump. In a deliberate reversal Conrad allows the sinking of the *Patna* to be narrated. In fact it is narrated twice. The first time is recounted by the raving chief engineer from his hospital bed, ' "I saw her go down." . . . "They turned me out of my bunk in the middle watch to look at her sinking," . . . "Only my eyes were good enough to see. I am famous for my eyesight." '[102] The abstraction of language from things recurs again in Jim's recollection of the chief engineer's words:

> A faint voice said, 'You there?' Another cried out shakily, 'She's gone!' and they all stood up together to look astern. They saw no lights. All was black. A thin cold drizzle was driving into their faces. The boat lurched slightly. The teeth chattered faster, stopped, and began again twice before the man could master his shiver sufficiently to say, 'Ju-ju-st in ti-ti-me . . . . Brrrr.' He recognised the voice of the chief engineer saying surlily, 'I saw her go down. I happened to turn my head.' The wind had dropped almost completely.[103]

The absent event, the sinking of the *Patna*, which in its avowed fictionality, points to the abstraction of language from things, refuses itself to the present moment in the stuttered 'Ju-ju-st in ti-ti-me' which enacts on a textual level exactly that dislocation of language and event that Blanchot discusses when he considers the twofold nature of the 'This' that denotes both here and now. The stuttered announcement is, as Derrida puts it, 'discrepant by the time of a breath – from the order of the signifier.'[104]

Conrad's presentation of Jim's leap as a point at which the novel resists the totalizing demands of narrative is prefigured by Marlow's relation to Jim. Marlow's final words on Jim are to describe him as 'inscrutable at heart', words that locate him as the inscrutable heart of a novel that repeatedly resists interpretation.[105] Throughout *Lord Jim* Marlow is conscious that he is unable to see his subject with any degree of accuracy, Jim is only ever seen as if through a haze. This 'haze' is one of the novel's recurring motifs; Jim is most often partially obscured by a metaphorical mist or fog: 'I saw his form pass by – appealing – significant – under a cloud', 'The views he let me have of himself were like those glimpses through the shifting rents in a thick fog', 'It was one of those bizarre and exciting glimpses through the fog', 'The mists were closing again . . . even as I looked at him the mists rolled into the rent', 'The mist of his feelings shifted between us', these images recur throughout the novel and to his listeners Marlow can only say, 'I cannot say I had ever seen him distinctly'.[106]

The first encounter between Marlow and Jim sets up this pattern of non-recognition. It is nothing more than a glance, narrated twice. Initially it is recounted in the voice of the narrator of the first four chapters,

> He [Jim] met the eyes of the white man. The glance directed at him was not the fascinated stare of the others. It was an act of intelligent volition. Jim between two questions forgot himself so far as to find leisure for a thought. This fellow – ran the thought – looks at me as though he could see somebody or something past my shoulder. He had come across that man before – in the street perhaps. He was positive he had never spoken to him.[107]

While Marlow's look is 'an act of intelligent volition' there is a sense in which it 'glances off' its subject to the 'somebody or something' that lies just past Jim's shoulder. More than this, the episode introduces the dialogue that both men will join and which will be questioned throughout the text. The exchange of looks occurs in a moment of silence: 'between two questions' Jim is confident that he has not spoken with Marlow. Later Marlow will recount this same moment, his words echoing Jim's thoughts: 'Then it was that our glances met. They met, and the look he gave me was discouraging of any intention I might have had to speak to him.'[108] This denial of speech, which characterises the opening section of *Lord Jim*, is played out in the apparently minor, but thematically central, passage in which Marlow first speaks to Jim. Outside the busy courtroom, an unnamed character trips over a stray dog and is overheard by Jim to remark, 'Look at that wretched cur'.[109] Jim turns to Marlow,

> 'Did you speak to me?' asked Jim very low, and bending forward, not so much towards me but at me, if you know what I mean. I said 'No' at once . . . 'You say you didn't,' he said, very sombre. 'But I heard.' 'Some mistake,' I protested, utterly at a loss.[110]

Like the chief engineer's account of the *Patna*'s last moments this dialogue circles around an event that did not happen. In these early encounters speech is problematic, misheard and denied, and glances appear to look beyond their subjects. This (non)exchange recurs towards the end of the novel in Jim's last words to Marlow:

> Jim, at the water's edge, raised his voice. 'Tell them . . .' he began. I signed to the men to cease rowing, and waited in wonder. Tell who? The half-submerged sun faced him; I could see its red gleam in his eyes that looked dumbly at me. . . . 'No – nothing,' he said, and with a slight wave of his hand motioned the boat away.[111]

The demand for narrative implied by Jim's 'tell them' is, paradoxically, what guarantees the 'no – nothing'. The transmission of the work, the necessity of language in the 'telling them', is what denies the possibility of the work appearing.

Early in this chapter I made the claim that Jim's death was a form of suicide. This claim followed Durkheim's definition of suicide as an act that included 'a purely negative attitude or mere abstention', a definition that takes on added significance when placed alongside a reading of *Lord Jim* that emphasizes the text's points of negativity and abstention.[112] While he doesn't shoot himself, Jim's death is not the result of 'mere abstention', nor can it be described as a 'purely negative' event: it is a conscious act of will that can be regarded as an attempt to atone for both his perceived misconduct as first mate of the *Patna* and his failure to protect the people of Patusan from Gentleman Brown. Introducing the second part of his story, Marlow, presumably with Jim's death in mind, writes: 'One wonders whether this was perhaps that supreme opportunity, that last and satisfying test for which I had always suspected him to be waiting, before he could frame a message to the impeccable world.'[113] This suggestion appears to subscribe to the idea that death will somehow validate Jim's life. John Batchelor, who concurs with Marlow's reading, suggests that 'to die thus is a test of strength. And it has a fine symmetry: destiny, which is personality, has again tripped him up. To defeat the destiny he will destroy the personality.'[114] What this idea of redemption, which might be phrased as rewriting, fails to account for is the impossibility of relating to death, an idea that might be inferred from the distinction that Batchelor makes between 'external' honour (the relation to the death of the other) and his 'inner' honour (the possibility of relating to 'my death') but which is closed down by his conclusion that 'the balance . . . is in favour of the judgement that both the inner and the outer honour have been retrieved'.[115] In a novel which constantly challenges this kind of finality it is no surprise that Marlow continues: 'there shall be nothing more; there shall be no message'.[116] *The Oxford Reader's Companion to Conrad*, which I cite here for the specifics of its wording, describes what happens as follows: 'Jim has pledged his own life to guarantee the safety of the Patusan community and chooses to redeem his pledge (and his lost honour) by walking to his death, to be shot by the grieving Doramin.'[117] This summary encapsulates the two approaches to death/meaning that appear in the novel. On the one hand there is the first death, the authorising death, and this appears here in the idea of Jim 'walking to his death' – a sentence that locates death spatially as something that the subject can approach and also picks out the notion of ownership, this is 'his death' and it is the death that Jim selects in Patusan. With Blanchot's reversal of this first death to something that cannot be approached in the second death, there is a sense that the 'to be shot by the grieving Doramin' should be prefaced by an 'only': in the second death the direction is reversed, death comes too soon and Jim's 'suicide' becomes a misrecognition of death, he walks towards it only to have it arrive, as otherness, inappropriately (a word which emphasises the impossibility of a proprietorial relation to death) soon.

The presentation of Jim's final moments is characterised by silence, by a refusal (or inability) to speak. And this reflects the impossibility of the demands placed on suicide. When Jim hears that Dain Waris has been killed Marlow remarks: 'I believe that in that very moment he had decided to defy the disaster in the only way it occurred to him such a disaster could be defied', words that suggest a requirement that his death be made part of life, a suggestion that is denied when he continues, 'but all I know is that, without a word, he came out of his room and sat before the long table, at the head of which he was accustomed to regulate the affairs of his world, proclaiming daily the truth.'[118] This silence, the inability to 'proclaim the truth' acknowledges death's quality of absolute otherness; Jim rebuffs all attempts to make him fight against his end: ' "There is nothing to fight for," he said; "nothing is lost." . . . "There is no escape," . . . "Nothing can touch me." '[119] His final action symbolises the incommunicable nature of death: 'with his hand over his lips', as if silencing himself, 'he fell forward, dead'.[120] According to this reading, any attempt to read Jim's self-sacrifice as an attempt to atone for his perceived misconduct fails to account for the impossibility of relating, and relating to, death. In the ending of *Lord Jim* there is a denial even of the 'cry' voiced by Kurtz in *Heart of Darkness* and Jewel's retreat into 'soundless, inert life' is a more appropriate reaction to this essential incommunicability than the impassioned plea of Kurtz's Intended for a 'last word – to live with'.[121]

This reading of *Lord Jim* as a novel that is centred around an absence suggests, and my reading of *Heart of Darkness* made a similar point, that in its failure to relate the events even of its own story, literary narrative reveals the nature of language as negation. As the point at which this occurs literary language is described as the site of double negation. Thus in the omission of Jim's jump (which is symptomatic of Marlow's inability to speak of Jim), or the lack of access to Kurtz's death, what appears is narrative as narrative, an idea embodied in these texts in the figure of Marlow. Read in this way, *Lord Jim* provides a clear illustration of Blanchot's description of the writing process: the attempt made by the writer to create the work and the resulting failure that is the production of the book. To claim this is to prefer a reading of *Lord Jim* that diverges from the story that is suggested by the title. The title directs the reader to expect, and find, a story that describes the adventures of Jim, the shamed water clerk, and his achievement of mastery, 'lordship'. The real interest of the story, read in terms of Blanchot's work on writing, is narrative. Put another way, the interest is in Marlow, and *Lord Jim* becomes a story about the possibility of storytelling.

Notes

1 Jeffrey Berman, *Writing as Rescue* (New York: Astra Books, 1977), p. 24; Todd G. Willy, 'Measures of the Heart and of the Darkness: Conrad and the Suicides of "New Imperialism"', *Conradiana*, 14 (1982), pp. 189–98, p. 189; Ian Watt, *Conrad in the Nineteenth Century* (London: Chatto & Windus, 1980), p. 14.

2 Jocelyn Baines, *Joseph Conrad: A Critical Biography* (London: Wiedenfeld, 1993), p. 54; C. B. Cox, *Joseph Conrad: The Modern Imagination* (London: J.M. Dent and Sons Ltd, 1974), p. 4; Bernard C. Meyer, *Joseph Conrad: A Psychoanalytic Biography* (Princeton, NJ: Princeton University Press, 1697), p. 274n.

3 Joseph Conrad, *The Shadow-Line and Within the Tides* (London: J. M. Dent and Sons Ltd, 1950), pp. 44, 85.

4 Émile Durkheim, *Suicide: A Study in Sociology*, 1897, trans. John A. Spaulding and George Simpson, introd. George Simpson (London: Routledge, 1952), p. 42.

5 Willy, 'Measures of the Heart and of the Darkness', p. 189.

6 Willy, 'Measures of the Heart and of the Darkness', p. 193.

7 Joseph Conrad, *Lord Jim* (London: J. M. Dent and Sons Ltd, 1946), p. 412.

8 Conrad, *Lord Jim,* p. 415.

9 Conrad, *Lord Jim*, pp. 57, 59.

10 Harold Bloom (ed.), *Marlow* (New York: Chelsea House Publishers, 1992), p. 187.

11 Conrad, *Lord Jim*, pp. ix, 68.

12 Conrad, *Lord Jim*, p. 68.

13 John Batchelor, *Lord Jim* (London: Unwin Hyman, 1988), p. 151.

14 Stephen K. Land, *Conrad and the Paradox of Plot* (London: Macmillan, 1984), p. 88.

15 Conrad, *Lord Jim*, p. 387.

16 Conrad, *Lord Jim*, pp. 131, 352.

17 Conrad, *Lord Jim*, p. 259. In a similar way Heyst and Peyrol's deaths can be read as suicides, just as, in *Under Western Eyes*, Razumov's confession to the Russian revolutionaries might be described as a suicidal act that almost literally, and certainly symbolically, costs him his life.

18 C. B. Cox, *Joseph Conrad: The Modern Imagination* (London: J.M. Dent and Sons Ltd., 1974), p. 4.

19 Joseph Conrad, *The Secret Agent: A Simple Tale*, ed. Bruce Harkness and S. W. Reid (Cambridge: Cambridge University Press, 1990), p. 55.

20 Conrad, *The Secret Agent*, p. 56.

21 Conrad, *The Secret Agent*, pp. 56–7.

22 Maurice Blanchot, *The Space of Literature*, trans. and introd. Ann Smock (Lincoln: Nebraska University Press, 1982), p. 103.

23 Joseph Conrad, *Chance: A Tale in Two Parts* (London: J. M. Dent and Sons Ltd, 1949), p. 183.

24 Simon Critchley, *Very Little ... Almost Nothing: Death, Philosophy, Literature* (London Routledge, 1997), p. 69.

25 Blanchot, *The Space of Literature*, p. 96.

26 Blanchot, *The Space of Literature*, p. 99.

27 Blanchot, *The Space of Literature*, p. 117.

28 Martin Heidegger, *Being and Time*, trans. J. Macquarrie and E. Robinson (Oxford: Blackwell, 1962), p. 40.

29 Heidegger, *Being and Time*, p. 379.

30 Jacques Derrida, *Aporias*, trans. Thomas Dutoit (Stanford, CA: Stanford University Press, 1993), p. 76.

31 Blanchot, *The Space of Literature*, pp. 125–6.

32 Blanchot, *The Space of Literature*, p. 104.

33 Maurice Blanchot, *The Station Hill Blanchot Reader: Fiction and Literary Essays*, ed. George Quasha, trans. Lydia Davis, Paul Auster and Robert Lamberton (New York: Station Hill Press, 1999), p. 392.

34 Derrida, *Aporias*, p. 22.

35 Blanchot, *The Station Hill Blanchot Reader*, p. 392.

36 Derrida, *Aporias*, p. 22.

37 Maurice Blanchot, *The Writing of the Disaster*, trans. Ann Smock (Lincoln: Nebraska University Press, 1995), p. 70.

38 Blanchot, *The Space of Literature*, p. 103.

39 Blanchot, *The Station Hill Blanchot Reader*, p. 378.

40 Blanchot, *The Station Hill Blanchot Reader*, pp. 380, 379.

41 G.W.F. Hegel, *Phenomenology of Spirit*, trans. A.V. Miller (Oxford: Clarendon, 1979), p. 66.

42 Blanchot, *The Station Hill Blanchot Reader*, p. 380.

43 Blanchot, *The Space of Literature*, p. 255.

44 Blanchot, *The Space of Literature*, p. 255.
45 Blanchot, *The Space of Literature*, p. 255.
46 Leslie Hill, *Blanchot: Extreme Contemporary* (London: Routledge, 1997), pp. 64–5.
47 Blanchot, *The Space of Literature*, pp. 255–6.
48 Blanchot, *The Station Hill Blanchot Reader*, p. 386.
49 Blanchot, *The Station Hill Blanchot Reader*, pp. 388, 396.
50 Ullrich Haase and William Large, *Maurice Blanchot* (London: Routledge, 2001), p. 30.
51 Blanchot, *The Station Hill Blanchot Reader*, pp. 366, 365.
52 Blanchot, *The Space of Literature*, p. 105.
53 Blanchot, *The Station Hill Blanchot Reader*, p. 364.
54 Blanchot, *The Station Hill Blanchot Reader*, p. 363.
55 Blanchot, *The Station Hill Blanchot Reader*, p. 363.
56 Blanchot, *The Station Hill Blanchot Reader*, p. 381.
57 Blanchot, *The Space of Literature*, pp. 255–6.
58 Blanchot, *The Station Hill Blanchot Reader, p. 385*
59 Frank Kermode, *The Sense of an Ending: Studies in the Theory of Fiction, With a New Epilogue* (Oxford: Oxford University Press, 2000), p. 138.
60 Zdzisław Nadjer, *Joseph Conrad: A Chronicle*, trans. Halina Carroll-Nadjer (Cambridge: Cambridge University Press, 1983), p. 39.
61 Najder, *Joseph Conrad,* p. 39.
62 Joseph Conrad, *The Arrow of Gold; A Story Between two Notes* (London: J. M. Dent and Sons Ltd, 1947), p. 346.
63 Zdzisław Nadjer, *Conrad's Polish Background: Letters to and From Polish Friends*, trans. Halina Carroll (London: Oxford University Press, 1964), p. 177.
64 Nadjer, *Joseph Conrad,* p. 39.
65 Nadjer, *Joseph Conrad,* pp. 46–7.
66 Najder, *Joseph Conrad,* p. 39.
67 Najder, *Joseph Conrad,* p. 53.
68 Frederick R. Karl, 'Three Problematical Areas of Conrad Biography', *Conrad Revisited: Essays For The Eighties*, ed. Ross C. Murfin (Alabama: Alabama University Press, 1985), p. 17.
69 Baines, *Joseph Conrad: A Critical Biography* (London: Wiedenfeld, 1993), p. 54.
70 Frederick Karl, *Joseph Conrad: The Three Lives* (London: Faber and Faber, 1979), p. 84n.
71 Karl, *Joseph Conrad: Three Lives*, p. 156n.
72 Karl, *Joseph Conrad: Three Lives*, p. 157.
73 Baines, *Joseph Conrad*, p. 53.
74 Blanchot, *The Space of Literature*, p. 103.
75 Blanchot, *The Station Hill Blanchot Reader*, p. 361.
76 Joseph Conrad, *Lord Jim* (London: Penguin, 1989), p. 11.
77 Brooks, *Reading for the Plot*, p. 351n.

78 Cedric Watts, 'Bakhtin's Monologism and the Endings of *Crime and Punishment* and *Lord Jim*', *The Conradian*, 25:1 (Spring 2000) pp. 15–30, p. 28.

79 Conrad, *Lord Jim*, p. 337.

80 Brooks, *Reading for the Plot*, p. 254.

81 F. R. Leavis, *The Great Tradition: George Eliot, Henry James, Joseph Conrad* (London: Chatto & Windus, 1962), p. 190.

82 Bruce Henricksen, *Nomadic Voices: Conrad and the Subject of Narrative* (Urbana and Chicago: University of Illinois Press, 1992), p. 87.

83 Henricksen, *Nomadic Voices*, p. 98. See also: Linda Dryden, *Joseph Conrad and the Imperial Romance* (Houndmills: Palgrave, 2000), Robert Hampson, *Cross-Cultural Encounters in Joseph Conrad's Malay Fiction* (Houndmills: Palgrave, 2000), and Andrea White, *Joseph Conrad and the Adventure Tradition: Constructing and Deconstructing the Imperial Subject* (Cambridge: Cambridge University Press, 1993).

84 Conrad, *Lord Jim*, p. 336.

85 Conrad, *Lord Jim*, p. 337.

86 Julian Wolfreys, *Deconstruction: Derrida* (Houndmills: Macmillan, 1998), pp. 158–81.

87 Conrad, *Lord Jim*, pp. 29–30.

88 Jocelyn Baines, 'Guilt and Atonement in *Lord Jim*', *Twentieth Century Interpretations of Lord Jim*, ed. Robert E. Kuehn (Eaglewood Cliffs, NJ: Prentice Hall Inc, 1969), p. 38.

89 Conrad, *Lord Jim*, pp. 110–11.

90 Conrad, *Lord Jim*, p. 111.

91 'The pluperfect or past perfect form of a verb is a combination of past and perfect, expressing a kind of pastness that is typically further back in time than what is expressed by the simple past tense, and expressing the kind of completeness associated with the perfect tense.' James R. Hurford, *Grammar: A Student's Guide* (Cambridge: Cambridge University Press, 1994), p. 175.

92 For further discussion of Conrad's use of time, succession and duration in *Lord Jim* see André Topia's 'The Impossible Present; A Flaubertian Reading of *Lord Jim*', *The Conradian*, 31:1 (Spring 2006), pp.37–51.

93 Conrad, *Lord Jim*, p. 116.

94 Conrad, *Lord Jim*, pp. 116–17.

95 H. M. Daleski, *Joseph Conrad: The Way of Dispossession* (London: Faber and Faber, 1977), pp. 78–9.

96 Conrad, *Lord Jim*, p. 35.

97 Daleski, *Joseph Conrad*, p. 79.

98 Berman, *Joseph Conrad*, p. 73.

99 Allan H. Simmons, ' "He was Misleading": Frustrated gestures in *Lord Jim*', *The Conradian*, 25:1 (Spring 2000) pp. 31–47, pp. 32, 31; Gail Fincham, 'The Dialogism of *Lord Jim*', *The Conradian*, 22:1/2 (Spring/Winter 1997) pp. 58–74, p. 59; Cedric Watts, 'Bakhtin's Monologism and the Endings of *Crime and Punishment* and *Lord Jim*', *The Conradian*, 25:1 (Spring 2000) pp. 15–30.

100 Henricksen, *Nomadic Voices*, p. 104.
101 Blanchot, *The Space of Literature*, pp. 255–6.
102 Conrad, *Lord Jim*, pp. 51–2.
103 Conrad, *Lord Jim*, p. 113.
104 Jacques Derrida, *Of Grammatology*, trans. Gayatri Chakravorty Spivak (Baltimore: The Johns Hopkins University Press, 1976), p. 18.
105 Conrad, *Lord Jim*, p. 416.
106 Conrad, *Lord Jim*, pp. ix, 76, 114, 128–9, 133, 221.
107 Conrad, *Lord Jim*, pp. 32–3.
108 Conrad, *Lord Jim*, p. 69.
109 Conrad, *Lord Jim*, p. 70.
110 Conrad, *Lord Jim*, pp. 70–1.
111 Conrad, *Lord Jim*, p. 335.
112 Durkheim, *Suicide*, p. 41.
113 Conrad, *Lord Jim*, p. 339.
114 Batchelor, *Lord Jim*, p. 155.
115 Batchelor, *Lord Jim*, p. 158.
116 Conrad, *Lord Jim*, p. 340.
117 Owen Knowles and Gene M. Moore (eds), *Oxford Reader's Companion to Conrad* (Oxford: Oxford University Press, 2000), p. 212.
118 Conrad *Lord Jim*, p. 409.
119 Conrad *Lord Jim*, pp. 412–13.
120 Conrad, *Lord Jim*, p. 351.
121 Conrad, Lord Jim, p. 416; *Conrad, Youth, Heart of Darkness, The End of the Tether*, p. 161.

4

Chance and the truth of literature

Half the words we use have no meaning whatever and of the other half each man understands each word after the fashion of his own folly and conceit. Faith is a myth and beliefs shift like mists on the shore; thoughts vanish; words, once pronounced, die; and the memory of yesterday is as shadowy as the hope of to-morrow. (Joseph Conrad, *Letters to Cunninghame Graham*)

Introduction: the 'illusion' of literature

Conrad's conception of the artist's work as an act of 'translation' in which the writer wrestles with words 'worn thin, defaced by ages of careless usage' evinces a similar concern to that of the Russian formalists who set literature the task of responding to the 'habituation' of perception and an everyday language that, through its very overuse, 'devours works, clothes, furniture, one's wife, and the fear of war'.[1] In his attempts to 'appeal to the senses', which are close to the formalist notion of defamiliarization, Conrad repeatedly allies the processes of reading with the processes of perception – making the manner in which objects are apprehended central to his literary endeavour.[2] This works to good effect in the Marlow novels which, in foregrounding their own linguistic practices, alert the reader to her/his role in the interpretive process. In making the transmission of narrative so central, which requires a language common to both narrator and narratee, or to writer and reader, Conrad's fiction also points up the impossibility inherent in the attempt to revivify language. As Marlow's frequent complaints about the difficulties of storytelling indicate, his 'No, it is impossible . . . We live, as we dream – alone', the project of communication must ceaselessly fall back onto these 'thin' and 'defaced' words: thin and defaced because they are common property.[3]

Maurice Blanchot describes this struggle against habituation as the 'illusion' of the literary work in which writers 'fight against common-place expressions and language by the very same means which engender language and commonplace expressions'.[4] For Blanchot the writer 'gives birth to art by a vain and blind struggle against it,' only to find 'that the work he thinks he has wrested from common, vulgar language exists thanks to the vulgarization of the virgin language he had imagined, through an excess of impurity and debasement'.[5] A conclusion that might be inferred from Conrad's remark in *A Personal Record* that 'a handful of pages, no matter how much you have made them your own, are at best but an obscure and questionable spoil . . . a mere rustle and flutter of pieces of paper settling down in the night, and indistinguishable, like the snowflakes of a great drift destined to melt away in sunshine.'[6] The artist's desire to make language 'his own', to write in a 'virgin' language that allows direct connection to individual Being, gives way to a necessary 'settling down', a 'melting', into the 'vulgar' common language that makes the transmission of narrative possible while negating, or annihilating, to use Blanchot's term, the objects of that narrative.

This apparent paradox in the literary project does not mean that literary narratives are without meaning. Quite the opposite: as I shall go on to suggest in my reading of *Chance*, meaning can be recovered in the appearance of this paradox in Conrad's work where it emerges as a consciousness of his own representative strategies. As Ullrich Haase and William Large suggest, 'The absence of meaning at the centre of the literary text should not be interpreted as nonsense . . . It is not because we have too little knowledge that we cannot comprehend the text, rather the text's resistance to comprehension belongs intrinsically to the experience of reading.'[7] This is a useful, if somewhat belated, caveat to the argument that has been developed in the preceding chapters of this book which might otherwise be seen to promote a view of literature as uninterpretable, if not impossible. On the contrary, the lack of a centre in narrative not only generates the possibility of a plurality of interpretations but it also demands a reflection on the nature of interpretation itself, directing attention to the reception of narrative: as Mary Ann Caws puts it, 'the study of the frame is always a self-study of our reading habits as well as of the picture itself.'[8] It is with this in mind that I now turn to Conrad's last Marlow novel, *Chance*, a text which, in its exploration of gender, demonstrates the very productive connection between literature's 'illusion' and textual meaning.

The narrative of *Chance*

Frederick R. Karl remarks that '*Chance* is, for all its trappings, thematically one of Conrad's most straightforward novels.'[9] Its story (to use Gérard Genette's terminology) is certainly straightforward. Flora is the daughter of the disgraced financier Mr de Barral who, at the start of the story, has been jailed for fraud. The destitute young woman subsequently elopes with Captain Anthony, the brother of one of her protectors, the feminist Mrs Fyne. At the behest of his wife, Mr Fyne attempts to intervene in the marriage and as a result Captain Anthony comes to believe that Flora does not love him whilst Flora remains under the impression, gained during a painful childhood, that no-one could possibly love her. At this point Flora's father is released from prison and joins the couple aboard the *Ferndale*, and for a time there is an atmosphere of despair as the young couple retreat into their own worlds of isolation and depression. Events come to a head when Mr de Barral attempts to poison Captain Anthony and, when this fails, drinks the poison himself and dies. Freed from the shadow of de Barral, Flora and Captain Anthony discover their love for one another and live happily together until the time of Captain Anthony's death in a shipping accident six years later.

Despite this relatively straightforward story *Chance* is an extremely complex text, as Robert Lynd put it in his *Daily Mail* review (15 January 1914): 'If Mr. Conrad had chosen to introduce us to his characters in the ordinary way, he could have told us their story in about 200 pages instead of the 406 pages of the present book.'[10] Conrad's novel, however, does not proceed in the 'ordinary way' and even the briefest survey of its structure makes clear the extent to which summaries like the above simplify the narrative through a number of silent omissions and by prioritising just one of the text's numerous narrative levels. *Chance* is subtitled 'A Tale in Two Parts' and correspondingly the novel is divided into two sections: 'The Damsel' and 'The Knight'. As with Conrad's other Marlow narratives this story is presented by an unnamed narrator who delivers Marlow's oral narrative in readable form, including in his narrative the scene of its original transmission. In a similar way to *Lord Jim*, *Chance* contains the narratives of a number of characters but employs the frame narrator to a larger extent, while eschewing the apparently omniscient narrator who figures in the earlier text, commenting extensively on both Flora's story and Marlow's narration. Uniquely, in *Chance* two narrators are introduced: Marlow and Charles Powell. In the first chapter Powell delivers a second-level narrative (i.e. it is contained within the controlling narrative of the first narrator) about his early days as a sailor. The significance of Powell's story lies in the effect it has on Marlow, who shortly after this begins his own second-level narrative about a character mentioned in Powell's story: Captain Anthony. This narrative is introduced in the same way as Powell's: it is initially recounted by the first narrator before, after a few pages, he yields, at least partially, to Marlow. Marlow's narrative is homodiegetic (he appears as a minor

character in the story) and narritized (there is little attempt at verisimili-
tude by way of minimising the evidence of the narrating act). Marlow's
narritized narrative contrasts with the first-narrator's reported narrative
(his narrative is 'reported' in that it pretends to reproduce Marlow's
narrative accurately without drawing attention to its own status as
narrative). What links the two narrative levels is that, like Marlow in the
second level, the first narrator is also homodiegetic, frequently appearing
in his narrative as a character who interacts with Marlow, but only in this
first-level narrative. To be able to say this is to identify two stories in
Chance, the story of Flora *and* the story of transmission enacted variously
at the 'river-side inn' and in the first narrator's 'rooms'.[11] In the second
section of the novel, 'The Knight', the first narrator reproduces Marlow's
continuation of the tale taken from a later time of telling. In this section,
pieced together by Marlow from his discussions with Powell, Marlow is
absent as a character and so the narrative can be classed as autodiegetic,
the only such section in any of the Marlow texts. This is significant in that
the narrative is a reproduction of an earlier reproduction. The first
narrator reproduces, in this second half of *Chance*, Marlow's narrative,
which is itself taken from the story told by Powell. Thus the second section
of the novel has three levels of narrative which might be diagrammed:

First narrator's narrative [Marlow's narrative [Powell's narrative.

Flora's story is then concluded in a rather perfunctory manner when
Marlow rejoins it as a character to arrange the marriage between Powell
and Flora.

The apparent disparity between the novel's rather conventional
romance plot and the complexities of its presentation has generated a
good deal of critical comment and, given the novel's complex narrative
structure, there is a certain disingenuousness in Marlow's remark that
'The means don't concern you except in so far as they belong to the
story.'[12] Responses to the novel that agree with Marlow about the primacy
of story (content) over narration (form) tend to take an evaluative stance.
Jocelyn Baines concludes that 'there are only rare occasions when anything
is gained from this cumbersome method of presentation' whilst Karl
complains that, 'the vast scaffolding of method is perhaps more distracting
than edifying, more detrimental than constructive.'[13] Other readers have
made a virtue of the structure, regarding it not so much as distracting but
rather as forming an integral part of the meaning of the text. Daniel R.
Schwartz is a case in point, sitting somewhere between these two schools
of thought: while he agrees that 'The tale is undermined – "deadened"
might be a better word – by the elaborate narrative technique', he goes on
to suggest that whilst the 'wreckage and clutter' of the novel's 'almost

geometric form threatens to snuff out content' it also, 'like a series of Chinese boxes, imprisons the characters and mirrors their repression'.[14] The 'mirroring' by which form and content are reconciled allows for more nuanced readings of the text in which the 'cumbersome', 'distracting', and 'deadening' structure of the novel might be regarded as both 'edifying' and 'constructive' in the way in which it directs attention towards the 'scaffolding of method'. This double-focus on form and (as distinct from) content and form *as* content allows Andrew Michael Roberts to argue that in *Chance*,

> the presence of narrative chains implicates the male reader and critic most challengingly . . . it draws the male reader, through its narrative strategy, into a dialectic of understanding and ignorance, of superiority and self-accusation in relation to the gender conceptions of other men – a dialectic of liberating self-criticism and inescapable complicity.[15]

As these divergent readings of *Chance* suggest, Flora's story may be a simple one, but that story is greatly complicated, and developed, by the addition of the second-level story of its subsequent narration and reception. Identifying these two narrative levels as the 'two parts' of *Chance* might prove to be a productive reading of the novel's subtitle and one that would suggest that Marlow is perhaps too reductive in his dismissal of 'means' in favour of 'story'. To suggest instead that what is at one point the 'means' can be the 'story' at another is not a radical claim, Genette makes it clear in *Narrative Discourse* that the interrelation of narrative levels and the relative positions of narrators are essential to the study of narrative. What is remarkable is the realisation that meaning emerges in these intersections. It is in the intersection between narrative levels that form and content (narrative, narrating and story) can be seen not only to reflect one another but, to a certain extent at least, to merge.

Marlow's handprints

Marlow's appearance in *Chance* recalls a quotation from Walter Benjamin's 'The Storyteller': 'it is', he writes, 'half the art of storytelling to keep a story free from explanation as one recounts it', a statement that initially seems to be at odds with his suggestion that a story will exhibit the 'handprints' of its many tellers, that 'traces of the storyteller cling to a story the way the handprints of the potter cling to a clay vessel'. [16] On closer inspection these handprints turn out to be evidence of repeated transmission rather than the reduction of story to information. Such handprints are readily observed in *Chance* where Conrad employs the frame narrator to a larger extent than in any of the other Marlow texts, commenting on both Flora's story and Marlow's narration. Contrary to expectation the insertion of the Marlow story, and the excess of interpretation that accompanies it, has the surprising effect of making interpretation not easier but harder. Marlow has already been shown to be an exemplary figure for the 'handprints' of narration and there is a certain irony in the fact that his first narrator often evokes him only to emphasize his apparent withdrawal from the story, he is 'nearly invisible' speaking 'out of the shadow of the bookcase', similarly in *Heart of Darkness* he is described as 'sitting apart . . . no more to us than a voice', 'indistinct and silent'. [17] It is at these points of apparent disappearance that Marlow appears as a character, as a narrator and as the physical embodiment of narrative technique. At such moments, which tend to occur when the story reaches a point of particular significance (Marlow disappears into the shadows of the bookcase just as he reveals that Mr de Barral has discovered Flora's marriage), there is an incongruous emphasis on Marlow's narration, the competing story.

Marlow's 'handprints' are not the only marks of narration in *Chance*. The novel's structure is well described as polyphonic: Flora's story is transmitted to the first narrator through various characters of whom Marlow and Powell are the principal, but not only, voices. The effect of this is to lose the story itself amongst an overabundance of voices that variously transmit and interpret it to, and for, one another. A close reading of the opening sequence quickly reveals this aspect of the text as it shifts rapidly from the voice of the unnamed narrator, to Powell and then Marlow: moving, in the space of four pages, from the unnamed narrator's 'I BELIEVE', to Powell's 'If we at sea', through the unnamed narrator's self-contradictory rewriting of Powell's speech, '*In his own words*: he might just as well have dropped them all properly addressed and stamped into the sewer grating' [my emphasis], to the introduction of Marlow who, 'with a slight reminiscent smile murmured that he "remembered him very well." '[18] From the second chapter onwards Marlow is the main narrator, but he is far from being the only one. Just as the first narrator recalls Marlow's tale, Marlow himself pieces together his tale from the narratives of others, including Flora, Powell, Mr and Mrs Fyne, and Mr Franklin. The following passage rewards close attention in this respect:

> [']I mention these curtains because at this point Mr. Powell himself recalled the existence of that unusual arrangement to my mind.
>
> 'He recalled them with simple-minded compunction at that distance of time. He said: "You understand that directly I stooped to pick up that coil of running gear – the spanker foot-outhaul, it was – I perceived that I could see right into that part of the saloon the curtains were meant to make particularly private. Do you understand me?" He insisted.[']¹⁹

This is the text provided by the first narrator – hence the quotation marks introducing the passage denote the fact that he is quoting, supposedly verbatim, the narrative supplied to him by Marlow who at this point is quoting the narrative he has heard from Powell.[20] This in itself is fairly typical of the narrative of *Chance* and this particular passage is made complex as much by *what* is being narrated as by *whom* it is narrated. In other words, this case is complicated by the fact that the narrative of one narrator is often composed of the narrating act of another. Immediately prior to the quotation the curtains under discussion have been narrated by the first narrator as curtains that exist at the first-level narrative, the extradiegetic level. The first sentence, 'I mention these . . . ', is a second-level narrative, the diegetic level in which the first narrator heard Marlow's narrative as he explains his motives for what he has included, *and*, in turn, that second-level narrative contains an almost identical moment in which Powell interrupted his telling of the first-level narrative, thus making a third-level, metadiegetic, narrative. The second sentence, 'He recalled . . .' belongs more straightforwardly to the story in which the narrator hears Flora's story whilst the third contains three levels of story: 'He said' belongs to the story of Marlow's narration, 'You understand that' is part of Powell's narration, and 'directly I stooped' returns to the earlier story of Powell's life on the *Ferndale*. Finally, Powell's 'Do you understand me?' returns to the story of Powell's narrating act. This brief extract, one of many possible examples, institutes a process by which the reader is placed at the end of a sequence of other readers, a process that makes very clear the relational aspect of language. Significantly, in this extract the 'story' of each narrative level concerns narrating, with only Powell's 'I stooped . . .' actually belonging to the level of Flora's story. This abundance of narrating activity aside, little actually happens, and instead of activity at the level of Flora's story what is presented is a series of narrative handprints that work to obscure that story.

Such examples make it clear that rather than fixing meaning, the great number of commentators in *Chance* makes the informational aspect of the story recede. As Leslie Hill notes, writing of a similarly paradoxical effect at work in Blanchot's *Thomas the Obscure*, 'The bizarre result [of the novel's excess of commentary, interpretation and gloss] is a writing in which everything seems to possess somewhere in the novel its own implicit or explicit interpretation, except for the process of commentary itself, which remains uninterpreted and, one might add, boundlessly uninterpretable'.[21] In the same way, the polyphonic structure of *Chance* affords the numerous characters involved with ample opportunity to interpret, filter and translate the events they recount, explaining everything away except for the very activity of their narrating – an act comprised of their constant commentary and critiques of events. Thus, in Benjamin's terms, the volume of 'handprints' exhibited by the text is exactly what answers his demand that the storyteller keep the story free from 'information'. Pursuing the connection between Benjamin and Blanchot, the appearance of language as language, the appearance of absence in language, is what might be called the essence of literature. Language, 'this excess of handprints', is thus revealed in and of itself, revealing the process by which meaning is structured, as Roberts puts it, the self reflexivity of the text involves the reader in 'a dialectic of liberating self-criticism and inescapable complicity'.[22]

The sense that *Chance* is a self-reflexive text comprised of its own critique is heightened by the fact that it is a novel populated by writers and narrators. There is, as Robert Hampson puts it, 'a literary self-consciousness in *Chance*' that appears in the fact that almost every character is engaged at some point in narrating, writing or reading.[23] In this way the story itself becomes infected with the same concerns that are so clear in the narrative. Within the story, both of the Fynes have published books: Mr Fyne 'wrote once a little book called the "Tramp's Itinerary"' and Marlow later learns, 'that his wife had been very much engaged in a certain work. I had always wondered how she occupied her time. It was in writing. Like her husband, she too published a little book.'[24] The actions of Flora come to be based, at least in part, on Mrs Fyne's book, 'a sort of handbook for women with grievances (and all women had them), a sort of compendious theory and practice of feminine free morality.'[25] Captain Anthony is, as Mr Fyne persists in pointing out, 'The son of Carleon Anthony, the poet' and both he and Mr Powell are shown to have a fondness for reading, as Powell remarks, 'Captain Anthony was a great reader just about that time; and I, too, I have a great liking for books.'[26] Beyond his own propensity for storytelling Marlow makes several references to literature that suggest a fondness for literature and language, describing Flora and her father as they stand by her mother's grave as 'Figures from Dickens – pregnant with pathos', jokingly referring to Captain Anthony's marriage to Flora as the 'affair of the purloined brother', an allusion to Poe that usefully recalls the mysterious letter that Flora sent to the Fynes, and delivering his narrative from the shadows of a bookcase.[27] Through these repeated references to reading and writing the story of *Chance*, that is what might be called the story of Flora, mirrors the concern with the narrating act that is so clear at the extradiegetic level. This parallel makes any claims that the novel is simple, which tend to arise from a focus on story to the exclusion of narrative and narrating, difficult to sustain. In terms of narrative and narrating *Chance* is an extremely complex text indeed.

It is the 'double negation' of literary language that guarantees that the notion of the story as information will be challenged, a double negation that becomes evident when the narrating act appears *as* story. Not only is the object negated and replaced by its image but the image with which the initial negation was masked is revealed in its emptiness. Accordingly, Marlow's reading of Anthony's narrative draws attention to the way in which the narrating act is emphasized to the point at which the narrated act itself becomes increasingly hard to locate. Later in the same chapter, having prevented Captain Anthony's poisoning, Powell remarks: 'I thought Captain Anthony was a man of iron till I saw him suddenly fling his head to the right and to the left fiercely, like a wild animal at bay not knowing which way to break out . . . .'[28] Marlow's narrative continues to be comprised of a discussion of Powell's narrating act, ' "Truly," commented Marlow, "brought to bay was not a bad comparison" ', what occurs in this instance is a focus on language at the level of the narrating act rather than the act of being 'brought to bay' in the story.[29] This can be better understood in terms of narrative levels. It is at the third level, the metadiegesis, that Captain Anthony 'fling[s] his head to the right and to the left fiercely, like a wild animal at bay'.[30] The next level of story, the diegesis, comments on the narration of Powell's story. It also serves to reintroduce Marlow as the narrator of the diegesis, asserting his authority with his judgement of Powell's storytelling. Thus the story at this point of the narrative concerns Powell's act of 'comparison' rather than his encounter with Captain Anthony. Such comments are plentiful in *Chance*, where Marlow regularly comments on Powell's choice of words: 'Fancied's the very word to use in this connection'; later, 'This is his own word. Bounded!'; and often on his own narrative, 'By accident I mean that which happens blindly and without intelligent design.'[31] It is clear that not only is Marlow's narrative a linguistic construct but that his narrative is concerned with interpreting and judging other narratives. Nowhere is this clearer than when, after recounting Powell's narrative, Marlow claims that Powell's statements about himself were the least interesting part of his story:

> They were also the least interesting part. The interest was elsewhere, and there of course all he could do was to look at the surface. The inwardness of what was passing before his eyes was hidden from him, who had looked on, more impenetrably than from me who at a distance of years was listening to his words.[32]

What emerges from this passage is a tangible sense of literary communication as an interpretative process. Marlow comments very directly on this process, and the implied relation between writer, reader and text anticipates, even in the metaphors of surface and depth that it employs, Roland Barthes's 'The Death of the Author'. As an author, Powell is denied control of the 'inwardness' of the text, what *was* his text. What remains is the play of surfaces, freed of this 'hidden' meaning and open to interpretation by Marlow and the subsequent readers of his text. Conrad's deployment of Marlow as narrator, framed as he is within the narrative of the unnamed narrator, only adds to the sense that the text exceeds the authority of its author by making the process of transmission integral to the text itself. Positioned as both character and narrator, Marlow goes beyond the role of Barthes's 'scriptor', the producer of texts, and unsettles the role of the 'reader' who, for Barthes, is 'without history, biography, psychology; he is simply *someone* who holds together in a single field all the traces by which the written text is constituted'.[33] There is, in fact, nothing 'simple' about it as Marlow effects a blurring of the two positions as if to challenge Ricoeur's suggestion that 'the book divides the act of writing and reading into two sides, between which there is no communication'.[34] Of course this challenge falters when Marlow is recognized as another part of what Barthes calls the 'multi-dimensional space in which a variety of writings, none of them original, blend and clash'.[35] But what makes *Chance* so effective a demonstration of this play of surfaces is the way in which Marlow's narrative, and its relation to the first-narrator's narrative, situates itself so firmly as a 'tissue of quotations' in its repeated comments that draw attention to its relation to itself.

The centre of *Chance*

Any attempt to move beyond this shifting 'tissue of quotations' in order to locate a central meaning of *Chance* might be well advised to heed Laurence Davies who cautions that, 'Finding the moral centre of *Chance* is notoriously hard.'[36] As Schwartz notes, '*Chance* lacks a radial centre' a fact he attributes to its 'seemingly baroque form' which confounds attempts to get to grips with the story itself.[37] This said, it is perhaps possible to say that there is an emerging consensus that the 'centre' of the novel is not chance, as the title suggests and which the epigram from Sir Thomas Browne ('Those that hold that all things are governed by fortune had not erred, had they not persisted there'), disavows, but gender.[38] Conrad himself was certainly concerned with the novel's depiction of women, in whom he recognized a large potential readership, writing: 'It's the sort of stuff that *may* have a chance with the public. All of it about a girl and with a steady run of references to women in general all along, some sarcastic, others sentimental, it ought to go down,' an expectation confirmed by the *New York Herald* who ran an interview promoting the novel's serialisation under the heading: 'World's Most Famous Author of Sea Stories Has Written "Chance," a Deliciously Characteristic Tale in Which, He Says, He Aimed to Interest Women Particularly'.[39] *Chance* is certainly unusual amongst Conrad's novels for its distinct interest in female characters and issues of gender. Hawthorn suggests that 'feminism and women's rights are confronted as a central issue in the novel' while Roberts widens the scope of his analysis, describing *Chance* as 'the novel in which Conrad seems most explicitly engaged with feminist issues and gender relations.'[40]

Given the fact that *Chance* displays such a keen interest in women, both as characters within the novel and as consumers of the novel, it is surprising that even the most casual of readings reveals a large degree of animosity towards women on the part of Marlow. His disparaging attitude towards women, which builds with cumulative effect, is clearly evident:

> As to honour – you know – it's a very fine mediaeval inheritance which women never got hold of. It wasn't theirs. Since it may be laid as a general principle that women always get what they want, we must suppose they didn't want it. In addition they are devoid of decency. I mean masculine decency.[41]

Similar statements occur throughout the text: 'I call a woman sincere when she volunteers a statement resembling remotely in form what she really would like to say'; 'They are too passionate. Too pedantic.'; 'What is delightful in women is that they so often resemble intelligent children'; 'Women can stand anything. The dear creatures have no imagination when it comes to solid facts of life.'; 'Women are more loyal, not to each other, but to their common femininity which they behold triumphant with a secret and proud satisfaction.'[42] Whilst Marlow's statements are remarkable for their misogyny it is, however, questionable simply to equate his views with those of Conrad. As Baines cautions: 'Marlow is a character in the book, and not necessarily Conrad's mouthpiece.'[43] Despite this Baines later allows that in certain passages 'he sums up what are undoubtedly Conrad's own views on women's predicament'.[44] It is certainly true that Conrad has been widely regarded as a writer of 'manly' stories, a perception that Susan Jones sums up with reference to Graham Hough, Edward Said and Joyce Carol Oates: 'Drawn in by his lasting reputation, critics have dismissed the possibility that women have had any positive impact on Conrad's creative life, that they have taken a valid position in his fiction, or that Conrad spoke to women readers.'[45] As Jones goes on to show, and I will say more about this later, the issue is far more complex than such an approach takes into account. In fact, a reading that focuses on the question of gender in *Chance* inevitably brings up the carefully constructed conflict between the novel's narrators, a conflict that is typical of a narrative strategy that foregrounds technique over story.

The contradictory relation between Marlow and the unnamed narrator, indeed the instability of Marlow as he appears throughout *Chance*, supports Davies's suggestion that finding the moral centre of *Chance* is 'notoriously difficult'. Karl proceeds with no such circumspection, describing *Chance* as, 'thematically one of Conrad's most straightforward novels', going on to conclude that 'If human relationships are the centre of the novel, then they are relationships responsible only to the consciences of individuals, never to the dictates of God.'[46] A similar conclusion is offered by Baines, stated in a slightly different form: 'The main theme is once again emotional isolation.'[47] Neither Karl nor Baines offer a close reading of the text, it is the nature of their books to offer broader studies of the novels they include, and neither critic undertakes to study the relation between the structure of the novel and the centres they determine for it. This omission is made all the more conspicuous by the fact that both critics reach the conclusion that the novel's structure confuses the story. Karl rejects outright the suggestion that the structure might support the novel's meaning: 'In parts of *Under Western Eyes* and *The Secret Agent*, the shape is the very stuff of the story, and the material allows no other method. *Chance*, on the other hand, ostensibly gains little from its tortured sequences.'[48] Indeed for Karl, apparently anxious to minimise the significance of *Chance*, the novel's structure, which he acknowledges as 'Conrad's most elaborately designed', is cited with the sole intention of revealing its flaws.[49] Despite the distraction of this 'clutter' Karl readily identifies the meaning of *Chance*: it is 'married love', 'the maturing of a girl to a young lady', 'Flora is the center', 'it was truly a woman-and man-centered universe', 'human relationships are the center', 'man [not God] as center'.[50] In a sense, Karl's reading, by not paying close attention to the novel's narrative structure, maintains the sexual stereotyping with which Marlow attempts to position Flora in the text, in terms of marriage, of the role of 'girls' and 'ladies', and the relation of these positions to the novel's male characters.

Two readings of *Chance* that do approach the 'moral centre' through a consideration of narrative are Hawthorn's *Joseph Conrad: Narrative Technique and Ideological Commitment*, which isolates the contradictory nature of *Chance*'s narrative for discussion and Jones's extremely persuasive discussion of *Chance* in *Conrad and Women*, which complements Hawthorn's work by re-reading the contradictions which he regards as a failure of ideological vision, making of those contradictions a powerful feminist reading of the novel.

It is clear from Hawthorn's chapter heading, '*Chance*: Conrad's Anti-feminine Feminist Novel', that his reading will engage with the novel's contradictory nature. This leads him to identify the book as 'among those works of Conrad's in which a lack of ideological coherence is related to narrative confusions'.[51] This statement is worthy of consideration because it puts what follows into context. Taking the latter half of the sentence first, Hawthorn joins Baines and Karl in condemning the narrative structure of *Chance*: 'the narrative chain is unnecessarily complicated and seems unproductive: moreover it leads Conrad into a number of impossibilities.'[52] He continues, again echoing Karl's sentiments, 'But this is also true of other of his novels – *Under Western Eyes*, for instance, a novel which retains its artistic power and cohesion in spite of such technical impossibilities.'[53] Hawthorn's disapproval of the 'narrative confusions' makes clear a similar dismay at the 'lack of ideological coherence' that he finds in *Chance*. Hawthorn demands this ideological coherence not simply from the text but from the text as it represents the ideology of Conrad as the author of *Chance*. In his introduction Hawthorn pre-empts the obvious criticism such a move might draw:

> Did not such theorists as Roland Barthes and Michel Foucault long ago announce the death of the author and conclude that the ceremony of the funeral was over?
>
> Nevertheless, I start not just with Conrad's fiction, but with Conrad and (and in) his fiction.[54]

While questions of authorial intention remain problematic, Hawthorn's approach implies a useful widening of perspective that, while paying close attention to the text itself, moves away from a purely formalist textual analysis in order to make a connection between the historical specificity of text and author, the text itself and its readers – all of which become elements (morally according to Hawthorn's analysis) in the interpretive process.[55] Texts thus become 'processes of mediation, transformations of vision, which join the human beings and the writer's insights and ideologies'.[56]

Hawthorn's argument begins by identifying the ways in which *Chance* can be read as an attack, albeit a rather veiled one, on the patriarchal structures of Victorian society. To this end, a series of parallels are traced out between the poet Carleon Anthony, Captain Anthony's father, and Coventry Patmore, the author of 'The Angel in the House' (1854), that famous celebration of Victorian ideals of womanhood. This connection, which is made both through close textual parallels between the narrator's description of Carleon Anthony and Patmore's poem as well as by noting the similarities between Patmore's biography and the life of Conrad's character (Hawthorn does not argue for a one to one correlation between Patmore and Anthony) is convincing and demonstrates the way in which Conrad's character, who adopts 'certain characteristics of the Victorian patriarch', is typical of a text that takes as its interest the inequities of Victorian patriarchy.[57] Hawthorn's next move is to argue for a connection between Conrad's work and the work of Charles Dickens. By comparing the portrayal of women in *Chance* with the treatment of women in Dickens's novels, where 'certain patriarchal myths [appear] in unusually pure form', Hawthorn indicates that the novel presents for critique a stiflingly patriarchal society that situates women, as daughters and wives, in a series of dependant relationships that function in terms of imprisonment.[58] By making these connections Hawthorn suggests the ways in which it is possible to marshal internal textual evidence to support the thesis that *Chance*, figured as an 'interrogation of Dickensian stereotypes', was an attack on Victorian patriarchal views of women.[59]

This reading of *Chance* is, at least in part, a rhetorical move that sets up the argument that follows, namely that Conrad's novel is incoherent in the presentation of its 'message' which becomes problematic when this implied critique of patriarchy is set alongside Marlow's obvious misogyny: 'Readers of *Chance* have either tended to have taken the novel to be an anti-feminist tract, or they have found its engagement with the issue of women's rights at best contradictory and at worst blurred and unsatisfactory.'[60] In Hawthorn's reading of *Chance*, which focuses on the need for a coherent ideology, this lack of a clear moral centre is seen as a serious flaw in the novel. The blurriness that Hawthorn finds in the novel results from the 'complicating factor' that the novel 'has no authorial narrator'.[61] Instead it has an unnamed narrator and Marlow who, as I indicated above, argue throughout the text about Marlow's misogynistic comments. The disagreement between the two narrators is regarded as symptomatic of the novel's fragmented and disjointed story and, according to Hawthorn, the novel is ultimately incoherent not because the two narrators disagree but because the presentation of Flora and her story is so vague that it becomes impossible to arrive at a stable reading of the text.

As has already been suggested, in the examination of the novel's narrative structure, narrating is often emphasized whilst the story is neglected. It is this relation between narrating and story that leads Hawthorn to claim, 'Such generalizations, however, need to be more than stated in a novel,' referring to the way in which the narrative is largely comprised of a discussion about narrating rather than actually narrating the story, 'they need to be dramatized'.[62] In other words they must exist as story: 'We need to be able to witness how Flora's isolation is compounded by her being a woman. And yet she is hard to see that clearly through the fog of Marlow's descriptions of her ... it is as if Conrad's narrative technique in *Chance* is somehow inappropriate.'[63] Read as a novel about gender, there is a benefit to reading Hawthorn's inappropriateness alongside Karl's claim that 'the novel's machinery becomes oppressive'.[64] The inappropriate and oppressive machinery, the overt nature of the novel's structure, introduces a way of reading *Chance* that interrogates the connection between language, gender and power.

Jones's reading of *Chance*, which focuses on the complexity of Conrad's narrative strategy and the 'oblique presentation of Flora', is as much a reading of the novel's 'machinery' as it is of its story.[65] In many ways Jones's initial position is in accord with that set out by Hawthorn. Her reading of *Chance* begins by considering the relationship between Conrad's writings and those of Marguerite Poradowska, a Polish author and one of his longest standing literary correspondences, suggesting her *Demoiselle Micia* (1888) as a major source for *Chance*. Focusing on the treatment of gender, Jones catalogues the parallels between the two novels to establish a position close to that from which Hawthorn begins his reading. Namely, both critics place *Chance* in relation to conventional Victorian representations of women in order to indicate the ways in which they are interrogated in Conrad's text. Jones makes a productive connection between gender and genre, suggesting that *Chance* draws on 'a number of sub-genres: the romance ... the detective novel ... the sensation novel and melodrama', and arguing that Flora is constructed in terms of a predominantly male discourse that imposes upon her 'the traditional characteristics of the romance heroine'.[66] There are, of course, a number of such stereotypical postures: the novel's two sections 'The Damsel' and 'The Knight' point to the key motifs that are simultaneously employed and critiqued. Accordingly, when Anthony is described as 'the rescuer of the most forlorn damsels of modern times,' the narrative deliberately undercuts this convention by indicating the male dominance that is inherent in such a 'knightly' role: as rescuer of damsels, Anthony is, 'the man of *violence*, gentleness and generosity' [my emphasis].[67] The multiple narrative voices of *Chance*, as Jones suggests, make it clear that this is 'a male construction of romance'.[68] The enigmatic presentation of Flora's 'suicide attempt' typifies Marlow's attempts to apprehend her along conventional lines and leads to one of the rare occasions where he interacts directly with his subject. Flora refutes his version of events, thereby destabilising the 'knight' and 'damsel' roles that it implies: 'I see you will have it that you saved my life. Nothing of the kind.'[69]

Similarities to Hawthorn's conclusions are also found in Jones's discussion of the novel's serial publication in *The New York Herald*, a paper which 'encouraged a female readership with women's pages presenting topical issues and romance fiction alongside advertisements for fashion, beauty aids, and domestic appliances . . . carefully censored by a patronising editorial tone which endorsed woman's role as nurturer, idealising her beauty and domesticity'.[70] It is in this context that Conrad's story comes to offer a critique of the very images that construct *The New York Herald*'s female readership, and so, the conflict that leads Hawthorn to identify *Chance* as an 'anti-feminine feminist novel' is extended beyond the confines of the novel to its context – a move that supports similar non-contextual readings of the story in its final published version.

Jones's argument breaks with Hawthorn's by taking the novel's rather schizophrenic presentation of women as the starting point for a further consideration of its presentation of gender in language. By exploring the ways in which *Chance* diverges from Poradowska's relatively traditional romance Jones considers the implications of the way in which the narrative of *Chance* appears *as* narrative, arguing that rather than being a conservative 'manly' writer, Conrad uses the romance formula provided by Poradowska to examine the ways in which such texts, and by extension society, position women, using 'the medium of Marlow's oscillating voice to demonstrate the range of possible interpretations, breaking through generic restrictions that classify women according to received definitions'.[71] For Jones this development of Poradowska's romantic set pieces foregrounds the inscription of women in masculine discourse by drawing attention to the process of narrative construction. The most obvious instance of this process of inscription is the debate about women carried on between Marlow and the unnamed narrator. The challenge to narrative authority, which operates through a questioning of the narratives of both Marlow and the unnamed narrator, situates the reader as the last in a series of critical interpreters of the text's authority. Jones notes that in the serialised version of *Chance* Marlow's misogynistic comments were usually accompanied by an immediate apology, 'when he relates Flora's response to the boarding of her husband's ship, he dilutes his acid tone "it is very lucky that small things please women" with a placatory remark: "because without it their lot would be even harder than it is." '[72] This is not the case in the novel where Marlow's misogyny is left to stand without apology, but where it is instead questioned by the unnamed narrator. The direct questioning of the narrator draws attention to the subjective nature of the picture of Flora that is presented and, coupled with the suggestion that Marlow himself doesn't take his words seriously ('Marlow paused with a whimsical look at me'; 'there was the flicker of a smile on his lips'), instigates a series of questions about this narrative in particular and narrative in general.[73] If, as the evidence cited by Davies and Jones suggests, *Chance* was written with a female audience in mind it would make sense to assume that Conrad expected his readers to challenge the narrator. More usefully, given the vagaries necessitated by attempts to grapple with authorial intention, one need only appeal to the structure of the text which, by foregrounding storytelling and the reception of story, emphasizes the active role of the reader in the interpretative process.

Questioning the narrator and the status of the narrative opens up the possibility of reading *Chance* in a way that recovers meaning from what Blanchot identifies as the double negation of literary language. Jones undertakes such a reading of *Chance*, describing the many voices that attempt, and fail, to describe Flora. As Jones illustrates, the polyphonic structure of the novel makes it increasingly difficult to locate Flora, ostensibly the subject of the novel, as she is variously mediated through the voices of others, rarely if ever appearing in person and almost always the subject of male discourse. The effect of this recalls Conrad's note to the novel in which he says: 'Flora de Barral passed before me, but so swiftly that I failed at first to get hold of her.'[74] Whilst George Gissing, one of Conrad's earliest and most generous critics, would write in a letter dated the 9th May 1903, 'Wonderful, I say, your mute, or all but mute, women. How in Satan's name do you make their souls speak through their silence?' it seems that the opposite is in fact the case.[75] The strange result of the numerous narratives that surround Flora is that she recedes from the reader with the increasing attempts to bring her to the fore. Jones writes:

> In the final version [of *Chance*] it is Flora herself who has become the 'text', the location of endless interpretations of the 'damsel's' part.
>   Yet her failure to inhabit fully the role of heroine simultaneously creates an ellipse at the centre of the narrative.[76]

According to this reading of *Chance*, Flora disappears; or rather the impossibility of adequately representing women within the genre of romance appears. Like the meaning at the heart of darkness and like Jim's absent leap from the *Patna*, Flora appears in *Chance* as her own refusal to appear and so, in this sense, her silence does 'speak'. Jones reads Conrad as deliberately dramatising the male-constructions of language and genre and applauds the way in which his technique, whilst belonging to male-centred discourse, clearly questions its own foundations:

> by limiting Marlow's voice so that it never achieves final authority, Conrad registers the dilemma of women who are unable to form identities untrammelled by plots, poses, gestures that have not already been invented for them, and that are not already entrenched at a cultural level.[77]

In its positioning of Flora as the ungraspable subject of a male discourse that is foregrounded in Conrad's text, Jones's reading of *Chance* can be refigured in terms of Blanchot's notion of literature as the site at which language reveals itself as negation, recalling Blanchot's claim, already quoted, that, 'For me to be able to say, "This woman" I must somehow take her flesh and blood reality away from her, cause her to be absent, annihilate her. The word gives me the being, but it gives it to me deprived of being.'[78] However Jones's critique of *Chance* only partially reflects Blanchot's statement about the annihilation of 'this woman'. According to Blanchot's reworking of Hegel, the negation that arises in literary language is not gendered. Blanchot's 'this woman' is a substitute, dramatic but not necessary, for Hegel's 'this tree', the logic of which turns on the word 'this' and not on the noun 'tree'. Thus Jones's reading might be regarded as one possible and extremely productive reading of the absence at the heart of literary language, one that does not contradict, and is not contradicted by, Robert Hampson's claim that the Marlow he finds in *Chance* 'is a Marlow who, for undisclosed reasons, is clearly hostile towards women – but it is also a Marlow who is also, though less obviously, hostile towards men.'[79] Without wishing to pursue Hampson's reading in detail, I cite it here in order to identify another possible interpretation of the text, it is helpful in pointing up the non-gendered nature of literary negation. In the same volume of *The Conradian*, Davies writes, 'If this text teaches anything, it is the inadequacy of those who teach – an unbearable paradox only if we insist, as the book is careful not to do, on absolute categories.'[80] What should be made clear is that whilst these readings might be shown to have their origins in the absent centre of literature they do not explicitly explore this aspect of narrative. This claim does not contradict their readings of *Chance* but, maintaining the focus on narrative, it is with a study of this aspect of *Chance* that I will end this study, considering the ways in which Marlow, as a figure standing for narrative, relates to the uncertainty at the centre of the novel.

The truth of literature

Readings such as that undertaken by Jones are made possible by the negation that Blanchot identifies at the heart of literature. The truth of literature, its aim, is to speak in order to say nothing, a negation that answers Benjamin's call for a storytelling that is free from information. It is to this negation that I turn now, pursuing a reading of the novel that builds upon a study of the trustworthiness of Marlow's narrative to consider the ways in which *Chance* parallels *Heart of Darkness* in its investigation of the notion of truth in literature through its presentation of lies.

In the same way that Marlow has no access to Flora beyond the conventions of male discourse it is apparent that he has no access to the truth of his narrative other than through the addition of further narrative. When Marlow interrupts his story, his 'tone between grim jest and grim earnest', to inform his interlocutor, 'Perhaps you didn't know that my character is upon the whole rather vindictive', it is clear that he is not to be regarded as a source of truth, whilst, significantly, he *is* a source of narrative.[81] Addressing the unnamed narrator directly, attempting to verify his narrative with additional narrative, Marlow's words break the continuity of his story bringing his status as character to the fore. In this way, and this is true of all four of the Marlow texts, Conrad institutes a questioning of the relationship between narrator and narrative. In this case the specific questions attached to the fact that the narrator is vindictive are not as significant as the notion that the narrator is open to questioning.

Once this questioning has begun, it becomes increasingly clear that as a narrator Marlow is unsure of his facts. The lack of narrative stability is exemplified when, towards the end of the novel, he tries to describe Captain Anthony's first meeting with his father-in-law. The passage is problematic because Marlow has no way of knowing why Captain Anthony decided to meet Mr de Barral in private:

'*Why* Anthony *appeared* to shrink from the contact . . . *is difficult to explain. Perhaps . . . Possibly . . .* he *may well have been* dismayed
'In short, we'll say *if you like* that *for various reasons* . . . [my emphasis]'[82]

The unnamed narrator refuses the attempt to make him party to the creation of the narrative, an attempt that is implicit in Marlow's 'if you like', inquiring, 'Why do you say this?'[83] Marlow is frequently challenged by the unnamed narrator who retells his narrative whose reactions of disbelief recur throughout the text: ' "Come, Marlow," I said, "you exaggerate surely – if only by your way of putting things. It's too startling." '; ' "You have a ghastly imagination," I said with a cheerfully sceptical smile.'; ' "How do you know all this?" I interrupted.'[84] Marlow's usual reaction is one of irritation: 'No! I don't exaggerate.'; 'You smile?'; 'What the devil are you laughing at?'[85] These disputes find their best illustration in an early exchange:

'Do you expect me to agree with all this?' I interrupted.
'No, it isn't necessary,' said Marlow feeling the check to his eloquence, but with a great effort at amiability. 'You need not even understand it.'[86]

This check to Marlow's eloquence is symptomatic of a narrative that interrogates itself through the repeated appearance of its own narrating act. Following this check, Marlow's assertion that his narrative requires neither agreement nor understanding is remarkable. What Marlow demands, and here he is in accord with Benjamin's storyteller, is that his story is transmitted. Comprehension, in terms of what Benjamin would call information, is not necessary. The realisation of the inaccessibility of information, equated with the negation that is central to literary language, is what marks *Chance* as a work which renders the speaking and writing of truth impossible.

This problem with truth, which emerges in narrative and narrating, can be seen to occur within the story of *Chance* as a very direct concern with lies which are, as Roberts points out, an 'important mode of communication in these works'.[87] It will be recalled that the Marlow of *Heart of Darkness* 'hate[s], detest[s], and can't bear' lies which, he says, contain 'a taint of death, a flavour of mortality' and, without wishing to pursue the claim that the Marlow of *Heart of Darkness* is identical to the Marlow of *Chance*, the connection that he makes between dying and lying suggests a way of reading the novels alongside one another in terms of the possibility of truth in, and of, literature.[88] This is made possible when lying is identified as a common theme and practice of both texts: Marlow excludes both Kurtz's Intended and Flora de Barral from the truth of his narratives, lying to both women about death only to retell the same stories not only intact but with the additional scenes of their original mistelling.

There is a highly suggestive near parallel between the two novels in the way that they treat the possibility of truth in connection to gender. In *Heart of Darkness* Marlow remarks:

> It's queer how out of touch with truth women are. They live in a world of their own, and there had never been anything like it, and never can be. It is too beautiful altogether, and if they were to set it up it would go to pieces before the first sunset. Some confounded fact we men have been living contentedly with ever since the day of creation would start up and knock the whole thing over.[89]

In *Chance* Marlow's patronising remark is restated in reverse, men are the idealists whilst:

> The women's rougher, simpler, more upright judgement, embraces the whole truth, which their tact, their mistrust of masculine idealism, ever prevents them from speaking in its entirety. And their tact is unerring. We could not stand women speaking the truth. We could not bear it.[90]

These statements have been usefully interrogated in terms of the narrative's gender positioning as is seen in the work of, for example, Nina Pelikan Straus, Jones and Roberts.[91] Without wishing to 'rescue' Conrad's work from charges of misogyny, it is hard to disagree with Straus's judgement that 'the artistic conventions of *Heart of Darkness* are brutally sexist', the negation that I am identifying as inherent in literary language is not necessarily gendered, at least not in biological terms.[92] Although it does, of course, generate the possibility that language, divorced from some absolute correlation with real-world referents, should, like the 'knowledge' that it bears, become a site at which power is generated and exerted. For this reason it is useful here that Conrad presents the impossibility of bearing truth both as knocking 'the whole thing [the world of women] over' and as unbearable to men.[93] My interest is in the question, what kind of truth is unbearable?

This unbearable truth, and the connection between literature and death appears in another parallel between *Chance* and *Heart of Darkness*. Both novels include final interviews between Marlow and their bereaved female characters in which the discussion of death is couched in terms of untruth. The Intended has lost Kurtz and her final interview with Marlow, in which he substitutes 'your name' for Kurtz's 'The horror!', was discussed in chapter 2, whilst Flora loses both Captain Anthony and her father.[94] Reading *Chance* alongside *Heart of Darkness* it becomes clear that there is a close correspondence between the presentation of the deaths of Kurtz and Mr de Barral. Just as Marlow lies to the Intended when she asks him to repeat Kurtz's last words, Flora is lied to about her father's suicide when Anthony and Powell allow her to believe that he has died from natural causes: 'Flora de Barral had been saved from *that* sinister shadow at least falling upon her path.'[95] Of course the reader, like Marlow's narrator, is well aware of both de Barral's suicide *and* of its misrepresentation to his daughter. In Flora's final interview with Marlow he maintains the lie:

> 'That night when my poor father died suddenly I am certain they had some sort of discussion about me. But I did not want to hold out any longer against my own heart! I could not.'
> 'She stopped short, then impulsively –
> 'Truth will out, Mr. Marlow.'
> 'Yes,' I said.[96]

The truth of which Flora speaks is the truth of her love for Anthony, but her words recall the unspoken lie about her father's suicide and it is this reference to which Marlow's 'yes' seems most fitting as a response. That *Chance* and *Heart of Darkness* end with lies about death not only suggests the inadequacy of narrative in assimilating and communicating death but also reveals the mechanisms by which language seeks to conceal the 'separation of signs from things' whilst at the same time exposing the referential function by which that separation is concealed.[97] Accordingly, whilst speaking of death is characterised as a stalling point in these two texts, the narratological conclusions that emerge from the connection between death and lies go beyond the identification of the problems associated, notably by Derrida, with laying claim to the phrase 'my death'. At the level of story these acknowledged lies, like literature, reveal the double negation of literary language which was described by Blanchot as 'a warning that at this very moment death is loose in the world, that it has suddenly appeared between me, as I speak, and the being I address'.[98] In other words, it might be possible to make a connection between the unacknowledged lie and Blanchot's description of 'everyday language'. The lie, like everyday language, is at once a negation of the truth and the masking of this negation (or substitution), which is its essence, by its own appearance as truth. This remains the case whilst the lie is allowed to stand in the place of truth, unrecognized in its very nature as untruth. Conversely, the lie that is recognized as a lie performs a similar function to literary language, paradoxically revealing (in the revealing of its nature as untruth), the double negation that is at the heart of language. Blanchot makes a similar connection between language and lying in 'Literature and the Right to Death' where he writes: 'there is a time when art realizes that everyday speech is dishonest and abandons it.'[99] In making this claim Blanchot marks the essential distinction between literary and everyday language, a distinction that can be understood in terms of the presentation of lying in *Chance* and *Heart of Darkness*. With this in mind *Chance* and *Heart of Darkness*, as attempts to tell their stories truthfully, in the way in which they acknowledge the process of lying, can be seen to enact at the level of story an identical problemetising of language.

The mistelling of de Barral's death is not the only lie in *Chance*.[100] The narrative also exposes as lies the promises, made and broken by both Powell and Marlow, concerning the novel's two suicides. Begged by Flora to keep her suicide attempt secret, Marlow, 'assured her that she could depend on my absolute silence'.[101] Later Powell promises Captain Anthony that he will keep de Barral's suicide a secret, 'Silence! Silence forever about this.'[102] Neither man keeps his word, and the text, in its presentation of the breaking of these promises of silence, enacts an extremely complex exploration of the relation between truth, literature and death. This breaking of the promise of silence marks both *Chance* and *Heart of Darkness* as retellings of stories that have been mistold: including in the retelling the instance of the initial mistelling. Accordingly, *Heart of Darkness* includes the scene with the Intended which is an earlier version of the transmission of Kurtz's story, while *Chance* recreates for the 'privileged listener', the unnamed narrator, a retelling not of Flora's life but of Mr de Barral's death. As an attempt to tell the truth of their subjects these retellings have the opposite effect, reinscribing their original failures by the very possibility of translation. The possibility of retelling, of translation, invokes the possibility of infinite substitution upon which language depends. Thus, when the unnamed narrator of *Chance* prefaces his summary of Powell's words with 'In his own words' a contradiction arises that can be seen as typical of the literary endeavour.[103] Once the process of questioning and interrogating narrative has begun, *Chance* is revealed to be a novel that is extremely conscious of the problems of narrative. There is a sense that the abundance of commentary on its own story leaves the reader with little to do but, as I have suggested in this chapter, rather than fixing the meaning of the story, this opens the text up to further interpretation. Through its own self-examination, *Chance* becomes a site of endless speculation that insistently reveals the complicity of the reader in the interpretative process at the same time as it refutes the possibility of 'fixing' textual meaning. This Blanchotian reading of narrative opens up the possibility of approaching the Marlow texts from what are extremely profitable angles and recovering meaning from what Blanchot identifies as the double negation of literary language. The identification of the various ellipses in the Marlow stories: Flora in *Chance*, the wisdom of Kurtz in *Heart of Darkness*, or Jim's absent jump from the *Patna* in *Lord Jim*, allows meaning to emerge from the narrating act itself. My conclusion is a return to the question of what occurs when narrating becomes story: it would appear that it is in this intersection that the work of the storyteller is located, where the meaning of the literary emerges. Put another way, this emphasis on negation in language does not make meaning impossible but rather generates the possibility of multiple readings of a single text and it is in this way that the Marlow narratives, which already include the scene of their own transmission, situate their readers and critics as part of an ongoing process of interpretation and refiguration.

Notes

1 Joseph Conrad, *The Nigger of the 'Narcissus'* (London: J. M. Dent and Sons Ltd, 1950), p. ix; Victor Shklovsky, 'Art as technique', in Lee T. Lemon and Marion J. Reis (eds), *Russian Formalist Criticism: Four Essays*, trans. Lee T. Lemon and Marion J. Reis (Lincoln: Nebraska University Press, 1965), pp. 3–24, p. 12.

2 Anthony Fothergill offers a useful consideration of Conrad's defamiliarization in his book *Heart of Darkness* (Milton Keynes, Open University Press, 1989), pp. 41–6. Similar ideas are also explored in terms of what has come to be called, following Ian Watt, 'delayed decoding'. For further discussion of delayed decoding see: Ian Watt, *Conrad in the Nineteenth Century* (London: Chatto & Windus, 1980) and Cedric Watts, *The Deceptive*

Text: An Introduction to Covert Plots (Brighton: The Harvester Press Ltd, 1984).

3 Joseph Conrad, *Youth, Heart of Darkness, The End of the Tether* (London: J. M. Dent and Sons Ltd, 1946), p. 82.

4 Maurice Blanchot, *The Blanchot Reader* (Oxford: Blackwell, 1995), p. 58.

5 Blanchot, *The Blanchot Reader*, p. 58.

6 Joseph Conrad, *The Mirror of the Sea: Memories and Impressions; A Personal Record: Some Reminiscences* (London: J. M. Dent and Sons Ltd, 1946), p. 99.

7 Ullrich Haase and William Large, *Maurice Blanchot* (London: Routledge, 2001), p. 34.

8 Mary Ann Caws, *Reading Frames in Modern Fiction* (Princeton, NJ: Princeton University Press, 1985), p. 265.

9 Frederick R. Karl, *A Reader's Guide to Joseph Conrad* (Syracuse, NY: Syracuse University Press, 1997), p. 242.

10 Norman Sherry (ed.), *Conrad: The Critical Heritage* (London: Routledge & Kegan Paul, 1973), p. 271.

11 Joseph Conrad, *Chance: A Tale in Two Parts* (London: J. M. Dent and Sons Ltd, 1949), pp. 3, 257.

12 Conrad, *Chance*, p. 326.

13 Jocelyn Baines, *Joseph Conrad* (London: Wiedenfeld, 1993), p. 382; Karl, *A Reader's Guide to Joseph Conrad*, p. 242.

14 Daniel R. Schwartz, *Conrad: The Later Fiction* (London and Basingstoke: Macmillan, 1982), pp. 44, 46.

15 Andrew Michael Roberts, *Conrad and Masculinity* (London: Macmillan 2000), p.161.

16 Walter Benjamin, *Selected Writings: Volume Three 1935–1938*, trans. Edmund Jephcott, Howard Eiland *et al.*, ed. Howard Eiland and Michael W. Jennings (Cambridge, MA: The Belknap Press of Harvard University Press, 2002), pp. 148, 149.

17 Conrad, *Chance*, p. 359; *Conrad, Youth, Heart of Darkness, The End of the Tether*, pp. 83, 162.

18 Conrad, *Chance*, pp. 3, 6, 7.

19 Conrad, *Chance*, pp. 410–11.

20 As was outlined in the preface, for practical reasons I have omitted these quotation marks from the majority of the quotations taken from Conrad's Marlow novels.

21 Leslie Hill, *Blanchot: Extreme Contemporary* (London: Routledge, 1997), p. 65.

22 Roberts, *Conrad and Masculinity*, p. 161.

23 Robert Hampson, '*Chance*: The Affair of the Purloined Brother', *The Conradian*, 6:2 (1980), pp. 5–15, p. 6.

24 Conrad, *Chance*, pp. 37, 65.

25 Conrad, *Chance*, pp. 65–6.

26 Conrad, *Chance*, pp. 38, 413.

27 Conrad, *Chance*, pp. 148, 162.

28 Conrad, *Chance*, p. 422.

29 Conrad, *Chance*, p. 422.

30 Conrad, *Chance*, p. 422.

31 Conrad, *Chance*, pp. 33, 36, 125.

32 Conrad, *Chance*, p. 426.

33 Roland Barthes, *Image, Music, Text*, trans. Stephen Heath (London: Fontana, 1977), p. 148.

34 Paul Ricoeur, *Hermeneutics and the Human Sciences: Essays on Language, Action and Interpretation*, ed. and trans. John B. Thompson (Cambridge: Cambridge University Press, 1981), p. 146.

35 Barthes, *Image, Music, Text*, p. 146.

36 Laurence Davies, 'Conrad, *Chance*, and Women Readers', *The Conradian*, 17:2 (Spring 1993), pp. 75–88, p. 84.

37 Schwartz, *Conrad: The Later Fiction*, p. 46.

38 Conrad, *Chance*, p. ii.

39 Frederick R. Karl and Laurence Davies (eds), *The Collected Letters of Joseph Conrad, Volume Five 1912–1916* (Cambridge: Cambridge University Press, 1996), p. 208; *The New York Herald*, 14 January 1912, Sunday Magazine. Quoted in Susan Jones, *Conrad and Women* (Oxford: Clarendon, 1999), p. 147. For further discussion of the marketing of *Chance* see Laurence Davies, 'Conrad, *Chance*, and Women Readers', *The Conradian*, 17:2 (Spring 1993), pp. 75–88.

40 Andrew Michael Roberts, 'Introduction', *The Conradian*, 21:1 (1996), pp. v–xi, p. vi; Jeremy Hawthorn, *Joseph Conrad: Narrative Technique and Ideological Commitment* (London: Edward Arnold, 1990), p. 133.

41 Conrad, *Chance*, p. 63.

42 Conrad, *Chance*, pp. 144, 159, 171, 352, 371.

43 Baines, *Joseph Conrad*, p. 382.

44 Baines, *Joseph Conrad*, p. 386.

45 Jones, *Conrad and Women*, pp. 7–8.

46 Karl, *A Reader's Guide to Joseph Conrad*, pp. 242, 239.

47 Baines, *Joseph Conrad*, p. 387.

48 Karl, *A Reader's Guide to Joseph Conrad*, p. 243.

49 Karl, *A Reader's Guide to Joseph Conrad*, p. 236.

50 Karl, *A Reader's Guide to Joseph Conrad*, pp. 242, 236, 237, 239, 240.

51 Hawthorn, *Joseph Conrad: Narrative Technique*, p. 133.

52 Hawthorn, *Joseph Conrad: Narrative Technique*, p. 154.

53 Hawthorn, *Joseph Conrad: Narrative Technique*, p. 154.

54 Hawthorn, *Joseph Conrad: Narrative Technique*, p. x.

55 Paul Ricoeur's 'What is a text?' (Ricoeur, *Hermeneutics and the Human Sciences*) offers an in-depth discussion of the relationship between studies that 'explain the text in terms of its internal relations' (p. 152) and move from this 'explanatory attitude' (p. 153) towards what he describes as the 'interpretation' of text, a model of criticism that widens the model of

reading to include the reader and which would 'fulfil the text in present speech' (p. 158).

56 Hawthorn, *Joseph Conrad: Narrative Technique*, p. xi.
57 Hawthorn, *Joseph Conrad: Narrative Technique*, p. 135.
58 Hawthorn, *Joseph Conrad: Narrative Technique*, p. 136.
59 Hawthorn, *Joseph Conrad: Narrative Technique*, p. 135.
60 Hawthorn, *Joseph Conrad: Narrative Technique*, p. 140.
61 Hawthorn, *Joseph Conrad: Narrative Technique*, p. 140.
62 Hawthorn, *Joseph Conrad: Narrative Technique*, p. 145.
63 Hawthorn, *Joseph Conrad: Narrative Technique*, pp. 145–6.
64 Karl, *A Reader's Guide to Joseph Conrad*, p. 244.
65 Jones, *Conrad and Women*, p. 105.
66 Jones, *Conrad and Women*, pp. 104, 105.
67 Conrad, *Chance*, p. 238.
68 Jones, *Conrad and Women*, p. 145.
69 Conrad, *Chance*, p. 213.
70 Jones, *Conrad and Women*, p.148.
71 Jones, *Conrad and Women*, p. 83.
72 Jones, *Conrad and Women*, p. 154.
73 Conrad, *Chance*, pp. 127, 292.
74 Conrad, *Chance*, p. vii.
75 Paul F. Mattheisen, Arthur C. Young and Pierre Coustillas (eds), *The Collected Letters of George Gissing, 1902–3, Volume Nine* (Ohio: Ohio University Press, 1997), p. 84.
76 Jones, *Conrad and Women*, pp. 159–60.
77 Jones, *Conrad and Women*, p. 115.
78 Maurice Blanchot, *The Station Hill Blanchot Reader: Fiction and Literary Essays*, trans. Lydia Davis, Paul Auster and Robert Lamberton, ed. George Quasha (New York: Station Hill Press, 1999), p. 379.
79 Robert Hampson, '*Chance* and the Secret Life: Conrad, Thackeray, Stevenson', *The Conradian*, 17:2 (1993), pp. 105–22, p. 116.
80 Davies, 'Conrad, *Chance*, and Women Readers', p. 88.
81 Conrad, *Chance*, p. 150.
82 Conrad, *Chance*, p. 350.
83 Conrad, *Chance*, p. 350.
84 Conrad, *Chance*, pp. 80, 102, 264.
85 Conrad, *Chance*, pp.136, 145, 353.
86 Conrad, *Chance*, p. 63.
87 Roberts, *Conrad and Masculinity*, p. 124.
88 Conrad, *Youth, Heart of Darkness, The End of the Tether*, p. 82.
89 Conrad, *Youth, Heart of Darkness, The End of the Tether*, p. 59.
90 Conrad, *Chance*, p. 144.
91 See Nina Pelikan Straus, 'The Exclusion of the Intended from Secret Sharing', *Joseph Conrad: Contemporary Critical Essays*, ed. Elaine Jordan (Houndmills: Macmillan, 1996), pp. 48–66; Roberts, *Conrad and Masculinity*; and, Jones, *Conrad and Women*.

92 Jordan, *Joseph Conrad: Contemporary Critical Essays*, p. 50.
93 Conrad, *Youth, Heart of Darkness, The End of the Tether*, p. 59.
94 Conrad, *Youth, Heart of Darkness, The End of the Tether*, p. 161.
95 Conrad, *Chance*, p. 435.
96 Conrad, *Chance*, p. 444.
97 Ricoeur, *Essays on Language, Action and Interpretation*, p. 148.
98 Blanchot, *The Station Hill Blanchot Reader*, p. 380.
99 Blanchot, *The Station Hill Blanchot Reader*, p. 388.
100 *Chance* starts with a lie, or more precisely an untold truth, when Powell goes along with the Shipping Master's suggestion that they are related: 'His name's Powell' (p. 18). Later Powell will lie directly, feigning illness in order to enter Captain Anthony's cabin (p. 418).
101 Conrad, *Chance*, p. 236.
102 Conrad, *Chance*, p. 434.
103 Conrad, *Chance*, p. 6.

Epilogue: the sense of an ending

The end – this thing has no end,' he clamoured, unexpectedly. 'Can't you understand that? I can . . . The beginning . . . (Joseph Conrad, 'The Return')

The sense of an ending

Who exactly is Charlie Marlow? Or, is it perhaps more appropriate to ask 'what' exactly is Charlie Marlow? In its attempts to get to grips with Conrad's most famous creation, this study has certainly approached Marlow in both senses: asking of him both who and what. Is Marlow a character or a narrator, a biographer or an autobiographical screen, a messenger or an interpreter, a bearer of the truth or a misguided liar? It might be expected of a conclusion to offer a definitive answer to one, or all, of these questions, but following an argument that has been concerned with the problematic nature of narrative completion, any gesture towards a conclusion can only be offered with a certain degree of caution. In this awareness, what is offered here can only be, recalling Frank Kermode, the 'sense' of an ending. Hence its designation as an epilogue rather than a conclusion is a deliberate attempt to sidestep the expectations of summative closure in favour of an ending that is a form of address, literally a 'speaking upon', that assumes and recognizes its audience and thus implies the possibility of further dialogue. So ending here returns us, in the manner that a dramatic epilogue might recall the audience to the prologue, to the questions with which this study began.

The refiguration of conclusion as a necessary reflection on beginnings, is central to what Heidegger calls hermeneutics' 'virtuous' circle – the productive circle of interpretation that enables and demands a reflection on the point from which it began in order to begin again. In this spirit, this final chapter is phrased in terms of a return to the point at which my argument began. In effect this return to beginning was inevitable: it is the 'puzzling paradox' of narrative hermeneutics that, to quote Richard E. Palmer, 'in order to read, it is necessary to understand in advance what will be said, and yet this understanding must come from the reading.'[1] Accordingly, what follows returns to the connection made between Marlow and Hermes and the reading that emerges from that pairing – the suggestion that 'Youth', *Heart of Darkness*, *Lord Jim* and *Chance*, all texts that foreground their own transmission, should be read in terms of a self-conscious narrative hermeneutics for which the emergence of meaning is connected at all points with the transmission of that meaning.

From the outset this study has been concerned with questions of narration and has, quite deliberately, positioned Marlow as a figure who, both as a character and as a narrative device, represents a certain anxiety about the possibility of narrative transmission. The connection made between Marlow and Hermes was equally deliberate, for in the figure of the ancient Greek herald we see the convergence of the themes that have been central to my argument – the transmission and translation of narrative, a liminality found in the traversing of boundaries and, in his role as psychopompus, the guide to Hades, a certain relation to death. Approaching Marlow through this connection with Hermes and through close narratological readings of the texts, as has been done here, brings out the frequently shifting position that he occupies in these texts and in which he appears as narrator and character; as generator, transmitter and translator of narrative. In this way, just as Heidegger suggests of Hermes, Marlow too might be seen as a figure for hermeneutics which, as the etymology of the term suggests, contains both the senses of expression (utterance, speaking) and explication (interpretation, translation).[2] Marlow both provides us with narrative and, entering into a dialogue not only with his characters and narrators, but also with earlier versions of his own split-personality, provides a commentary (that itself provokes further commentary) on that narrative. In this way Hermes brings together the ideas that inform my reading of Marlow, central to which is the suggestion that his identity might be divided along similar lines and that a determination to fix him in place would be to misrecognize his status in Conrad's narratives. With this in mind, it is in the very multiplicity of the possible responses to the question(s) 'who/what is Charlie Marlow?' that an answer begins to emerge. Marlow's essence is liminality – the constant shifting of position, both within and across the individual texts, which places his different roles in dialogue with one another. It is in this manner that he has been approached in this study: as a figure that crosses, or invokes the crossing of, numerous boundaries. In the same way, the text, which in any case can never really be separated from Marlow, is mobilised to resist the boundaries within which it might be contained.

There are numerous indicators that problematise Marlow's narratives and demand further interpretation. His narratives are characterised by a questioning of the reliability of language; by a concern with translating that appears both in the obvious sense of the translation from one language to another and in a solipsistic uncertainty about the possibility of relating the experience of an individual to others; through a questioning of the connection between words and things that manifests itself most obviously in an uncertainty about proper names; in the 'adjectival insistence' that loses objects behind a chain of non-description; in an abundance of ellipses that repeatedly fracture the move towards completion; and, most obviously, in the complex narrative structures that have been the central interest of this book. Namely, the clear indication that the texts exist in a problematic dialogue between Marlow and his auditors – and particularly the unnamed narrator.

All four texts make a point of exploring the limits of representation and the very nature of the finite. As such, the presentation of death, figured, with reference to Heidegger, Derrida and Blanchot, as the limit of the traversable, has been central to their study. The negotiation of this border, which, says Derrida, 'would be more essential, more originary, and more proper than those of any other territory in the world,' is one of the more obvious connections with Hermes.[3] In this case, the mythic connection is made for us by Conrad who has Marlow, en route to the Congo, visit the 'whited sepulchre' of the Company Offices.[4] In a building that is as 'still as a house in a city of the dead', he is confronted by the sight of two women, 'one fat and the other slim, sat on straw-bottomed chairs, knitting black wool'.[5] The significance of this pair is not lost on Marlow to whom they seem 'eerie', 'uncanny and fateful':

> Often far away I thought of these two, guarding the door of Darkness, knitting black wool as for a warm pall, one introducing, introducing continuously to the unknown, the other scrutinizing the cheery and foolish faces with unconcerned old eyes. *Ave!* Old knitter of black wool. *Morituri te salutant.* Not many of those she looked at ever saw her again – not half by a long way.[6]

As Anthony Fothergill and others have noted, these two knitters, along with the 'compassionate secretary', whose gender remains unspecified and whose 'skinny forefinger' beckons Marlow into the 'sanctuary', recall the Fates of ancient Greece: Clotho, Lachesis and Atropos, the three goddesses who spun, measured and cut the threads of life.[7] But if Marlow is allowed to enter the realm of the dead, he, unlike Hermes, who retrieved the abducted Persephone, is unable to bring anyone back. This is the point at which the connection to Hermes appears to break down. For Marlow, access to death is an impossibility, and so the attempt to tell the story of Kurtz becomes the story of 'something' buried 'in a muddy hole'.[8] The demand that an authentic encounter with death will produce words of wisdom, the necessity of 'something to live with', is reversed and replaced with 'a dying vibration ... without any kind of sense'.[9] All four texts evince a similar refusal to allow a relation to death that would guarantee meaning and, in this way access to being is refused to language. This would appear to be the message that Marlow delivers in his narratives and it is in this sense that Marlow becomes a messenger whose message is the inappropriateness of the demands placed on language.

Yet for all this there is a sense in which death does appear in Marlow's stories. Marlow's comment that there is 'a flavour of mortality in lies' directs our attention to his own untruths which, in his stories, are afforded a double status.[10] Retold and unmasked they become truths – lies recognized as lies. So Marlow's lies to the Intended and to Flora, which are both refusals to speak of death, are retold truthfully, accorded their position in this latest version of the tale. In this way the Marlow narratives comment on the connection between death and language more generally and reading them alongside Blanchot's notion of the double death suggests literature, which has a very specific relation to truth, as the site at which death emerges. Literary language in recognising its status as fictional reveals the death that everyday language masks: it does, as Blanchot tells us, announce real death. Death therefore circulates at the level of literary language because of the recognition that language not only fails to guarantee access to Being but that it guarantees the opposite – it is the guarantee of the absolute loss of Being. This, it could be said, is the 'truth of literature', a somewhat misleading phrase that pretends to find the truth in the appearance of a death that is itself the impossibility of meaning.

An understandable response to the deconstructive position that might be inferred from this connection between narrative and death might lead the critic to insist, along with Alvan Hervey, the jilted husband in Conrad's 'The Return', that 'This is awful! ... Words? Yes, words. Words mean something – yes – they do – for all this infernal affectation. They mean something to me – to everybody – to you.'[11] Notably for Hervey it is his wife's refusal to enter into dialogue, her disavowal of language, that drives him from his house. Of course it is the recognition that words mean something 'to everybody' that identifies language as a process of exchange in which access to some fundamental meaning finds itself replaced by a dialogic model in which the very transmittability of language guarantees its dislocation from the individual instance. This determination of narrative as a dialogic act is central to the Marlow texts which place, in both their style and content, notions of language alongside Marlow's nihilistic claim that 'We live, as we dream – alone'.[12] The conclusion of the oral narrative of *Lord Jim* appears to bear this out. The narrator,

picking up the story in the second section recalls that at the conclusion of
Marlow's tale:

> Men drifted off the verandah in pairs or alone without loss of time, without
> offering a remark, as if the last image of that incomplete story, its
> incompleteness itself, and the very tone of the speaker, had made discussion
> vain and comment impossible.[13]

These lines, which preface the resumption of Marlow's story, should not
be read as affirming the impossibility of discussion. The narrator's 'as if'
indicates the very possibility of interpretative engagement with the text.
Indeed, the very form of the Marlow texts insists that storytelling is
conceived as a process of exchange. Everything in these novels, which, it
should be recalled, retell Marlow's own interpretative act *with* comments,
refutes the suggestion that their narratives preclude discussion.

Rather than being impossible, commentary and dialogue are the
defining features of the Marlow texts in which they appear as a very
deliberately staged concern with the genesis, transmission and interpretation of narrative. 'Youth', *Heart of Darkness*, *Lord Jim* and *Chance*
refuse to be reduced to an 'informational' reading by which they could be
said to be completed, and the desire to resolve the plots of these texts, and
the subsequent frustration of that desire, leads to a certain anxiety at the
impossibility of moving beyond their 'incompleteness'. Consequently,
while Marlow's fictional auditors find 'discussion vain and comment
impossible', Conrad's critics have found his narratives to be an 'odd mix
of clarity and obscurity'.[14] The presence of Marlow as narrator ensures
this deferral of resolution: he is 'very much a muddler' whose framed
narratives lack the authority of an omniscient narrator with the result
that Conrad's texts are 'ridden,' in the words of Henry James, 'by such
a danger of steeping his matter in perfect eventual obscuration as we
recall no other artist's consenting to with equal grace.'[15] Contrary to
expectation, it is an excess of 'comment' and 'discussion', those traces of
the storyteller that Walter Benjamin likens so poetically to the 'handprints
of the potter', that makes the Marlow texts so complex.[16] It is increasingly
evident that the need for interpretive action that is so clearly indicated
by the texts is indicated by nothing so much as by the appearance
of, the abundance of, interpretative action within the text. The act of
interpretation is exactly what reveals the parabolic nature of the text –
interpretation simultaneously demands and forestalls interpretation. The
relationship between Marlow's handprints and the vessels they shape is
best characterised as dialogue: dialogue between Marlow, his characters
and his narrator, and, just as significantly, between the various 'Marlows'
that simultaneously occupy, create and constitute the texts. The resultant

ambiguity is well described by Roland Barthes's famous declaration that 'a text is not a line of words releasing a single theological meaning (the "message" of the Author-God) but a multi-dimensional space in which a variety of writings, none of them original, blend and clash.'[17] The many-layered structuring of Conrad's fictions, and consequently the necessarily liminal status of their narrator who must traverse these layers, can be seen as a model of the 'multidimensional space' through which Marlow moves almost as a fictional precursor to Barthes's thesis. In an unexpected reversal, whilst Barthes attributes this textual mobility to the 'removal' of the author, Conrad's almost obsessive/excessive placement of the character-author within these texts, which could be read as a fictional notation of the displacement of the 'real' author, generates an almost identical effect. In the Marlow texts, where the supplier of the narrative is also the first reader of that narrative, it is fair to say that meaning, that is to say fixed meaning, is most deliberately subverted: Marlow's 'Do you see the story? Do you see anything?' is not so much a question as a statement of the fact that final disclosure is impossible.[18]

Reading Conrad's texts in this way, as hermeneutic dialogues in which the possibility of linear fixity is replaced by a more dynamic circularity, introduces a multiplying of meanings that emerge through dialogue. More correctly, these readings emerge through a number of dialogues that the reader encounters in her/his interaction with the text, and recognizes in the dialogues between the text and other texts and, as is clear in the Marlow novels, the multiple layers of narrative that make up the text itself. In the words of Frances Wentworth Cutler, one of Marlow's early critics, 'with Conrad we actually enter into the creative process: we grope with him through blinding mists, we catch fleeting glimpses and thrill with sudden illuminations.'[19] Cutler continues,

> For the art of Conrad is literally a social art – the collaboration of many tellers and of many listeners: –
> 'In time the story shaped itself before me out of the listless answers to my questions, out of the indifferent words heard in wayside inns . . . People confirmed and completed the story.'
> Thus we, the listeners, not only share in the creation, but verily 'confirm and complete' these stories, whose aim is the search itself and not its ending. For the verdict on Jim and on Flora rests with us at last.[20]

Like Barthes who, some fifty years later, would suggest that 'a text's unity lies not in its origin but in its destination', Cutler implies that it is the reader who holds the text together.[21] But the 'confirmation and completion' that Cutler finds in this, slightly adapted, quotation from 'The Idiots' (1896) should not be thought in terms of a singular meaning but in its multiplicity. The verdict on Jim and Flora may rest with the reader as interpreter, but as the role of interpreter merges into that of narrator, it is increasingly difficult to regard this as being, in some way, the final verdict.

From this viewpoint, Marlow's sense that 'the meaning of an episode was not inside like a kernel but outside, enveloping the tale' takes on new resonance, and can be read as placing an emphasis on the role of the recipients of his tales in generating their meanings.[22] This insistence on dialogue recalls the distinction made by Benjamin between 'information' and 'wisdom'. Information, that closed reading that Conrad's texts disavow, is replaced by a wisdom that demands participation and which, in its form, reflects the project of hermeneutics. To this dialogic hermeneutics Benjamin gives the name 'counsel': 'counsel is less an answer to a question than a proposal concerning the continuation of a story which is in the process of unfolding. To seek this counsel, one would first have to be able to tell the story.'[23] The structure of this approach to wisdom is enacted within the texts by the unnamed narrator who, as Marlow's first reader, holds together his stories without reducing them to a single meaning, thus providing a model by which we might approach the Marlow texts. At this point, with the recognition that in the case of Marlow to talk about character is to talk about function, the critical emphasis might usefully be shifted towards the other participants in his dialogues: towards Marlow's unnamed and barely characterised narrators, or beyond the text towards a narrative hermeneutics that includes the reader in its field of study. In this way we return to the questions with which this study began, asking them of a Marlow who assumes an almost metaphorical role in which he becomes a figure for the processes of narrative communication.

Notes

1 Richard E. Palmer, *Hermeneutics: Interpretation Theory in Schleiermacher, Dilthey, Heidegger, and Gadamer* (Evanston: Northwestern University Press, 1969), p. 16.

2 See Jean Grondin, *Introduction to Philosophical Hermeneutics*, trans. Joel Weinsheimer (New Haven and London: Yale University Press, 1994), pp. 17–44, for a detailed discussion of the etymology of the term.

3 Jacques Derrida, *Aporias*, trans. Thomas Dutoit (Stanford, CA: Stanford University Press, 1993), p. 3.

4 Joseph Conrad, *Youth, Heart of Darkness, The End of the Tether* (London: J. M. Dent and Sons Ltd, 1946), p. 55.

5 Conrad, *Youth, Heart of Darkness, The End of the Tether*, pp. 57, 55.

6 Conrad, *Youth, Heart of Darkness, The End of the Tether*, p. 57.

7   Anthony Fothergill, *Heart of Darkness* (Milton Keynes: Open University Press, 1989), pp. 31–2; Conrad, *Youth, Heart of Darkness, The End of the Tether*, p. 56.
8   Conrad, *Youth, Heart of Darkness, The End of the Tether*, p. 150.
9   Conrad, *Youth, Heart of Darkness, The End of the Tether*, pp. 115, 161.
10 Conrad, *Youth, Heart of Darkness, The End of the Tether*, p. 82.
11 Joseph Conrad, *Almayer's Folly and Tales of Unrest* (London: J. M. Dent and Sons Ltd, 1947), p. 163.
12 Conrad, *Youth, Heart of Darkness, The End of the Tether*, p. 82.
13 Joseph Conrad, *Lord Jim* (London: J. M. Dent and Sons Ltd, 1946), p. 337.
14 Conrad, *Lord Jim*, p. 337; Harold Bloom (ed.), *Marlow* (New York: Chelsea House Publishers, 1992), p. 146.
15 Bloom (ed.), *Marlow*, pp. 3, 6.
16 Walter Benjamin, *Selected Writings: Volume Three: 1935–1938*, trans. Edmund Jephcott, Howard Eiland *et al.*, ed. Howard Eiland and Michael W. Jennings (Cambridge, MA: The Belknap Press of Harvard University Press, 2002), p. 149.
17 Roland Barthes, *Image, Music, Text*, trans. Stephen Heath (London: Fontana, 1977), p. 146.
18 Conrad, *Youth, Heart of Darkness, The End of the Tether*, p. 82.
19 Bloom (ed.), *Marlow*, p. 10.
20 Bloom (ed.), *Marlow*, p. 10.
21 Barthes, *Image, Music, Text*, p. 148.
22 Conrad, *Youth, Heart of Darkness, The End of the Tether*, p. 48.
23 Benjamin, *Selected Writings: Volume Three*, pp. 145–6.

Bibliography

Achebe, Chinua, *Hopes and Impediments: Selected Essays* (London: Heinemann, 1988)

Ariès, Philippe, *Western Attitudes Towards Death: From the Middle Ages to the Present*, trans. Patricia M. Ranum (London: Marion Boyars Publishers, 1994)

Aristotle, *Poetics*, trans. Malcolm Heath (London: Penguin, 1996)

Baines, Jocelyn, *Joseph Conrad: A Critical Biography* (London: Wiedenfeld, 1993)

Bakhtin, Mikhail, *The Dialogic Imagination: Four Essays*, ed. Michael Holquist, trans. Caryl Emerson and Michael Holquist (Austin, TX: Texas University Press, 1981)

Barthes, Roland, *Writing Degree Zero*, trans. Annette Lavers and Colin Smith (London: Jonathan Cape, 1967)

—— *Image, Music, Text*, trans. Stephen Heath (London: Fontana, 1977)

—— *S/Z*, trans. Richard Miller (Oxford: Blackwell, 1990)

Batchelor, John, *The Life of Joseph Conrad: A Critical Biography* (Oxford: Blackwell, 1994)

—— *Lord Jim* (London: Unwin Hyman, 1988)

Bender, Todd K., *A Concordance to Conrad's Heart of Darkness* (New York: Garland Publishing Inc, 1979)

Benjamin, Walter, *Selected Writings: Volume Three: 1935–1938*, trans. Edmund Jephcott, Howard Eiland *et al.*, ed. Howard Eiland and Michael W. Jennings (Cambridge, MA: The Belknap Press of Harvard University Press, 2002)

Berman, Jeffrey, *Joseph Conrad: Writing as Rescue* (New York: Astra Books, 1977)

Blackburn, William (ed.), *Joseph Conrad: Letters to William Blackwood and David S. Meldrum* (Durham, NC: Duke University Press, 1958)

Blackwood, William (ed.), *Blackwood's Edinburgh Magazine* (Edinburgh & London)

Blanchot, Maurice, *The Space of Literature*, trans. and introd. Ann Smock (Lincoln: Nebraska University Press, 1982)

—— *The Blanchot Reader*, ed. and introd. Michael Holland (Oxford: Blackwell, 1995)

—— *The Writing of the Disaster*, trans. Ann Smock (Lincoln: Nebraska University Press, 1995)

—— *The Station Hill Blanchot Reader: Fiction and Literary Essays*, trans. Lydia Davis, Paul Auster and Robert Lamberton, ed. George Quasha (New York: Station Hill Press, 1999)

Bloom, Harold (ed.), *Marlow* (New York: Chelsea House Publishers, 1992)

Booth, Wayne C., *The Rhetoric of Fiction* (Chicago and London: Chicago University Press, 1961)

Brooks, Peter, *Reading for the Plot: Design and Intention in Narrative* (Oxford: Clarendon, 1984)

Caserio, Robert L., 'Joseph Conrad, Dickensian Novelist of the Nineteenth Century: A Dissent from Ian Watt,' *Nineteenth Century Fiction*, 36:3 (Dec. 1981), pp. 337–47

Caws, Mary Ann, *Reading Frames in Modern Fiction* (Princeton, NJ: Princeton University Press, 1985)

Clark, Timothy, *Derrida, Heidegger, Blanchot: Sources of Derrida's Notion and Practice of Literature* (Cambridge: Cambridge University Press, 1992)

Cobley, Paul, *Narrative* (London: Routledge, 2001)

Conrad, Joseph, *Lord Jim* (London: J. M. Dent and Sons Ltd, 1946)

—— *The Mirror of the Sea: Memories and Impressions; A Personal Record: Some Reminiscences* (London: J. M. Dent and Sons Ltd, 1946)

—— *Youth, Heart of Darkness, The End of the Tether* (London: J. M. Dent and Sons Ltd, 1946)

—— *Almayer's Folly and Tales of Unrest* (London: J. M. Dent and Sons Ltd, 1947)

—— *The Arrow of Gold; A Story Between two Notes* (London: J. M. Dent and Sons Ltd, 1947)

—— *Under Western Eyes* (London: J. M. Dent and Sons Ltd, 1947)

—— *Victory: An Island Tale* (London: J. M. Dent and Sons Ltd, 1948)

—— *An Outcast of the Islands* (London: J. M. Dent and Sons Ltd, 1949)

—— *Chance: A Tale in Two Parts* (London: J. M. Dent and Sons Ltd, 1949)

—— *The Nigger of the 'Narcissus'* (London: J. M. Dent and Sons Ltd, 1950)

—— *The Shadow-Line and Within the Tides* (London: J. M. Dent and Sons Ltd, 1950)

—— *The Secret Agent: A Simple Tale*, ed. Bruce Harkness and S. W. Reid (Cambridge: Cambridge University Press, 1990)

Coroneos, Con, *Space, Conrad, and Modernity* (Oxford: Oxford University Press, 2002)

Cox, C. B., *Joseph Conrad: The Modern Imagination* (London: J. M. Dent and Sons Ltd, 1974)

Critchley, Simon, *Very Little . . . Almost Nothing: Death, Philosophy, Literature* (London Routledge, 1997)

Curle, Richard, *Joseph Conrad and his Characters: A Study of Six Novels* (New York: Russell & Russell, 1957)

Daleski, H. M., *Joseph Conrad: The Way of Dispossession* (London: Faber & Faber, 1977)

Davies, Laurence, 'Conrad, *Chance*, and Women Readers,' *The Conradian*, 17:2 (1993), pp. 75–88

Derrida, Jacques, *Of Grammatology*, trans. Gayatri Chakravorty Spivak (Baltimore: The Johns Hopkins University Press, 1976)

—— *Aporias*, trans. Thomas Dutoit (Stanford, CA: Stanford University Press, 1993)

Dryden, Linda, *Joseph Conrad and the Imperial Romance* (Houndmills: Palgrave, 2000)

Durkheim, Émile, *Suicide: A Study in Sociology*, 1897, trans. John A. Spaulding and George Simpson, introd. George Simpson (London: Routledge, 1952)

Fincham, Gail, 'The Dialogism of *Lord Jim*,' *The Conradian*, 22:1/2 (Spring/Winter 1997) pp. 58–74

Fothergill, Anthony, *Heart of Darkness* (Milton Keynes: Open University Press, 1989)

Genette, Gérard, *Narrative Discourse: An Essay in Method*, trans. Jane E. Lewin (Oxford: Blackwell, 1980)

Gibson, Andrew, 'Ethics and Unrepresentability in *Heart of Darkness*,' *The Conradian*, 22:1/2 (1997), pp. 113–37

Gill, Carolyn Bailey (ed.), *Maurice Blanchot: The Demand of Writing* (London: Routledge, 1996)

Glassman, Peter J., *Language and Being: Joseph Conrad and the Literature of Personality* (New York: Columbia University Press, 1976)

Graham, Kenneth, *Indirections of the Novel: James, Conrad, and Forster* (Cambridge: Cambridge University Press, 1988)

Greaney, Michael, *Conrad, Language and Narrative* (Cambridge: Cambridge University Press, 2002)

Grondin, Jean, *Introduction to Philosophical Hermeneutics*, trans. Joel Weinsheimer (New Haven and London: Yale University Press, 1994)

Guerard, Albert J., *Conrad the Novelist* (Cambridge, MA: Harvard University Press, 1958)

Haase, Ullrich, and William Large, *Maurice Blanchot* (London: Routledge, 2001)

Hampson, Robert, '*Chance*: The Affair of the Purloined Brother,' *The Conradian* 6:2 (1980), pp. 5–15

—— '"Heart of Darkness" and "The Speech that Cannot be Silenced",' *English*, 39:163 (Spring 1990), pp. 15–32

—— '*Chance* and the Secret Life: Conrad, Thackeray, Stevenson,' *The Conradian* 17:2 (1993): pp. 105–22

—— *Cross-Cultural Encounters in Joseph Conrad's Malay Fiction* (Houndmills: Palgrave, 2000)

Hansford, James, 'Reflection and Self Consumption in "Youth"', *The Conradian*, 12:2 (1987), pp. 150–65

Harpham, Geoffrey Galt, *One of Us: The Mastery of Joseph Conrad* (Chicago: Chicago University Press, 1996)

Hawthorn, Jeremy, *Joseph Conrad: Language and Fictional Self-Consciousness* (London: Edward Arnold, 1979)

—— *Joseph Conrad: Narrative Technique and Ideological Commitment* (London: Edward Arnold, 1990)

Hegel, G.W.F. *Phenomenology of Spirit*, 1807, trans. A.V. Miller (Oxford: Clarendon, 1979)

Heidegger, Martin, *Being and Time* [1927], trans. J. Macquarrie and E. Robinson (Oxford: Blackwell, 1962)

—— *On the Way to Language*, trans. Peter D. Hertz (New York: Harper, 1971)

Henricksen, Bruce, *Nomadic Voices: Conrad and the Subject of Narrative* (Urbana and Chicago: University of Illinois Press, 1992)

Hill, Leslie, *Blanchot: Extreme Contemporary* (London: Routledge, 1997)

Houghton, Walter E. (ed.), *The Wellesley Index to Victorian Periodicals 1824–1900: Tables of Contents and Identification of Contributors with Bibliographies of their Articles and Stories, Volume One* (Toronto: University of Toronto Press, 1966)

Hurford, James R., *Grammar: A Student's Guide* (Cambridge: Cambridge University Press, 1994)

Jameson, Fredric, *The Political Unconscious: Narrative as a Socially Symbolic Act* (London: Methuen, 1981)

Jones, Susan, *Conrad and Women* (Oxford: Clarendon, 1999)

Jordan, Elaine (ed.), *Joseph Conrad: Contemporary Critical Essays* (Houndmills: Macmillan, 1996)

Karl, Frederick R., *Joseph Conrad: The Three Lives* (London: Faber and Faber, 1979)

—— and Laurence Davies (eds), *The Collected Letters of Joseph Conrad, Volume Two 1898–1902* (Cambridge: Cambridge University Press, 1986)

—— *The Collected Letters of Joseph Conrad, Volume Three 1903–1907* (Cambridge: Cambridge University Press, 1988)

—— *The Collected Letters of Joseph Conrad, Volume Four 1908–1911* (Cambridge: Cambridge University Press, 1990)

—— *The Collected Letters of Joseph Conrad, Volume Five 1912–1916* (Cambridge: Cambridge University Press, 1996)

—— *A Reader's Guide to Joseph Conrad* (Syracuse, NY: Syracuse University Press, 1997)

Kermode, Frank, *The Genesis of Secrecy: On the Interpretation of Narrative* (Cambridge, MA: Harvard University Press, 1979)

—— *The Sense of an Ending: Studies in the Theory of Fiction, With a New Epilogue* (Oxford: Oxford University Press, 2000)

Knowles, Owen and Gene M. Moore (eds), *Oxford Reader's Companion to Conrad* (Oxford: Oxford University Press, 2000)

Kuehn, Robert E. (ed.), *Twentieth Century Interpretations of Lord Jim* (Eaglewood Cliffs, NJ: Prentice Hall Inc, 1969)

Land, Stephen K., *Conrad and the Paradox of Plot* (London: Macmillan, 1984)

Leavis, F.R., *The Great Tradition: George Eliot, Henry James, Joseph Conrad* (London: Chatto and Windus, 1962)

Lemon, Lee T. and Marion J. Reis (eds), *Russian Formalist Criticism: Four Essays*, trans. Lee T. Lemon and Marion J. Reis (Lincoln: Nebraska University Press, 1965)

Levenson, Michael H., *A Genealogy of Modernism: A Study of English Literary Doctrine 1908–1922* (Cambridge: Cambridge University Press, 1984)

Levine, George, *The Realistic Imagination: English Fiction from Frankenstein to Lady Chatterley* (Chicago and London: University of Chicago Press, 1981)

Lothe, Jakob, *Conrad's Narrative Method* (Oxford: Clarendon, 1989)

Lyon, John, 'Introduction' to Conrad, *Youth/Heart of Darkness/The End of the Tether*, ed. John Lyon (London: Penguin, 1995)

Maclean, Marie, *Narrative as Performance: The Baudelairean Experiment* (London: Routledge, 1988)

Matthiesen, Paul F., Arthur C. Young and Pierre Coustillas (eds), *The Collected Letters of George Gissing, 1902–3, Volume Nine* (Ohio: Ohio University Press, 1997)

Meyer, Bernard C., *Joseph Conrad: A Psychoanalytic Biography* (Princeton, NJ: Princeton University Press, 1697)

Meyers, Jeffrey, *Joseph Conrad: A Biography* (New York: Charles Schribner's Sons, 1991)

Miller, J. Hillis, *Poets of Reality: Six Twentieth Century Writers* (Cambridge, MA: Belknap, Harvard University Press, 1966)

Moran, Dermot, *Introduction to Phenomenology* (London: Routledge, 2000)

Moser, Thomas, *Joseph Conrad: Achievement and Decline* (Cambridge, MA: Harvard University Press, 1957)

Mulhall, Stephen, *Heidegger and Being and Time* (London: Routledge, 1996)

Murfin, Ross C. (ed.), *Conrad Revisited: Essays for the Eighties* (Alabama: Alabama University Press, 1985)

Najder, Zdzisław, *Conrad's Polish Background: Letters to and from Polish Friends*, trans. Halina Carroll (Oxford: Oxford University Press, 1964)

—— *Joseph Conrad: A Chronicle*, trans. Halina Carroll-Najder (Cambridge: Cambridge University Press, 1983)

Niland, Richard, 'Aging and Individual Experience in "Youth" and "Heart of Darkness,"' *The Conradian*, 29.1 (2004), pp. 99–118

Palmer, Richard E., *Hermeneutics: Interpretation Theory in Schleiermacher, Dilthey, Heidegger, and Gadamer* (Evanston: Northwestern University Press, 1969)

—— 'The Liminality of Hermes and the Meaning of Hermeneutics,' *MacMurray College Homepage* (2001), 23 April 2006. <http://www.mac.edu/faculty/richardpalmer/liminality.html>

Paris, Bernard J., *Conrad's Charlie Marlow: A New Approach to 'Heart of Darkness' and Lord Jim* (Houndmills, Basingstoke: Palgrave Macmillan, 2005)

Pettersson, Torsten, *Consciousness and Time: A Study in the Philosophy and Narrative Technique of Joseph Conrad* (Abo: Abo Akademi, 1982)

Ray, Martin, 'Introduction' to Conrad, *Chance: A Tale in Two Parts*, ed. Martin Ray (Oxford: Oxford University Press, 1999)

Ricoeur, Paul, *The Symbolism of Evil*, trans. Emerson Buchanan (Boston: Beacon Press, 1969)

—— *Hermeneutics and the Human Sciences: Essays on Language, Action and Interpretation*, ed. and trans. John B. Thompson (Cambridge: Cambridge University Press, 1981)

—— *Time and Narrative: Volume One*, trans. Kathleen McLaughlin and David Pellauer (Chicago: Chicago University Press, 1984)

—— *Time and Narrative: Volume Two*, trans. Kathleen McLaughlin and David Pellauer (Chicago: Chicago University Press, 1985)

—— *Time and Narrative: Volume Three*, trans. Kathleen Blamey and David Pellauer (Chicago: Chicago University Press, 1988)

Rignall, John (ed.), *Oxford Reader's Companion to George Eliot* (Oxford: Oxford University Press, 2000)

Roberts, Andrew Michael, 'Introduction,' *The Conradian*, 17:2 (1993), pp. v-xi

—— *Conrad and Masculinity* (London: Macmillan, 2000)

Schneider, Lissa, *Conrad's Narratives of Difference: Not Exactly Tales for Boys* (London: Routledge, 2003)

Schuster, Joshua, 'Death Reckoning in the Thinking of Heidegger, Foucault, and Derrida,' *Other Voices* (1997), 14 Dec.1999 <http://dept.english.upenn.edu/~ov/jnschust/death.html>.

Schwartz, Daniel R., *Conrad: The Later Fiction* (London and Basingstoke: Macmillan, 1982)

Sherry, Norman *Conrad's Western World* (Cambridge: Cambridge University Press, 1971)

—— (ed.), *Conrad: The Critical Heritage* (London: Routledge & Kegan Paul, 1973)

Siegle, Robert, 'The Two Texts of *Chance*,' *Conradiana*, 16 (1984), pp. 83–101

Simmons, Allan H., ' "He was Misleading": Frustrated gestures in *Lord Jim*,' *The Conradian*, 25:1 (Spring 2000) pp. 31–47

—— *The Conradian*, 27:1 (2000, 2002, 2004)

—— 'The Art of Englishness: Identity and Representation in Conrad's Early Career,' *The Conradian*, 29:1 (Spring 2004), pp. 1–26

Simms, Karl, *Paul Ricoeur* (London: Routledge, 2003)

Stallman, R. W. (ed.), *Joseph Conrad a Critical Symposium* (Athens, OH: Ohio University Press, 1982)

Stape, J. H. (ed.), *The Cambridge Companion to Joseph Conrad* (Cambridge: Cambridge University Press, 1996)

Stevenson, John, *British Society 1914–45* (London: Penguin, 1990)

Stevenson, Randall, *Modernist Fiction: An Introduction* (London: Prentice Hall, 1998)

Stewart, Garrett, 'Lying as Dying in *Heart of Darkness*,' *PMLA*, 95:3 (1980), pp. 319–31

Topia, André, 'The Impossible Present; A Flaubertian Reading of *Lord Jim*,' *The Conradian*, 31:1 (Spring 2006) pp. 37–51

Tredell, Nicholas (ed.), *Joseph Conrad: Heart of Darkness* (Cambridge: Icon Books Ltd., 1998)

Van Ghent, Dorothy, *The English Novel: Form and Function* (New York: Holt, Rinehart and Winston, 1953).

Verleun-Van de Vriesenaerde, Jetty, *Conrad Criticism 1965–1985: Heart of Darkness* (Groningen: Phoenix Press, 1988)

Vitoux, Pierre, 'Marlow: The Changing Narrator of Conrad's Fiction,' *Cahiers Victoriens et Édouardiens*, 2 (1975), pp. 83–102

Watt, Ian, 'Conrad's Preface to *The Nigger of the "Narcissus"*', *Novel*, 7:2 (Winter 1974), pp. 101–15

—— *Conrad in the Nineteenth Century* (London: Chatto & Windus, 1980)

Watts, Cedric, (ed.), *Joseph Conrad's Letters to Cunninghame Graham* (Cambridge: Cambridge University Press, 1969)

—— *Conrad's Heart of Darkness: A Critical and Contextual Discussion* (Milan: Mursia, 1977)

—— *The Deceptive Text: An Introduction to Covert Plots* (Brighton: The Harvester Press Ltd, 1984)

—— 'Introduction' to Conrad, *Lord Jim*, ed. Robert Hampson (London: Penguin, 1989)

—— 'Introduction' to Conrad, *Heart of Darkness and Other Tales*, ed. Cedric Watts (Oxford: Oxford University Press, 1998)

—— 'Bakhtin's Monologism and the Endings of *Crime and Punishment* and *Lord Jim*', *The Conradian*, 25:1 (Spring 2000) pp. 15–30

Webster, Richard, 'New Ends for Old: Frank Kermode's *The Sense of an Ending*,' *richardwebster.net* (2003), 25 Aug 2003 <http://www.richardwebster.net/kermode.html>

White, Allon, *The Uses of Obscurity: The Fiction of Early Modernism* (London: Routledge & Kegan Paul, 1981)

White, Andrea, *Joseph Conrad and the Adventure Tradition: Constructing and Deconstructing the Imperial Subject* (Cambridge: Cambridge University Press, 1993)

Willy, Todd G., 'Measures of the Heart and of the Darkness: Conrad and the Suicides of "New Imperialism"', *Conradiana*, 14 (1982), pp. 189–98

Wolfreys, Julian, *Deconstruction: Derrida* (Houndmills: Macmillan, 1998)

Wood, David (ed.), *On Paul Ricoeur: Narrative and Interpretation* (London: Routledge, 1991)

Woolf, Virginia, *The Common Reader* (London: Hogarth Press, 1975)

Zyla, Wolodmymyr T. and Wendell M. Aycock (eds), *Joseph Conrad: Theory and World Fiction – Proceedings of the Comparative Literature Symposium, Vol VII* (Lubbock, TX: Interdepartmental Committee on Comparative Literature, Texas Tech University, 1974)

Index